FALLING IN LOVE

&c.

First Published 1889
Reprinted 1972

Library of Congress Cataloging in Publication Data

Allen, Grant, 1848-1899.
   Falling in love.

   (Essay index reprint series)
   Reprint of the 1889 ed.
   CONTENTS: Falling in love.--Right and left.--
Evolution. [etc.]
   1. Science--Addresses, essays, lectures. I. Title.
Q171.A42 1972   508'.1   72-3357
ISBN 0-8369-2884-9

FALLING IN LOVE

WITH OTHER ESSAYS

ON

MORE EXACT BRANCHES OF SCIENCE

BY

GRANT ALLEN

Essay Index Reprint Series

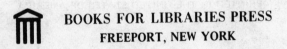

BOOKS FOR LIBRARIES PRESS
FREEPORT, NEW YORK

PREFACE

SOME people complain that science is dry. That is, of course, a matter of taste. For my own part, I like my science and my champagne as dry as I can get them. But the public thinks otherwise. So I have ventured to sweeten accompanying samples as far as possible to suit the demand, and trust they will meet with the approbation of consumers.

Of the specimens here selected for exhibition, my title piece originally appeared in the *Fortnightly Review*: 'Honey Dew' and 'The First Potter' were contributions to *Longman's Magazine*: and all the rest found friendly shelter between the familiar yellow covers of the good old *Cornhill*. My thanks are due to the proprietors and editors of those various periodicals for kind permission to reproduce them here.

G. A.

THE NOOK, DORKING:
September, 1889.

CONTENTS

FALLING IN LOVE

An ancient and famous human institution is in pressing danger. Sir George Campbell has set his face against the time-honoured practice of Falling in Love. Parents innumerable, it is true, have set their faces against it already from immemorial antiquity; but then they only attacked the particular instance, without venturing to impugn the institution itself on general principles. An old Indian administrator, however, goes to work in all things on a different pattern. He would always like to regulate human life generally as a department of the India Office; and so Sir George Campbell would fain have husbands and wives selected for one another (perhaps on Dr. Johnson's principle, by the Lord Chancellor) with a view to the future development of the race, in the process which he not very felicitously or elegantly describes as ' man-breeding.' ' Probably,' he says, as reported in *Nature*, ' we have enough physiological knowledge to effect a vast improvement in the pairing of individuals of the same or allied races if we could only apply that knowledge to make fitting marriages, instead of giving way to foolish ideas about love and the tastes of young people, whom we can hardly trust to choose their own bonnets, much less to choose in a graver matter in which they are most likely to be influenced by frivolous prejudices.' He wants us, in other words, to discard the deep-seated inner physiological promptings of inherited instinct, and to substitute for them some calm and dis-

B

passionate but artificial selection of a fitting partner as the
father or mother of future generations.

Now this is of course a serious subject, and it ought to be
treated seriously and reverently. But, it seems to me, Sir
George Campbell's conclusion is exactly the opposite one
from the conclusion now being forced upon men of science
by a study of the biological and psychological elements in
this very complex problem of heredity. So far from considering love as a ' foolish idea,' opposed to the best interests
of the race, I believe most competent physiologists and
psychologists, especially those of the modern evolutionary
school, would regard it rather as an essentially beneficent
and conservative instinct developed and maintained in us
by natural causes, for the very purpose of insuring just
those precise advantages and improvements which Sir
George Campbell thinks he could himself effect by a conscious and deliberate process of selection. More than that,
I believe, for my own part (and I feel sure most evolutionists would cordially agree with me), that this beneficent
inherited instinct of Falling in Love effects the object it
has in view far more admirably, subtly, and satisfactorily,
on the average of instances, than any clumsy human
selective substitute could possibly effect it.

In short, my doctrine is simply the old-fashioned and
confiding belief that marriages are made in heaven : with
the further corollary that heaven manages them, one time
with another, a great deal better than Sir George Campbell.

Let us first look how Falling in Love affects the
standard of human efficiency ; and then let us consider
what would be the probable result of any definite conscious
attempt to substitute for it some more deliberate external
agency.

Falling in Love, as modern biology teaches us to believe, is nothing more than the latest, highest, and most involved exemplification, in the human race, of that almost universal selective process which Mr. Darwin has enabled us to recognise throughout the whole long series of the animal kingdom. The butterfly that circles and eddies in his aerial dance around his observant mate is endeavouring to charm her by the delicacy of his colouring, and to overcome her coyness by the display of his skill. The peacock that struts about in imperial pride under the eyes of his attentive hens, is really contributing to the future beauty and strength of his race by collecting to himself a harem through whom he hands down to posterity the valuable qualities which have gained the admiration of his mates in his own person. Mr. Wallace has shown that to be beautiful is to be efficient; and sexual selection is thus, as it were, a mere lateral form of natural selection—a survival of the fittest in the guise of mutual attractiveness and mutual adaptability, producing on the average a maximum of the best properties of the race in the resulting offspring. I need not dwell here upon this aspect of the case, because it is one with which, since the publication of the 'Descent of Man,' all the world has been sufficiently familiar.

In our own species, the selective process is marked by all the features common to selection throughout the whole animal kingdom; but it is also, as might be expected, far more specialised, far more individualised, far more cognisant of personal traits and minor peculiarities. It is furthermore exerted to a far greater extent upon mental and moral as well as physical peculiarities in the individual.

We cannot fall in love with everybody alike. Some of us fall in love with one person, some with another. This instinctive and deep-seated differential feeling we may regard as the outcome of complementary features, mental, moral, or physical, in the two persons concerned; and experience shows us that, in nine cases out of ten, it is a reciprocal affection, that is to say, in other words, an affection roused in unison by varying qualities in the respective individuals.

Of its eminently conservative and even upward tendency very little doubt can be reasonably entertained. We *do* fall in love, taking us in the lump, with the young, the beautiful, the strong, and the healthy; we do *not* fall in love, taking us in the lump, with the aged, the ugly, the feeble, and the sickly. The prohibition of the Church is scarcely needed to prevent a man from marrying his grandmother. Moralists have always borne a special grudge to pretty faces; but, as Mr. Herbert Spencer admirably put it (long before the appearance of Darwin's selective theory), 'the saying that beauty is but skin-deep is itself but a skin-deep saying.' In reality, beauty is one of the very best guides we can possibly have to the desirability, so far as race-preservation is concerned, of any man or any woman as a partner in marriage. A fine form, a good figure, a beautiful bust, a round arm and neck, a fresh complexion, a lovely face, are all outward and visible signs of the physical qualities that on the whole conspire to make up a healthy and vigorous wife and mother; they imply soundness, fertility, a good circulation, a good digestion. Conversely, sallowness and paleness are roughly indicative of dyspepsia and anæmia; a flat chest is a symptom of deficient maternity; and what we call a bad figure is really, in one way or another, an unhealthy departure from the central norma and standard of the race. Good teeth mean good deglutition; a clear eye means an active liver; scrubbiness and undersizedness mean feeble virility. Nor are indications of mental and moral efficiency by any means wanting as recognised elements in personal beauty. A good-humoured face is in itself almost pretty,

A pleasant smile half redeems unattractive features. Low, receding foreheads strike us unfavourably. Heavy, stolid, half-idiotic countenances can never be beautiful, however regular their lines and contours. Intelligence and goodness are almost as necessary as health and vigour in order to make up our perfect ideal of a beautiful human face and figure. The Apollo Belvedere is no fool; the murderers in the Chamber of Horrors at Madame Tussaud's are for the most part no beauties.

What we all fall in love with, then, as a race, is in most cases efficiency and ability. What we each fall in love with individually is, I believe, our moral, mental, and physical complement. Not our like, not our counterpart; quite the contrary; within healthy limits, our unlike and our opposite. That this is so has long been more or less a commonplace of ordinary conversation; that it is scientifically true, one time with another, when we take an extended range of cases, may, I think, be almost demonstrated by sure and certain warranty of human nature.

Brothers and sisters have more in common, mentally and physically, than any other members of the same race can possibly have with one another. But nobody falls in love with his sister. A profound instinct has taught even the lower races of men (for the most part) to avoid such union of the all-but-identical. In the higher races the idea never so much as occurs to us. Even cousins seldom fall in love—seldom, that is to say, in comparison with the frequent opportunities of intercourse they enjoy, relatively to the remainder of general society. When they do, and when they carry out their perilous choice effectively by marriage, natural selection soon avenges Nature upon the offspring by cutting off the idiots, the consumptives, the weaklings, and the cripples, who often result from such consanguineous marriages. In narrow communities, where breeding in-and-in becomes almost inevitable, natural selection has similarly to exert itself upon a crowd of *crétins* and other hapless incapables. But in wide and open champaign countries, where individual choice has free room for exercise, men and women as a rule (if not constrained by parents and moralists) marry for love, and marry on the whole their natural complements. They prefer outsiders, fresh blood, somebody who comes from beyond the community, to the people of their own immediate surroundings. In many men the dislike to marrying among the folk with whom they have been brought up amounts almost to a positive instinct; they feel it as impossible to fall in love with a fellow-townswoman as to fall in love with their own first cousins. Among exogamous tribes such an instinct (aided, of course, by other extraneous causes) has hardened into custom; and there is reason to believe (from the universal traces among the higher civilisations of marriage by capture) that all the leading races of the world are ultimately derived from exogamous ancestors, possessing this healthy and excellent sentiment.

In minor matters, it is of course universally admitted that short men, as a rule, prefer tall women, while tall men admire little women. Dark pairs by preference with fair; the commonplace often runs after the original. People have long noticed that this attraction towards one's opposite tends to keep true the standard of the race; they have not, perhaps, so generally observed that it also indicates roughly the existence in either individual of a desire for its own natural complement. It is difficult here to give definite examples, but everybody knows how, in the subtle psychology of Falling in Love, there are involved innumerable minor elements, physical and mental, which strike us exactly because of their absolute adaptation to form with ourselves an adequate union. Of course we do not definitely seek out and discover such qualities ; instinct works far more intuitively than that ; but we find at last, by subsequent observation, how true and how trustworthy were its immediate indications. That is to say, those men do so who were wise enough or fortunate enough to follow the earliest promptings of their own hearts, and not to be ashamed of that divinest and deepest of human intuitions, love at first sight.

How very subtle this intuition is, we can only guess in part by the apparent capriciousness and incomprehensibility of its occasional action. We know that some men and women fall in love easily, while others are only moved to love by some very special and singular combination of peculiarities. We know that one man is readily stirred by every pretty face he sees, while another man can only be roused by intellectual qualities or by moral beauty. We know that sometimes we meet people possessing every virtue and grace under heaven, and yet for some unknown and incomprehensible reason we could no more fall in love with them than we could fall in love with the Ten Commandments. I don't, of course, for a moment accept the silly romantic notion that men and women fall in love only once in their lives, or that each one of us has somewhere on earth his or her exact affinity, whom we must sooner or later meet or else die unsatisfied. Almost every healthy normal man or woman has probably fallen in love over and over again in the course of a lifetime (except in case of very early marriage), and could easily find dozens of persons with whom they would be capable of falling in love again if due occasion offered. We are not all created in pairs, like the Exchequer tallies, exactly intended to fit into one another's minor idiosyncrasies. Men and women as a rule very sensibly fall in love with one another in the particular places and the particular

societies they happen to be cast among.   A man at Ashby-
de-la-Zouch does not hunt the world over to find his pre-
established harmony at Paray-le-Monial or at Denver,
Colorado.   But among the women he actually meets, a
vast number are purely indifferent to him ; only one or two,
here and there, strike him in the light of possible wives,
and only one in the last resort (outside Salt Lake City)
approves herself to his inmost nature as the actual wife of
his final selection.

Now this very indifference to the vast mass of our fellow-
countrymen or fellow-countrywomen, this extreme pitch
of selective preference in the human species, is just one
mark of our extraordinary specialisation, one stamp and
token of our high supremacy.   The brutes do not so pick
and choose, though even there, as Darwin has shown, selection plays a large part (for the very butterflies are coy, and
must be wooed and won).   It is only in the human race itself
that selection descends into such minute, such subtle, such
indefinable discriminations.   Why should a universal and
common impulse have in our case these special limits ?
Why should we be by nature so fastidious and so diversely
affected ?   Surely for some good and sufficient purpose.
No deep-seated want of our complex life would be so
narrowly restricted without a law and a meaning.   Sometimes we can in part explain its conditions.   Here, we see
that beauty plays a great *rôle* ; there, we recognise the
importance of strength, of manner, of grace, of moral
qualities.   Vivacity, as Mr. Galton justly remarks, is one
of the most powerful among human attractions, and often
accounts for what might otherwise seem unaccountable
preferences.   But after all is said and done, there remains
a vast mass of instinctive and inexplicable elements : a
power deeper and more marvellous in its inscrutable rami-
fications than human consciousness.   'What on earth,' we

say, ' could So-and-so see in So-and-so to fall in love with ? '
This very inexplicability I take to be the sign and seal of a
profound importance. An instinct so conditioned, so curious,
so vague, so unfathomable, as we may guess by analogy
with all other instincts, must be Nature's guiding voice
within us, speaking for the good of the human race in all
future generations.

On the other hand, let us suppose for a moment (impossible supposition !) that mankind could conceivably di-
vest itself of ' these foolish ideas about love and the tastes
of young people,' and could hand over the choice of partners
for life to a committee of anthropologists, presided over
by Sir George Campbell. Would the committee manage
things, I wonder, very much better than the Creator has
managed them ? Where would they obtain that intimate
knowledge of individual structures and functions and differences which would enable them to join together in holy
matrimony fitting and complementary idiosyncrasies ? Is
a living man, with all his organs, and powers, and faculties,
and dispositions, so simple and easy a problem to read that
anybody else can readily undertake to pick out off-hand a
help meet for him ? I trow not ! A man is not a horse
or a terrier. You cannot discern his ' points ' by simple
inspection. You cannot see *à priori* why a Hanoverian
bandsman and his heavy, ignorant, uncultured wife, should
conspire to produce a Sir William Herschel. If you tried
to improve the breed artificially, either by choice from
outside, or by the creation of an independent moral sentiment, irrespective of that instinctive preference which we
call Falling in Love, I believe that so far from improving
man, you would only do one of two things—either spoil his
constitution, or produce a tame stereotyped pattern of
amiable imbecility. You would crush out all initiative,
all spontaneity, all diversity, all originality ; you would

get an animated moral code instead of living men and
women.

Look at the analogy of domestic animals. That is the
analogy to which breeding reformers always point with
special pride : but what does it really teach us ? That you
can't improve the efficiency of animals in any one point to
any high degree, without upsetting the general balance of
their constitution. The race-horse can run a mile on a
particular day at a particular place, bar accidents, with
wonderful speed : but that is about all he is good for. His
health as a whole is so surprisingly feeble that he has to
be treated with as much care as a delicate exotic. ' In
regard to animals and plants,' says Sir George Campbell,
' we have very largely mastered the principles of heredity
and culture, and the modes by which good qualities may be
maximised, bad qualities minimised.' True, so far as concerns a few points prized by ourselves for our own purposes.
But in doing this, we have so lowered the general constitu-
tional vigour of the plants or animals that our vines fall an
easy prey to oidium and phylloxera, our potatoes to the
potato disease and the Colorado beetle ; our sheep are
stupid, our rabbits idiotic, our domestic breeds generally
threatened with dangers to life and limb unknown to their
wiry ancestors in the wild state. And when one comes to
deal with the infinitely more complex individuality of man,
what hope would there be of our improving the breed by
deliberate selection ? If we developed the intellect, we
would probably stunt the physique or the moral nature ; if
we aimed at a general culture of all faculties alike, we would
probably end by a Chinese uniformity of mediocre dead
level.

The balance of organs and faculties in a race is a very
delicate organic equilibrium. How delicate we now know
from thousands of examples, from the correlations of seem-

ingly unlike parts, from the wide-spread effects of small
conditions, from the utter dying out of races like the Tas-
manians or the Paraguay Indians under circumstances
different from those with which their ancestors were
familiar. What folly to interfere with a marvellous instinct
which now preserves this balance intact, in favour of an·
untried artificial system which would probably wreck it as
helplessly as the modern system of higher education for
women is wrecking the maternal powers of the best class
in our English community !

Indeed, within the race itself, as it now exists, free
choice, aided by natural selection, is actually improving
every good point, and is for ever weeding out all the occasional failures and shortcomings of nature. For weakly
children, feeble children, stupid children, heavy children,
are undoubtedly born under this very régime of falling in
love, whose average results I believe to be so highly bene-
ficial. How is this ? Well, one has to take into consideration two points in seeking for the solution of that obvious
problem.

In the first place, no instinct is absolutely perfect. All
of them necessarily fail at some points. If on the average
they do good, they are sufficiently justified. Now the
material with which you have to start in this case is not
perfect. Each man marries, even in favourable circum-·
stances, not the abstractly best adapted woman in the
world to supplement or counteract his individual peculiarities, but the best woman then and there obtainable for
him. The result is frequently far from perfect ; all I claim
is that it would be as bad or a good deal worse if somebody
else made the choice for him, or if he made the choice himself on abstract biological and ' eugenic ' principles. And,
indeed, the very existence of better and worse in the world
is a condition precedent of all upward evolution. Without

an overstocked world, with individual variations, some pro-
gressive, some retrograde, there could be no natural selection, no survival of the fittest.   That is the chief besetting
danger of cut-and-dried doctrinaire views.   Malthus was a
very great man ; but if his principle of prudential restraint
were fully carried out, the prudent would cease to reproduce
their like, and the world would be peopled in a few generations by the hereditarily reckless and dissolute and impru-
dent.   Even so, if eugenic principles were universally
adopted, the chance of exceptional and elevated natures
would be largely reduced, and natural selection would be
in so much interfered with or sensibly retarded.

In the second place, again, it must not be forgotten
that falling in love has never yet, among civilised men at
least, had a fair field and no favour.   Many marriages are
arranged on very different grounds—grounds of convenience,
grounds of cupidity, grounds of religion, grounds of snobbish-
ness.   In many cases it is clearly demonstrable that such
marriages are productive in the highest degree of evil con-
sequences.   Take the case of heiresses.   An heiress is
almost by necessity the one last feeble and flickering relic
of a moribund stock—often of a stock reduced by the sordid
pursuit of ill-gotten wealth almost to the very verge of
actual insanity.   But let her be ever so ugly, ever so unhealthy, ever so hysterical, ever so mad, somebody or other
will be ready and eager to marry her on any terms.   Considerations of this sort have helped to stock the world with
many feeble and unhealthy persons.   Among the middle
and upper classes it may be safely said only a very small
percentage of marriages is ever due to love alone ; in other
words, to instinctive feeling.   The remainder have been influenced by various side advantages, and nature has taken her
vengeance accordingly on the unhappy offspring.   Parents
and moralists are ever ready to drown her voice, and to

counsel marriage within one's own class, among nice people, with a really religious girl, and so forth *ad infinitum*. By many well-meaning young people these deadly interferences with natural impulse are accepted as part of a higher and nobler law of conduct. The wretched belief that one should subordinate the promptings of one's own soul to the dictates of a miscalculating and misdirecting prudence has been instilled into the minds of girls especially, until at last many of them have almost come to look upon their natural instincts as wrong, and the immoral, race-destructive counsels of their seniors or advisers as the truest and purest earthly wisdom. Among certain small religious sects, again, such as the Quakers, the duty of ' marrying in ' has been strenuously inculcated, and only the stronger-minded and more individualistic members have had courage and initiative enough to disregard precedent, and to follow the internal divine monitor, as against the externally-imposed law of their particular community. Even among wider bodies it is commonly held that Catholics must not marry Protestants.; and the admirable results obtained by the mixture of Jewish with European blood have almost all been reached by male Jews having the temerity to marry ' Christian ' women in the face of opposition and persecution from their co-nationalists. It is very rarely indeed that a Jewess will accept a European for a husband. In so many ways, and on so many grounds, does convention interfere with the plain and evident dictates of nature.

Against all such evil parental promptings, however, a great safeguard is afforded to society by the wholesome and essentially philosophical teaching of romance and poetry. I do not approve of novels. They are for the most part a futile and unprofitable form of literature ; and it may profoundly be regretted that the mere blind laws of supply and demand should have diverted such an immense number of the ablest minds in England, France, and America, from more serious subjects to the production of such very frivolous and, on the whole, ephemeral works of art. But the novel has this one great counterpoise of undoubted good to set against all the manifold disadvantages and short-comings of romantic literature—that it always appeals to the true internal promptings of inherited instinct, and opposes the foolish and selfish suggestions of interested outsiders. It is the perpetual protest of poor banished human nature against the expelling pitchfork of calculating expediency in the matrimonial market. While parents and moralists are for ever saying, ' Don't marry for beauty; don't marry for inclination ; don't marry for love : marry for money, marry for social position, marry for advancement, marry for our convenience, not for your own,' the romance-writer is for ever urging, on the other hand, ' Marry for love, and for love only.' His great theme in all ages has been the opposition between parental or other external wishes and the true promptings of the young and unsophisticated human heart. He has been the chief ally of sentiment and of nature. He has filled the heads of all our girls with what Sir George Campbell describes off-hand as ' foolish ideas about love.' He has preserved us from the hateful conventions of civilisation. He has exalted the claims of personal attraction, of the mysterious native yearning of heart for heart, of the indefinite and inde-scribable element of mutual selection ; and, in so doing, he has unconsciously proved himself the best friend of human improvement and the deadliest enemy of all those hideous ' social lies which warp us from the living truth.' His mission is to deliver the world from Dr. Johnson and Sir George Campbell.

For, strange to say, it is the moralists and the doc-trinaires who are always in the wrong : it is the sentimentalists and the rebels who are always in the right in this matter. If the common moral maxims of society could have had their way—if we had all chosen our wives and our husbands, not for their beauty or their manliness, not for their eyes or their moustaches, not for their attractiveness or their vivacity, but for their 'sterling qualities of mind and character,' we should now doubtless be a miserable race of prigs and bookworms, of martinets and puritans, of nervous invalids and feeble idiots. It is because our young men and maidens will not hearken to these penny-wise apophthegms of shallow sophistry—because they often prefer *Romeo and Juliet* to the 'Whole Duty of Man,' and a beautiful face to a round balance at Coutts's—that we still preserve some vitality and some individual features, in spite of our grinding and crushing civilisation. The men who marry balances, as Mr. Galton has shown, happily die out, leaving none to represent them : the men who marry women they have been weak enough and silly enough to fall in love with, recruit the race with fine and vigorous and intelligent children, fortunately compounded of the complementary traits derived from two fairly contrasted and mutually reinforcing individualities.

I have spoken throughout, for argument's sake, as though the only interest to be considered in the married relation were the interests of the offspring, and so ultimately of the race at large, rather than of the persons themselves who enter into it. But I do not quite see why each generation should thus be sacrificed to the welfare of the generations that afterwards succeed it. Now it is one of the strongest points in favour of the system of falling in love that it does, by common experience in the vast majority of instances, assort together persons who subsequently prove themselves thoroughly congenial and helpful to one another. And this result I look upon as one great proof of the real value and importance of the instinct. Most men and women select for themselves partners for life at an age when they know but little of the world, when they judge but superficially of characters and motives, when they still make many mistakes in the conduct of life and in the estimation of chances. Yet most of them find in after days that they have really chosen out of all the world one of the persons best adapted by native idiosyncrasy to make their joint lives enjoyable and useful. I make every allowance for the effects of habit, for the growth of sentiment, for the gradual approximation of tastes and sympathies; but surely, even so, it is a common consciousness with every one of us who has been long married, that we could hardly conceivably have made ourselves happy with any of the partners whom others have chosen; and that we have actually made ourselves so with the partners we chose for ourselves under the guidance of an almost unerring native instinct. Yet adaptation between husband and wife, so far as their own happiness is concerned, can have had comparatively little to do with the evolution of the instinct, as compared with adaptation for the joint production of vigorous and successful offspring. Natural selection lays almost all the stress on the last point, and hardly any at all upon the first one. If, then, the instinct is found on the whole so trustworthy in the minor matter, for which it has not specially been fashioned, how far more trustworthy and valuable must it probably prove in the greater matter—greater, I mean, as regards the interests of the race—for which it has been mainly or almost solely developed!

I do not doubt that, as the world goes on, a deeper sense of moral responsibility in the matter of marriage will grow up among us. But it will not take the false direction of ignoring these our profoundest and holiest instincts. Marriage for money may go; marriage for rank may go; marriage for position may go; but marriage for love, I believe and trust, will last for ever. Men in the future will probably feel that a union with their cousins or near relations is positively wicked; that a union with those too like them in person or disposition is at least undesirable; that a union based upon considerations of wealth or any other consideration save considerations of immediate natural impulse, is base and disgraceful. But to the end of time they will continue to feel, in spite of doctrinaires, that the voice of nature is better far than the voice of the Lord Chancellor or the Royal Society; and that the instinctive desire for a particular helpmate is a surer guide for the ultimate happiness, both of the race and of the individual, than any amount of deliberate consultation. It is not the foolish fancies of youth that will have to be got rid of, but the foolish, wicked, and mischievous interference of parents or outsiders.

RIGHT AND LEFT

ADULT man is the only animal who, in the familiar scriptural phrase, ' knoweth the right hand from the left.' This fact in his economy goes closely together with the other facts, that he is the only animal on this sublunary planet who habitually uses a knife and fork, articulate language, the art of cookery, the common pump, and the musical glasses. His right-handedness, in short, is part cause and part effect of his universal supremacy in animated nature. He is what he is, to a great extent, ' by his own right hand ; ' and his own right hand, we may shrewdly suspect, would never have differed at all from his left were it not for the manifold arts and trades and activities he practises.

It was not always so, when wild in woods the noble savage ran. Man was once, in his childhood on earth, what Charles Reade wanted him again to be in his maturer centuries, ambidextrous. And lest any lady readers of this volume— in the Cape of Good Hope, for example, or the remoter portions of the Australian bush, whither the culture of Girton and the familiar knowledge of the Latin language have not yet penetrated—should complain that I speak with unknown tongues, I will further explain for their special benefit that ambidextrous means equally-handed, using the right and the left indiscriminately. This, as Mr. Andrew Lang remarks in immortal verse, 'was the manner of Primitive Man.' He never minded twopence which hand he used, as long as he got the fruit or the scalp he wanted. How could he when twopence wasn't yet invented ? His mamma never said to him in early youth, ' Why-why,' or ' Tom-tom,' as the case might be, ' that's the wrong hand to hold your flint-scraper in.' He grew up to man's estate in happy ignorance of such minute and invidious distinctions between his anterior extremities. Enough for him that his hands could grasp the forest boughs or chip the stone into shapely arrows ; and he never even thought in his innocent soul which particular hand he did it with.

How can I make this confident assertion, you ask, about a gentleman whom I never personally saw, and whose habits the intervention of five hundred centuries has pre-cluded me from studying at close quarters ? At first sight, you would suppose the evidence on such a point must be purely negative. The reconstructive historian must surely be inventing *à priori* facts, evolved, *more Germanico*, from his inner consciousness. Not so. See how clever modern archæology has become ! I base my assertion upon solid evidence. I know that Primitive Man was ambidextrous, because he wrote and painted just as often with his left as with his right, and just as successfully.

This seems once more a hazardous statement to make about a remote ancestor, in the age before the great glacial epoch had furrowed the mountains of Northern Europe ; but, nevertheless, it is strictly true and strictly demon-strable. Just try, as you read, to draw with the forefinger and thumb of your right hand an imaginary human profile on the page on which these words are printed. Do you observe that (unless you are an artist, and therefore sophisticated) you naturally and instinctively draw it with the face turned towards your left shoulder ? Try now to draw it with the profile to the right, and you will find it requires a far greater effort of the thumb and fingers. The hand moves of its own accord from without inward, not from within outward. Then, again, draw with your left thumb and forefinger another imaginary profile, and you will find, for the same reason, that the face in this case looks rightward. Existing savages, and our own young children, whenever they draw a figure in profile, be it of man or beast, with their right hand, draw it almost always with the face or head turned to the left, in accordance with this natural human instinct. Their doing so is a test of their perfect right-handedness.

But Primitive Man, or at any rate the most primitive men we know personally, the carvers of the figures from the French bone-caves, drew men and beasts, on bone or mammoth-tusk, turned either way indiscriminately. The inference is obvious. They must have been ambidextrous. Only ambidextrous people draw so at the present day; and indeed to scrape a figure otherwise with a sharp flint on a piece of bone or tooth or mammoth-tusk would, even for a practised hand, be comparatively difficult.

I have begun my consideration of rights and lefts with this one very clear historical datum, because it is interesting to be able to say with tolerable certainty that there really was a period in our life as a species when man in the lump was ambidextrous. Why and how did he become otherwise? This question is not only of importance in itself, as helping to explain the origin and source of man's supremacy in nature—his tool-using faculty—but it is also of interest from the light it casts on that fallacy of poor Charles Reade's already alluded to—that we ought all of us in this respect to hark back to the condition of savages. I think when we have seen the reasons which make civilised man now right-handed, we shall also see why it would be highly undesirable for him to return, after so many ages of practice, to the condition of his undeveloped stone-age ancestors.

The very beginning of our modern right-handedness goes back, indeed, to the most primitive savagery. Why did one hand ever come to be different in use and function from another? The answer is, because man, in spite of all appearances to the contrary, is really one-sided. Externally, indeed, his congenital one-sidedness doesn't show: but it shows internally. We all of us know, in spite of Sganarelle's assertion to the contrary, that the apex of the heart inclines to the left side, and that the liver and other internal organs show a generous disregard for strict and formal symmetry. In this irregular distribution of those human organs which polite society agrees to ignore, we get the clue to the irregularity of right and left in the human arm, and finally even the particular direction of the printed letters now before you.

For primitive man did not belong to polite society. His manners were strikingly deficient in that repose which stamps the caste of Vere de Vere. When primitive man felt the tender passion steal over his soul, he lay in wait in the bush for the Phyllis or Daphne whose charms had inspired his heart with young desire; and when she passed his hiding-place, in maiden meditation, fancy free, he felled her with a club, caught her tight by the hair of her head, and dragged her off in triumph to his cave or his rock-shelter. (Marriage by capture, the learned call this simple mode of primeval courtship.) When he found some Strephon or Damœtas rival him in the affections of the dusky sex, he and that rival fought the matter out like two bulls in a field; and the victor and his Phyllis supped that evening off the roasted remains of the vanquished suitor. I don't say these habits and manners were pretty; but they were the custom of the time, and there's no good denying them.

Now, Primitive Man, being thus by nature a fighting animal, fought for the most part at first with his great canine teeth, his nails, and his fists ; till in process of time he added to these early and natural weapons the further persuasions of a club or shillelagh. He also fought, as Darwin has very conclusively shown, in the main for the possession of the ladies of his kind, against other members of his own sex and species. And if you fight, you soon learn to protect the most exposed and vulnerable portion of your body ; or, if you don't, natural selection manages it for you, by killing you off as an immediate consequence. To the boxer, wrestler, or hand-to-hand combatant, that most vulnerable portion is undoubtedly the heart. A hard blow, well delivered on the left breast, will easily kill, or at any rate stun, even a very strong man. Hence, from a very early period, men have used the right hand to fight with, and have employed the left arm chiefly to cover the heart and to parry a blow aimed at that specially vulnerable region. And when weapons of offence and defence supersede mere fists and teeth, it is the right hand that grasps the spear or sword, while the left holds over the heart for defence the shield or buckler.

From this simple origin, then, the whole vast difference of right and left in civilised life takes its beginning. At first, no doubt, the superiority of the right hand was only felt in the matter of fighting. But that alone gave it a distinct pull, and paved the way, at last, for its supremacy elsewhere. For when weapons came into use, the habitual employment of the right hand to grasp the spear, sword, or knife made the nerves and muscles of the right side far more obedient to the control of the will than those of the left. The dexterity thus acquired by the right—see how the very word ' dexterity ' implies this fact—made it more natural for the early hunter and artificer to employ the same hand preferentially in the manufacture of flint hatchets, bows and arrows, and in all the other manifold activities of savage life. It was the hand with which he grasped his weapon ; it was therefore the hand with which he chipped it. To the very end, however, the right hand remains especially ' the hand in which you hold your knife ; ' and that is exactly how our own children to this day decide the question which is which, when they begin to know their right hand from their left for practical purposes.

A difference like this, once set up, implies thereafter innumerable other differences which naturally flow from it. Some of them are extremely remote and derivative. Take, for example, the case of writing and printing. Why do these run from left to right ? At first sight such a practice seems clearly contrary to the instinctive tendency I noticed above—the tendency to draw from right to left, in accordance with the natural sweep of the hand and arm. And, indeed, it is a fact that all early writing habitually took the opposite direction from that which is now universal in western countries. Every schoolboy knows, for instance (or at least he would if he came up to the proper Macaulay standard), that Hebrew is written from right to left, and that each book begins at the wrong cover. The reason is that words, and letters, and hieroglyphics were originally carved, scratched, or incised, instead of being written with coloured ink, and the hand was thus allowed to follow its natural bent, and to proceed, as we all do in naïve drawing, with a free curve from the right leftward.

Nevertheless, the very same fact—that we use the right hand alone in writing—made the letters run the opposite way in the end ; and the change was due to the use of ink and other pigments for staining papyrus, parchment, or paper. If the hand in, this case moved from right to left it would of course smear what it had already written; and to prevent such untidy smudging of the words, the order of writing was reversed from left rightward. The use of wax tablets also, no doubt, helped forward the revolution, for in this case, too, the hand would cover and rub out the words written.

The strict dependence of writing, indeed, upon the material employed is nowhere better shown than in the case of the Assyrian cuneiform inscriptions. The ordinary substitute for cream-laid note in the Euphrates valley in its palmy days was a clay or terra-cotta tablet, on which the words to be recorded—usually a deed of sale or something of the sort—were impressed while it was wet and then baked in, solid. And the method of impressing them was very simple; the workman merely pressed the end of his graver or wedge into the moist clay, thus giving rise to triangular marks which were arranged in the shapes of various letters. When alabaster, or any other hard material, was substituted for clay, the sculptor imitated these natural dabs or triangular imprints; and that was the origin of those mysterious and very learned-looking cuneiforms. This, I admit, is a palpable digression; but inasmuch as it throws an indirect light on the simple reasons which sometimes bring about great results, I hold it not wholly alien to the present serious philosophical inquiry.

Printing, in turn, necessarily follows the rule of writing, so that in fact the order of letters and words on this page depends ultimately upon the remote fact that primitive man had to use his right hand to deliver a blow, and his left to parry, or to guard his heart.

Some curious and hardly noticeable results flow once more from this order of writing from left to right. You will find, if you watch yourself closely, that in examining a landscape, or the view from a hill-top, your eye naturally ranges from left to right ; and that you begin your survey, as you would begin reading a page of print, from the left-hand corner. Apparently, the now almost instinctive act of reading (for Dogberry was right after all, for the civilised infant) has accustomed our eyes to this particular movement, and has made it especially natural when we are trying to 'read' or take in at a glance the meaning of any complex and varied total.

In the matter of pictures, I notice, the correlation has even gone a step farther. Not only do we usually take in the episodes of a painting from left to right, but the painter definitely and deliberately intends us so to take them in. For wherever two or three distinct episodes in succession are represented on a single plane in the same picture—as happens often in early art—they are invariably represented in the precise order of the words on a written or printed page, beginning at the upper left-hand corner, and ending at the lower right-hand angle. I first noticed this curious extension of the common principle in the mediæval frescoes of the Campo Santo at Pisa ; and I have since verified it by observations on many other pictures elsewhere, both ancient and modern. The Campo Santo, however, forms an exceptionally good museum of such story-telling frescoes by various painters, as almost every picture consists of several successive episodes. The famous Benozzo Gozzoli, for example, of Noah's Vineyard represents on a single plane all the stages in that earliest drama of intoxication, from the first act of gathering the grapes on the top left, to the scandalised lady, the *vergognosa di Pisa*, who covers her face with her hands in shocked horror at the patriarch's disgrace in the lower right-hand corner.

Observe, too, that the very conditions of *technique* demand this order almost as rigorously in painting as in writing. For the painter will naturally so work as not to smudge over what he has already painted : and he will also naturally begin with the earliest episode in the story he unfolds, proceeding to the others in due succession. From which two principles it necessarily results that he will begin at the upper left, and end at the lower right-hand corner.

I have skipped lightly, I admit, over a considerable interval between primitive man and Benozzo Gozzoli. But consider further that during all that time the uses of the right and left hand were becoming by gradual degrees each day still further differentiated and specialised. Innumerable trades, occupations, and habits imply ever-widening differences in the way we use them. It is not the right hand alone that has undergone an education in this respect : the left, too, though subordinate, has still its own special functions to perform. If the savage chips his flints with a blow of the right, he holds the core, or main mass of stone from which he strikes it, firmly with his left. If one hand is specially devoted to the knife, the other grasps the fork to make up for it. In almost every act we do with both hands, each has a separate office to which it is best fitted. Take, for example, so simple a matter as buttoning one's coat, where a curious distinction between the habits of the sexes enables us to test the principle with ease and certainty. Men's clothes are always made with the buttons on the right side and the button-holes on the left. Women's, on the contrary, are always made with the buttons on the left side, and the button-holes on the right. (The occult reason for this curious distinction, which has long engaged the attention of philosophers, has never yet been discovered, but it is probably to be accounted for by the perversity of women.) Well, if a man tries to put on a woman's waterproof, or a woman to put on a man's ulster, each will find that neither hand is readily able to perform the part of the other. A man, in buttoning, grasps the button in his right hand, pushes it through with his right thumb, holds the button-hole open with his left, and pulls all straight with his right fore-finger. Reverse the sides, and both hands at once seem equally helpless.

It is curious to note how many little peculiarities of dress or manufacture are equally necessitated by this prime distinction of right and left. Here are a very few of them, which the reader can indefinitely increase for himself. (I leave out of consideration obvious cases like boots and gloves : to insult that proverbially intelligent person's intelligence with those were surely unpardonable.) A scarf habitually tied in a sailor's knot acquires one long side, left, and one short one, right, from the way it is manipulated by the right hand ; if it were tied by the left, the relations would be reversed. The spiral of corkscrews and of ordinary screws turned by hand goes in accordance with the natural twist of the right hand : try to drive in an imaginary corkscrew with the right hand, the opposite way, and you will see how utterly awkward and clumsy is the motion. The strap of the flap that covers the keyhole in trunks and portmanteaus always has its fixed side over to the right, and its buckle to the left ; in this way only can it be conveniently buckled by a right-handed person. The hands of watches and the numbers of dial-faced barometers run from left to right : this is a peculiarity dependent upon the left to right system of writing. A servant offers you dishes from the left side : you can't so readily help yourself from the right, unless left-handed. Schopenhauer despaired of the German race, because it could never be taught like the English to keep to the right side of the pavement in walking. A sword is worn at the left hip : a handkerchief is carried in the right pocket, if at the side ; in the left, if in the coat-tails : in either case for the right hand to get at it most easily. A watch-pocket is made in the left breast ; a pocket for railway tickets halfway down the right side. Try to reverse any one of these simple actions, and you will see at once that they are immediately implied in the very fact of our original right-handedness.

And herein, I think, we find the true answer to Charles Reade's mistaken notion of the advantages of ambidexterity. You couldn't make both hands do everything alike without a considerable loss of time, effort, efficiency, and convenience. Each hand learns to do its own work and to do it well ; if you made it do the other hand's into the bargain, it would have a great deal more to learn, and we should find it difficult even then to prevent specialisation. We should have to make things deliberately different for the two hands —to have rights and lefts in everything, as we have them now in boots and gloves—or else one hand must inevitably gain the supremacy. Sword-handles, shears, surgical instruments, and hundreds of other things have to be made right-handed, while palettes and a few like subsidiary objects are adapted to the left ; in each case for a perfectly sufficient reason. You can't upset all this without causing confusion. More than that, the division of labour thus brought about is certainly a gain to those who possess it : for if it were not so, the ambidextrous races would have beaten the dextro-sinistrals in the struggle for existence ; whereas we know that the exact opposite has been the case. Man's special use of the right hand is one of his points of superiority to the brutes. If ever his right hand should forget its cunning, his supremacy would indeed begin to totter. Depend upon it, Nature is wiser than even Charles Reade. What she finds most useful in the long run must certainly have many good points to recommend it.

And this last consideration suggests another aspect of right and left which must not be passed over without one word in this brief survey of the philosophy of the subject. The superiority of the right caused it early to be regarded as the fortunate, lucky, and trusty hand; the inferiority of the left caused it equally to be considered as ill-omened, unlucky, and, in one expressive word, sinister. Hence come innumerable phrases and superstitions. It is the right hand of friendship that we always grasp; it is with our own right hand that we vindicate our honour against sinister suspicions. On the other hand, it is 'over the left' that we believe a doubtful or incredible statement; a left-handed compliment or a left-handed marriage carry their own condemnation with them. On the right hand of the host is the seat of honour; it is to the left that the goats of ecclesiastical controversy are invariably relegated. The very notions of the right hand and ethical right have got mixed up inextricably in every language: *droit* and *la droite* display it in French as much as right and the right in English. But to be *gauche* is merely to be awkward and clumsy; while to be right is something far higher and more important.

So unlucky, indeed, does the left hand at last become that merely to mention it is an evil omen; and so the Greeks refused to use the true old Greek word for left at all, and preferred euphemistically to describe it as *euonymos*, the well-named or happy-omened. Our own *left* seems equally to mean the hand that is left after the right has been mentioned, or, in short, the other one. Many things which are lucky if seen on the right are fateful omens if seen to leftward. On the other hand, if you spill the salt, you propitiate destiny by tossing a pinch of it over the left shoulder. A murderer's left hand is said by good authorities to be an excellent thing to do magic with; but here I cannot speak from personal experience. Nor do I know why the wedding-ring is worn on the left hand; though it is significant, at any rate, that the mark of slavery should be put by the man with his own right upon the inferior member of the weaker vessel. Strong-minded ladies may get up an agitation if they like to alter this gross injustice of the centuries.

One curious minor application of rights and lefts is the rule of the road as it exists in England. How it arose I can't say, any more than I can say why a lady sits her side-saddle to the left. Coachmen, to be sure, are quite unanimous that the leftward route enables them to see how close they are passing to another carriage; but, as all continental authority is equally convinced the other way, I make no doubt this is a mere illusion of long-continued custom. It is curious, however, that the English usage, having once obtained in these islands, has influenced railways, not only in Britain, but over all Europe. Trains, like carriages, go to the left when they pass; and this habit, quite natural in England, was transplanted by the early engineers to the Continent, where ordinary carriages, of course, go to the right. In America, to be sure, the trains also go right like the carriages; but then, those Americans have such a curiously un-English way of being strictly consistent and logical in their doings. In Britain we should have compromised the matter by going sometimes one way and sometimes the other.

EVOLUTION

EVERYBODY nowadays talks about evolution. Like electricity, the cholera germ, woman's rights, the great mining boom, and the Eastern Question, it is 'in the air.' It pervades society everywhere with its subtle essence; it infects small-talk with its familiar catchwords and its slang phrases; it even permeates that last stronghold of rampant Philistinism, the third leader in the penny papers. Everybody believes he knows all about it, and discusses it as glibly in his everyday conversation as he discusses the points of race-horses he has never seen, the charms of peeresses he has never spoken to, and the demerits of authors he has never read. Everybody is aware, in a dim and nebulous semi-conscious fashion, that it was all invented by the late Mr. Darwin, and reduced to a system by Mr. Herbert Spencer—don't you know?—and a lot more of those scientific fellows. It is generally understood in the best-informed circles that evolutionism consists for the most part in a belief about nature at large essentially similar to that applied by Topsy to her own origin and early history. It is conceived, in short, that most things 'growed.' Especially is it known that in the opinion of the evolutionists as a body we are all of us ultimately descended from men with tails, who were the final offspring and improved edition of the common gorilla. That, very briefly put, is the popular conception of the various points in the great modern evolutionary programme.

It is scarcely necessary to inform the intelligent reader, who of course differs fundamentally from that inferior class of human beings known to all of us in our own minds as ' other people,' that almost every point in the catalogue thus briefly enumerated is a popular fallacy of the wildest description. Mr. Darwin did not invent evolution any more than George Stephenson invented the steam-engine, or Mr. Edison the electric telegraph. We are not descended from men with tails, any more than we are descended from Indian elephants. There is no evidence that we have anything in particular more than the remotest fiftieth cousinship with our poor relation the West African gorilla. Science is not in search of a ' missing link '; few links are anywhere missing, and those are for the most part wholly unimportant ones. If we found the imaginary link in question, he would not be a monkey, nor yet in any way a tailed man. And so forth generally through the whole list of popular beliefs and current fallacies as to the real meaning of evolutionary teaching. Whatever most people think evolutionary is for the most part a pure parody of the evolutionist's opinion.

But a more serious error than all these pervades what we may call the drawing-room view of the evolutionist theory. So far as Society with a big initial is concerned, evolutionism first began to be talked about, and therefore known (for Society does not read ; it listens, or rather it overhears and catches fragmentary echoes) when Darwin published his ' Origin of Species.' That great book consisted simply of a theory as to the causes which led to the distinctions of kind between plants and animals. With evolution at large it had nothing to do ; it took for granted the origin of sun, moon, and stars, planets and comets, the earth and all that in it is, the sea and the dry land, the mountains and the valleys, nay even life itself in the crude form, everything in fact, save the one point of the various types and species of living beings. Long before Darwin's book appeared evolution had been a recognised force in the moving world of science and philosophy. Kant and Laplace had worked out the development of suns and earths from white-hot star-clouds. Lyell had worked out the evolution of the earth's surface to its present highly complex geographical condition. Lamarck had worked out the descent of plants and animals from a common ancestor by slow modification. Herbert Spencer had worked out the growth of mind from its simplest beginnings to its highest outcome in human thought.

But Society, like Gallio, cared nothing for all these things. The evolutionary principles had never been put into a single big book, asked for at Mudie's, and permitted to lie on the drawing-room table side by side with the last new novel and the last fat volume of scandalous court memoirs. Therefore Society ignored them and knew them not ; the word evolution scarcely entered at all as yet into its polite and refined dinner-table vocabulary. It recognised only the ' Darwinian theory,' ' natural selection,' ' the missing link,' and the belief that men were merely monkeys who had lost their tails, presumably by sitting upon them. To the world at large that learned Mr. Darwin had invented and patented the entire business, including descent with modification, if such notions ever occurred at all to the world-at-large's speculative intelligence.

Now, evolutionism is really a thing of far deeper growth and older antecedents than this easy, superficial drawing-room view would lead us to imagine. It is a very ancient and respectable theory indeed, and it has an immense variety of minor developments. I am not going to push it back, in the fashionable modern scientific manner, to the vague and indefinite hints in our old friend Lucretius. The great original Roman poet—the only original poet in the

D

Latin language—did indeed hit out for himself a very good rough working sketch of a sort of nebulous and shapeless evolutionism. It was bold, it was consistent, for its time it was wonderful. But Lucretius's philosophy, like all the philosophies of the older world, was a mere speculative idea, a fancy picture of the development of things, not dependent upon observation of facts at all, but wholly evolved, like the German thinker's camel, out of its author's own pregnant inner consciousness. The Roman poet would no doubt have built an excellent superstructure if he had only possessed a little straw to make his bricks of. As it was, however, scientific brick-making being still in its infancy, he could only construct in a day a shadowy Aladdin's palace of pure fanciful Epicurean phantasms, an imaginary world of imaginary atoms, fortuitously concurring out of void chaos into an orderly universe, as though by miracle. It is not thus that systems arise which regenerate the thought of humanity ; he who would build for all time must make sure first of a solid foundation, and then use sound bricks in place of the airy nothings of metaphysical speculation.

It was in the last century that the evolutionary idea really began to take form and shape in the separate conceptions of Kant, Laplace, Lamarck, and Erasmus Darwin. These were the true founders of our modern evolutionism. Charles Darwin and Herbert Spencer were the Joshuas who led the chosen people into the land which more than one venturous Moses had already dimly descried afar off from the Pisgah top of the eighteenth century.

Kant and Laplace came first in time, as astronomy comes first in logical order. Stars and suns, and planets and satellites, necessarily precede in development plants and animals. You can have no cabbages without a world to grow them in. The science of the stars was therefore reduced to comparative system and order, while the sciences

of life, and mind, and matter were still a hopeless and inextricable muddle. It was no wonder, then, that the evolution
of the heavenly bodies should have been clearly apprehended
and definitely formulated while the evolution of the earth's
crust was still imperfectly understood, and the evolution of
living beings was only tentatively and hypothetically hinted
at in a timid whisper.

In the beginning, say the astronomical evolutionists,
not only this world, but all the other worlds in the universe,
existed potentially, as the poet justly remarks, in ' a haze of
fluid light,' a vast nebula of enormous extent and almost
inconceivable material thinness. The world arose out of a
sort of primitive world-gruel. The matter of which it was
composed was gas, of such an extraordinary and unimaginable gasiness that millions of cubic miles of it might easily
be compressed into a common antibilious pill-box. The
pill-box itself, in fact, is the net result of a prolonged
secular condensation of myriads of such enormous cubes of
this primæval matter. Slowly setting around common
centres, however, in anticipation of Sir Isaac Newton's
gravitative theories, the fluid haze gradually collected into
suns and stars, whose light and heat is presumably due to
the clashing together of their component atoms as they fall
perpetually towards the central mass. Just as in a burning
candle the impact of the oxygen atoms in the air against
the carbon and hydrogen atoms in the melted and rarefied
wax or tallow produces the light and heat of the flame, so
in nebula or sun the impact of the various gravitating atoms
one against the other produces the light and heat by whose
aid we are enabled to see and know those distant bodies.
The universe, according to this now fashionable nebular
theory, began as a single vast ocean of matter of immense
tenuity, spread all alike over all space as far as nowhere,
and comparatively little different within itself when looked

at side by side with its own final historical outcome. In Mr. Spencer's perspicuous phrase, evolution in this aspect is a change from the homogeneous to the heterogeneous, from the incoherent to the coherent, and from the indefinite to the definite condition. Difficult words at first to apprehend, no doubt, and therefore to many people, as to Mr. Matthew Arnold, very repellent, but full of meaning, lucidity, and suggestiveness, if only we once take the trouble fairly and squarely to understand them.

Every sun and every star thus formed is for ever gathering in the hem of its outer robe upon itself, for ever radiating off its light and heat into surrounding space, and for ever growing denser and colder as it sets slowly towards its centre of gravity. Our own sun and solar system may be taken as good typical working examples of how the stars thus constantly shrink into smaller and ever smaller dimensions around their own fixed centre. Naturally, we know more about our own solar system than about any other in our own universe, and it also possesses for us a greater practical and personal interest than any outside portion of the galaxy. Nobody can pretend to be profoundly immersed in the internal affairs of Sirius or of Alpha Centauri. A fiery revolution in the belt of Orion would affect us less than a passing finger-ache in a certain single terrestrial baby of our own household. Therefore I shall not apologise in any way for leaving the remainder of the sidereal universe to its unknown fate, and concentrating my attention mainly on the affairs of that solitary little, out-of-the-way, second-rate system, whereof we form an inappreciable portion. The matter which now composes the sun and its attendant bodies (the satellites included) was once spread out, according to Laplace, to at least the furthest orbit of the outermost planet—that is to say, so far as our present knowledge goes, the planet Neptune. Of course, when it was expanded to that immense distance, it must have been very thin indeed, thinner than our clumsy human senses can even conceive of. An American would say, too thin; but I put Americans out of court at once as mere irreverent scoffers. From the orbit of Neptune, or something outside it, the faint and cloud-like mass which bore within it Cæsar and his fortunes, not to mention the remainder of the earth and the solar system, began slowly to converge and gather itself in, growing denser and denser but smaller and smaller as it gradually neared its existing dimensions. How long a time it took to do it is for our present purpose relatively unimportant : the cruel physicists will only let us have a beggarly hundred million years or so for the process, while the grasping and extravagant evolutionary geologists beg with tears for at least double or even ten times that limited period. But at any rate it has taken a good long while, and, as far as most of us are personally concerned, the difference of one or two hundred millions, if it comes to that, is not really at all an appreci-able one.

As it condensed and lessened towards its central core, revolving rapidly on its great axis, the solar mist left behind at irregular intervals concentric rings or belts of cloud-like matter, cast off from its equator; which belts, once more undergoing a similar evolution on their own account, have hardened round their private centres of gravity into Jupiter or Saturn, the Earth or Venus. Round these again, minor belts or rings have sometimes formed, as in Saturn's girdle of petty satellites ; or subsidiary planets, thrown out into space, have circled round their own primaries, as the moon does around this sublunary world of ours. Meanwhile, the main central mass of all, retreating ever inward as it dropped behind it these occasional little reminders of its temporary stoppages, formed at last the sun itself, the

main luminary of our entire system. Now, I won't deny
that this primitive Kantian and Laplacian evolutionism,
this nebular theory of such exquisite concinnity, here
reduced to its simplest terms and most elementary
dimensions, has received many hard knocks from later
astronomers, and has been a good deal bowled over, both
on mathematical and astronomical grounds, by recent
investigators of nebulæ and meteors. Observations on
comets and on the sun's surface have lately shown that it
contains in all likelihood a very considerable fanciful
admixture. It isn't more than half true; and even the
half now totters in places. Still, as a vehicle of popular
exposition the crude nebular hypothesis in its rawest form
serves a great deal better than the truth, so far as yet
known, on the good old Greek principle of the half being
often more than the whole. The great point which it im-
presses on the mind is the cardinal idea of the sun and
planets, with their attendant satellites, not as turned out
like manufactured articles, ready made, at measured
intervals, in a vast and deliberate celestial Orrery, but as
due to the slow and gradual working of natural laws, in
accordance with which each has assumed by force of circumstances its existing place, weight, orbit, and motion.

The grand conception of a gradual becoming, instead
of a sudden making, which Kant and Laplace thus applied
to the component bodies of the universe at large, was
further applied by Lyell and his school to the outer crust
of this one particular petty planet of ours. While the
astronomers went in for the evolution of suns, stars, and
worlds, Lyell and his geological brethren went in for the
evolution of the earth's surface. As theirs was stellar, so
his was mundane. If the world began by being a red-hot
mass of planetary matter in a high state of internal excite-
ment, boiling and dancing with the heat of its emotions, it

gradually cooled down with age and experience, for growing old is growing cold, as every one of us in time, alas, discovers. As it passed from its fiery and volcanic youth to its staider and soberer middle age, a solid crust began to form in filmy fashion upon its cooling surface. The aqueous vapour that had floated at first as steam around its heated mass condensed with time into a wide ocean over the now hardened shell. Gradually this ocean shifted its bulk into two or three main bodies that sank into hollows of the viscid crust, the precursors of Atlantic, Pacific, and the Indian Seas. Wrinklings of the crust, produced by the cooling and consequent contraction, gave rise at first to baby mountain ranges, and afterwards to the earliest rough draughts of the still very vague and sketchy continents. The world grew daily more complex and more diverse; it progressed, in accordance with the Spencerian law, from the homogeneous to the heterogeneous, and so forth, as aforesaid, with delightful regularity.

At last, by long and graduated changes, seas and lands, peninsulas and islands, lakes and rivers, hills and mountains, were wrought out by internal or external energies on the crust thus generally fashioned. Evaporation from the oceans gave rise to clouds and rain and hailstorms; the water that fell upon the mountain tops cut out the valleys and river basins; rills gathered into brooks, brooks into streams, streams into primæval Niles, and Amazons, and Mississippis. Volcanic forces uplifted here an Alpine chain, or depressed there a deep-sea hollow. Sediment washed from the hills and plains, or formed from countless skeletons of marine creatures, gathered on the sinking bed of the ocean as soft ooze, or crumbling sand, or thick mud, or gravel and conglomerate. Now upheaved into an elevated table-land, now slowly carved again by rain and rill into valley and watershed, and now worn down once more into the mere degraded stump of a plateau, the crust underwent innumerable changes, but almost all of them exactly the same in kind, and mostly in degree, as those we still see at work imperceptibly in the world around us. Rain washing down the soil; weather crumbling the solid rock; waves dashing at the foot of the cliffs; rivers forming deltas at their barred mouths; shingle gathering on the low spits; floods sweeping before them the countryside; ice grinding ceaselessly at the mountain top; peat filling up the shallow lake—these are the chief factors which have gone to make the physical world as we now actually know it. Land and sea, coast and contour, hill and valley, dale and gorge, earth-sculpture generally—all are due to the ceaseless interaction of these separately small and unnoticeable causes, aided or retarded by the slow effects of elevation or depression from the earth's shrinkage towards its own centre. Geology, in short, has shown us that the world is what it is, not by virtue of a single sudden creative act, nor by virtue of successive terrible and recurrent cataclysms, but by virtue of the slow continuous action of causes still always equally operative.

Evolution in geology leads up naturally to evolution in the science of life. If the world itself grew, why not also the animals and plants that inhabit it? Already in the eager active eighteenth century this obvious idea had struck in the germ a large number of zoologists and botanists, and in the hands of Lamarck and Erasmus Darwin it took form as a distinct and elaborate system of organic evolution. Buffon had been the first to hint at the truth; but Buffon was an eminently respectable nobleman in the dubious days of the tottering monarchy, and he did not care personally for the Bastille, viewed as a place of permanent residence. In Louis Quinze's France, indeed, as things then went, a man who offended the orthodoxy of the Sorbonne was prone to find himself shortly ensconced in free quarters, and kept there for the term of his natural existence without expense to his heirs or executors. So Buffon did not venture to say outright that he thought all animals and plants were descended one from the other with slight modifications; that would have been wicked, and the Sorbonne would have proved its wickedness to him in a most conclusive fashion by promptly getting him imprisoned or silenced. It is so easy to confute your opponent when you are a hundred strong and he is one weak unit. Buffon merely said, therefore, that if we didn't know the contrary to be the case by sure warrant, we might easily have concluded (so fallible is our reason) that animals always varied slightly, and that such variations, indefinitely accumulated, would suffice to account for almost any amount of ultimate difference. A donkey might thus have grown into a horse, and a bird might have developed from a primitive lizard. Only we know it was quite otherwise! A quiet hint from Buffon was as good as a declaration from many less knowing or suggestive people. All over Europe, the wise took Buffon's hint for what he meant it; and the unwise blandly passed it by as a mere passing little foolish vagary of that great ironical writer and thinker.

Erasmus Darwin, the grandfather of his grandson, was no fool; on the contrary, he was the most far-sighted man of his day in England; he saw at once what Buffon was driving at; and he worked out ' Mr. Buffon's ' half-concealed hint to all its natural and legitimate conclusions. The great Count was always plain Mr. Buffon to his English contemporary. Life, said Erasmus Darwin nearly a century since, began in very minute marine forms, which gradually acquired fresh powers and larger bodies, so as imperceptibly to transform themselves into different creatures. Man, he remarked, anticipating his descendant, takes rabbits or pigeons, and alters them almost to his own fancy, by immensely changing their shapes and colours. If man can make a pouter or a fantail out of the common runt, if he can produce a piebald lop-ear from the brown wild rabbit, if he can transform Dorkings into Black Spanish, why cannot Nature, with longer time to work in, and endless lives to try with, produce all the varieties of vertebrate animals out of one single common ancestor ? It was a bold idea of the Lichfield doctor—bold, at least, for the times he lived in—when Sam Johnson was held a mighty sage, and physical speculation was regarded askance as having in it a dangerous touch of the devil. But the Darwins were always a bold folk, and had the courage of their opinions more than most men. So even in Lichfield, cathedral city as it was, and in the politely somnolent eighteenth century, Erasmus Darwin ventured to point out the probability that quadrupeds, birds, reptiles, and men were all mere divergent descendants of a single similar original form, and even that ' one and the same kind of living filament is, and has been, the cause of organic life.'

The eighteenth century laughed, of course. It always laughed at all reformers. It said Dr. Darwin was very clever, but really a most eccentric man. His ' Temple of Nature,' now, and his ' Botanic Garden,' were vastly fine and charming poems—those sweet lines, you know, about poor Eliza !—but his zoological theories were built of course upon a most absurd and uncertain foundation. In prose, no sensible person could ever take the doctor seriously. A freak of genius—nothing more ; a mere desire to seem clever and singular. But what a Nemesis the whirligig of time has brought around with it ! By a strange irony of fate, those admired verses are now almost entirely forgotten ; poor Eliza has survived only as our awful example of artificial pathos ; and the zoological heresies, at which the eighteenth century shrugged its fat shoulders and dimpled the corners of its ample mouth, have grown to be the chief cornerstone of all accepted modern zoological science.

In the first year of the present century, Lamarck followed Erasmus Darwin's lead with an open avowal that in his belief all animals and plants were really descended from one or a few common ancestors. He held that organisms were just as much the result of law, not of miraculous interposition, as suns and worlds and all the natural phenomena around us generally. He saw that what naturalists call a species differs from what naturalists call a variety, merely in the way of being a little more distinctly marked, a little less like its nearest congeners elsewhere. He recognised the perfect gradation of forms by which in many cases one species after another merges into the next on either side of it. He observed the analogy between the modifications induced by man and the modifications induced by nature. In fact, he was a thorough-going and convinced evolutionist, holding every salient opinion which Society still believes to have been due to the works of Charles Darwin. In one point only, a minor point to outsiders, though a point of cardinal importance to the inner brotherhood of evolutionism, he did not anticipate his more famous successor. He thought organic evolution was wholly due to the direct action of surrounding circumstances, to the intercrossing of existing forms, and above all to the actual efforts of animals themselves. In other words, he had not discovered natural selection, the cardinal idea of Charles Darwin's epoch-making book. For him, the giraffe had acquired its long neck by constant reaching up to the boughs of trees ; the monkey had acquired its opposable thumb by constant grasping at the neighbouring branches ; and the serpent had acquired its sinuous shape by constant wriggling through the grass of the meadows. Charles Darwin improved upon all that by his suggestive hint of survival of the fittest, and in so far, but in so far alone, he became the real father of modern biological evolutionism.

From the days of Lamarck, to the day when Charles Darwin himself published his wonderful ' Origin of Species,' this idea that plants and animals might really have grown, instead of having been made all of a piece, kept brewing everywhere in the minds and brains of scientific thinkers. The notions which to the outside public were startlingly new when Darwin's book took the world by storm, were old indeed to the thinkers and workers who had long been familiar with the principle of descent with modification and the speculations of the Lichfield doctor or the Paris philosopher. Long before Darwin wrote his great work, Herbert Spencer had put forth in plain language every idea which the drawing-room biologists attributed to Darwin. The supporters of the development hypothesis, he said seven years earlier—yes, he called it the ' development hypothesis ' in so many words—' can show that modification has effected and is effecting great changes in all organisms, subject to modifying influences.' They can show, he goes on (if I may venture to condense so great a thinker), that any existing plant or animal, placed under new conditions, begins to undergo adaptive changes of form and structure ; that in successive generations these changes continue, till the plant or animal acquires totally new habits ; that in cultivated plants and domesticated animals changes of the sort habitually occur ; that the differences thus caused, as for example in dogs, are often greater than those on which species in the wild state are founded, and that throughout all organic nature there *is* at work a modifying influence of the same sort as that which they believed to have caused the differences of species—' an influence which, to all appearance, would produce in the millions of years and under the great variety of conditions which geological records imply, any amount of change.' What is this but pure Darwinism, as the drawing-room philosopher still understands the word? And yet it was written seven years before Darwin published the ' Origin of Species.'

The fact is, one might draw up quite a long list of Darwinians before Darwin. Here are a few of them— Buffon, Lamarck, Goethe, Oken, Bates, Wallace, Lecoq, Von Baer, Robert Chambers, Matthew, and Herbert Spencer. Depend upon it, no one man ever yet of himself discovered anything. As well say that Luther made the German Reformation, that Lionardo made the Italian Renaissance, or that Robespierre made the French Revolution, as say that Charles Darwin, and Charles Darwin alone, made the evolutionary movement, even in the restricted field of life only. A thousand predecessors worked up towards him ; a thousand contemporaries helped to diffuse and to confirm his various principles.

Charles Darwin added to the primitive evolutionary idea the special notion of natural selection. That is to say, he pointed out that while plants and animals vary perpetually and vary indefinitely, all the varieties so produced are not equally adapted to the circumstances of the species. If the variation is a bad one, it tends to die out, because every point of disadvantage tells against the individual in the struggle for life. If the variation is a good one, it tends to persist, because every point of advantage similarly tells in the individual's favour in that ceaseless and viewless battle. It was this addition to the evolutionary concept, fortified by Darwin's powerful advocacy of the general principle of descent with modification, that won over the whole world to the 'Darwinian theory.' Before Darwin, many men of science were evolutionists : after Darwin, all men of science became so at once, and the rest of the world is rapidly preparing to follow their leadership.

As applied to life, then, the evolutionary idea is briefly this—that plants and animals have all a natural origin from a single primitive living creature, which itself was the product of light and heat acting on the special chemical constituents of an ancient ocean. Starting from that single early form, they have gone on developing ever since, from the homogeneous to the heterogeneous, assuming ever more varied shapes, till at last they have reached their present enormous variety of tree, and shrub, and herb, and seaweed, of beast, and bird, and fish, and creeping insect. Evolution throughout has been one and continuous, from nebula to sun, from gas-cloud to planet, from early jelly-speck to man or elephant. So at least evolutionists say—and of course they ought to know most about it.

But evolution, according to the evolutionists, does not even stop here. Psychology as well as biology has also its evolutionary explanation : mind is concerned as truly as matter. If the bodies of animals are evolved, their minds must be evolved likewise. Herbert Spencer and his followers have been mainly instrumental in elucidating this aspect of the case. They have shown, or they have tried to show (for I don't want to dogmatise on the subject), how mind is gradually built up from the simplest raw elements of sense and feeling ; how emotions and intellect slowly arise ; how the action of the environment on the organism begets a nervous system of ever greater and greater complexity, culminating at last in the brain of a Newton, a Shakespeare, or a Mendelssohn. Step by step, nerves have built themselves up out of the soft tissues as channels of communication between part and part. Sense-organs of extreme simplicity have first been formed on the outside of the body, where it comes most into contact with external nature. Use and wont have fashioned them through long ages into organs of taste and smell and touch; pigment spots, sensitive to light or shade, have grown by infinite gradations into the human eye or into the myriad facets of bee and beetle; tremulous nerve-ends, responsive sympathetically to waves of sound, have tuned themselves at last into a perfect gamut in the developed ear of men and mammals. Meanwhile corresponding percipient centres have grown up in the brain, so that the coloured picture flashed by an external scene upon the eye is telegraphed from the sensitive mirror of the retina, through the many-stranded cable of the optic nerve, straight up to the appropriate headquarters in the thinking brain. Stage by stage the continuous process has gone on unceasingly, from the jelly-fish with its tiny black specks of eyes, through infinite steps of progression, induced by ever-widening intercourse with the outer world, to the final outcome in the senses and the emotions, the intellect and the will, of civilised man. Mind begins as a vague consciousness of touch or pressure on the part of some primitive, shapeless, soft creature: it ends as an organised and co-ordinated reflection of the entire physical and psychical universe on the part of a great cosmical philosopher.

Last of all, like diners-out at dessert, the evolutionists take to politics. Having shown us entirely to their own satisfaction the growth of suns, and systems, and worlds, and continents, and oceans, and plants, and animals, and minds, they proceed to show us the exactly analogous and parallel growth of communities, and nations, and languages, and religions, and customs, and arts, and institutions, and literatures. Man, the evolving savage, as Tylor, Lubbock, and others have proved for us, slowly putting off his brute aspect derived from his early ape-like ancestors, learned by infinitesimal degrees the use of fire, the mode of manufacturing stone hatchets and flint arrowheads, the earliest beginnings of the art of pottery. With drill or flint he became the Prometheus to his own small heap of sticks and dry leaves among the tertiary forests. By his nightly camp-fire he beat out gradually his excited gesture-language and his oral speech. He tamed the dog, the horse, the cow, the camel. He taught himself to hew small clearings in the woodland, and to plant the banana, the yam, the bread-fruit, and the coco-nut. He picked and improved the seeds of his wild cereals till he made himself from grass-like grains his barley, his oats, his wheat, his Indian corn. In time, he dug out ore from mines, and learnt the use first of gold, next of silver, then of copper, tin, bronze, and iron. Side by side with these long secular changes, he evolved the family, communal or patriarchal, polygamic or monogamous. He built the hut, the house, and the palace. He clothed or adorned himself first in skins and leaves and feathers; next in woven wool and fibre; last of all in purple and fine linen, and fared sumptuously every day. He gathered into hordes, tribes, and nations; he chose himself a king, gave himself laws, and built up great empires in Egypt, Assyria, China, and Peru. He raised him altars, Stonehenges and Karnaks. His picture-writing grew into hieroglyphs and cuneiforms, and finally emerged, by imperceptible steps, into alphabetic symbols, the raw material of the art of printing. His dug-out canoe culminates in the iron-clad and the 'Great Eastern'; his boomerang and slingstone in the Woolwich infant; his boiling pipkin and his wheeled car in the locomotive engine; his picture-message in the telephone and the Atlantic cable. Here, where the course of evolution has really been most marvellous, its steps have been all more distinctly historical; so that nobody now doubts the true descent of Italian, French, and Spanish from provincial Latin, or the successive growth of the trireme, the 'Great Harry,' the 'Victory,'and the 'Minotaur' from the coracles or praus of prehistoric antiquity.

The grand conception of the uniform origin and development of all things, earthly or sidereal, thus summed up for us in the one word evolution, belongs by right neither to Charles Darwin nor to any other single thinker. It is the joint product of innumerable workers, all working up, though some of them unconsciously, towards a grand final unified philosophy of the cosmos. In astronomy, Kant, Laplace, and the Herschels; in geology, Hutton, Lyell, and the Geikies; in biology, Buffon, Lamarck, the Darwins, Huxley, and Spencer; in psychology, Spencer, Romanes, Sully, and Ribot; in sociology, Spencer, Tylor, Lubbock, and De Mortillet—these have been the chief evolutionary teachers and discoverers. But the use of the word evolution itself, and the establishment of the general evolutionary theory as a system of philosophy applicable to the entire universe, we owe to one man alone—Herbert Spencer. Many other minds —from Galileo and Copernicus, from Kepler and Newton, from Linnæus and Tournefort, from D'Alembert and Diderot, nay, even, in a sense, from Aristotle and Lucretius —had been piling together the vast collection of raw material from which that great and stately superstructure was to be finally edified. But the architect who placed each block in its proper niche, who planned and designed the whole elevation, who planted the building firmly on the rock and poised the coping-stone on the topmost pinnacle, was the author of the 'System of Synthetic Philosophy,' and none other. It is a strange proof of how little people know about their own ideas, that among the thousands who talk glibly every day of evolution, not ten per cent. are probably aware that both word and conception are alike due to the commanding intelligence and vast generalising power of Herbert Spencer.

STRICTLY INCOG.

AMONG the reefs of rock upon the Australian coast, an explorer's dredge often brings up to the surface some tangled tresses of reddish seaweed, which, when placed for a while in a bucket of water, begin slowly to uncoil themselves as if endowed with animal life, and finally to swim about with a gentle tremulous motion in a mute inquiring way from side to side of the pail that contains them. Looked at closely with an attentive eye, the complex moving mass gradually resolves itself into two parts : one a ruddy seaweed with long streaming fronds ; the other, a strangely misshapen and dishevelled pipe-fish, exactly imitating the weed itself in form and colour. When removed from the water, this queer pipe-fish proves in general outline somewhat to resemble the well-known hippocampus or sea-horse of the aquariums, whose dried remains, in a mummified state, form a standing wonder in many tiny domestic museums. But the Australian species, instead of merely mimicking the knight on a chess-board, looks rather like a hippocampus in the most advanced stage of lunacy, with its tail and fins and the appendages of its spines flattened out into long thin streaming filaments, utterly indistinguishable in hue and shape from the fucus round which the creature clings for support with its prehensile tail. Only a rude and shapeless rough draught of a head, vaguely horse-like in contour, and inconspicuously provided with an unobtrusive snout and a pair of very unnoticeable eyes, at all suggests to the most microscopic observer its animal nature. Taken as a whole, nobody could at first sight distinguish it in any way from the waving weed among which it vegetates.

Clearly, this curious Australian cousin of the Mediterranean sea-horses has acquired so marvellous a resemblance to a bit of fucus in order to deceive the eyes of its ever-watchful enemies, and to become indistinguishable from the uneatable weed whose colour and form it so surprisingly imitates. Protective resemblances of the sort are extremely common among the pipe-fish family, and the reason why they should be so is no doubt sufficiently obvious at first sight to any reflecting mind—such, for example, as the intelligent reader's. Pipe-fish, as everybody knows, are far from giddy. They do not swim in the vortex of piscine dissipation. Being mostly small and defenceless creatures, lurking among the marine vegetation of the shoals and reefs, they are usually accustomed to cling for support by their snake-like tails to the stalks or leaves of those submerged forests. The omniscient schoolboy must often have watched in aquariums the habits and manners of the common sea-horses, twisted together by their long thin bodies into one inextricable mass of living matwork, or anchored firmly with a treble serpentine coil to some projecting branch of coralline or of quivering sea-wrack. Bad swimmers by nature, utterly unarmed, and wholly undefended by protective mail, the pipe-fish generally can neither fight nor run away: and therefore they depend entirely for their lives upon their peculiar skulking and lurking habits. Their one mode of defence is not to show themselves; discretion is the better part of their valour; they hide as much as possible among the thickest seaweed, and trust to Providence to escape observation.

Now, with any animals thus constituted, cowards by

hereditary predilection, it must necessarily happen that the more brightly coloured or obtrusive individuals will most readily be spotted and most unceremoniously devoured by their sharp-sighted foes, the predatory fishes. On the other hand, just in proportion as any particular pipe-fish happens to display any chance resemblance in colour or appearance to the special seaweed in whose folds it lurks, to that extent will it be likely to escape detection, and to hand on its peculiarities to its future descendants. A long-continued course of the simple process thus roughly described must of necessity result at last in the elimination of all the most conspicuous pipe-fish, and the survival of all those unobtrusive and retiring individuals which in any respect happen to resemble the fucus or coralline among which they dwell. Hence, in many places, various kinds of pipe-fish exhibit an extraordinary amount of imitative likeness to the sargasso or seaweed to whose tags they cling ; and in the three most highly developed Australian species the likeness becomes so ridiculously close that it is with difficulty one can persuade oneself one is really and truly looking at a fish, and not at a piece of strangely animated and locomotive fucus.

Of course, the playful pipe-fish is by no means alone in his assumption of so neat and effective a disguise. Protective resemblances of just the same sort as that thus exhibited by this extraordinary little creature are common throughout the whole range of nature ; instances are to be found in abundance, not only among beasts, birds, reptiles, and fishes, but even among caterpillars, butterflies, and spiders, of species which preserve the strictest incognito. Everywhere in the world, animals and plants are perpetually masquerading in various assumed characters ; and sometimes their make-up is so exceedingly good as to take in for a while not merely the uninstructed ordinary observer, but even the scientific and systematic naturalist.

A few selected instances of such successful masquerading will perhaps best serve to introduce the general principles upon which all animal mimicry ultimately depends. Indeed, naturalists of late years have been largely employed in fishing up examples from the ends of the earth and from the depths of the sea for the elucidation of this very subject. There is a certain butterfly in the islands of the Malay Archipelago (its learned name, if anybody wishes to be formally introduced, is *Kallima paralekta*) which always rests among dead or dry leaves, and has itself leaf-like wings, all spotted over at intervals with wee speckles to imitate the tiny spots of fungi on the foliage it resembles. The well-known stick and leaf insects from the same rich neighbourhood in like manner exactly mimic the twigs and leaves of the forest among which they lurk : some of them look for all the world like little bits of walking bamboo, while others appear in all varieties of hue, as if opening buds and full-blown leaves and pieces of yellow foliage sprinkled with the tints and moulds of decay had of a sudden raised themselves erect upon six legs, and begun incontinently to perambulate the Malayan woodlands like vegetable Frankensteins in all their glory. The larva of one such deceptive insect, observed in Nicaragua by sharp-eyed Mr. Belt, appeared at first sight like a mere fragment of the moss on which it rested, its body being all prolonged into little thread-like green filaments, precisely imitating the foliage around it. Once more, there are common flies which secure protection for themselves by growing into the counterfeit presentment of wasps or hornets, and so obtaining immunity from the attacks of birds or animals. Many of these curiously mimetic insects are banded with yellow and black in the very image of their stinging originals, and have their tails sharpened, *in terrorem*, into a pretended sting, to give point and verisimilitude to the deceptive resemblance. More curious still, certain South American butterflies of a perfectly inoffensive and edible family mimic in every spot and line of colour sundry other butterflies of an utterly unrelated and fundamentally dissimilar type, but of so disagreeable a taste as never to be eaten by birds or lizards.` The origin of these curious resemblances I shall endeavour to explain (after Messrs. Bates and Wallace) a little farther on : for the present it is enough to observe that the extraordinary resemblances thus produced have often deceived the very elect, and have caused experienced naturalists for a time to stick some deceptive specimen of a fly among the wasps and hornets, or some masquerading cricket into the midst of a cabinet full of saw-flies or ichneumons.

Let us look briefly at the other instances of protective coloration in nature generally which lead up to these final bizarre exemplifications of the masquerading tendency.

Wherever all the world around is remarkably uniform in colour and appearance, all the animals, birds, and insects alike necessarily disguise themselves in its prevailing tint to escape observation. It does not matter in the least whether they are predatory or defenceless, the hunters or the hunted : if they are to escape destruction or starvation, as the case may be, they must assume the hue of all the rest of nature about them. In the arctic snows, for example, all animals, without exception, must needs be snow-white. The polar bear, if he were brown or black, would immediately be observed among the unvaried ice-fields by his expected prey, and could never get a chance of approaching his quarry unperceived at close quarters. On the other hand, the arctic hare must equally be dressed in a snow-white coat, or the arctic fox would too readily discover him and pounce down upon him off-hand; while, conversely, the fox himself, if red or brown, could never creep upon the unwary hare without previous detection, which would defeat his purpose. For this reason, the ptarmigan and the willow grouse become as white in winter as the vast snow-fields under which they burrow; the ermine changes his dusky summer coat for the expensive wintry suit beloved of British Themis; the snow-bunting acquires his milk-white plumage; and even the weasel assimilates himself more or less in hue to the unvarying garb of arctic nature. To be out of the fashion is there quite literally to be out of the world: no half-measures will suit the stern decree of polar biology; strict compliance with the law of winter change is absolutely necessary to success in the struggle for existence.

Now, how has this curious uniformity of dress in arctic animals been brought about? Why, simply by that un-yielding principle of Nature which condemns the less adapted for ever to extinction, and exalts the better adapted to the high places of her hierarchy in their stead. The ptarmigan and the snow-buntings that look most like the snow have for ages been least likely to attract the unfavourable atten-tion of arctic fox or prowling ermine; the fox or ermine that came most silently and most unperceived across the shifting drifts has been most likely to steal unawares upon the heedless flocks of ptarmigan and snow-bunting. In the one case protective colouring preserves the animal from himself being devoured; in the other case it enables him the more easily to devour others. And since 'Eat or be eaten' is the shrill sentence of Nature upon all animal life, the final result is the unbroken whiteness of the arctic fauna in all its developments of fur or feather.

Where the colouring of nature is absolutely uniform, as among the arctic snows or the chilly mountain tops, the colouring of the animals is uniform too. Where it is slightly diversified from point to point, as in the sands of the desert, the animals that imitate it are speckled or diversified with various soft neutral tints. All the birds, reptiles, and insects of Sahara, says Canon Tristram, copy closely the grey or isabelline colour of the boundless sands that stretch around them. Lord George Campbell, in his amusing 'Log Letters from the "Challenger,"' mentions a butterfly on the shore at Amboyna which looked exactly like a bit of the beach, until it spread its wings and fluttered away gaily to leeward. Soles and other flat-fish similarly resemble the sands or banks on which they lie, and accommodate themselves specifically to the particular colour of their special bottom. Thus the flounder imitates the muddy bars at the mouths of rivers, where he loves to half bury himself in the congenial ooze; the sole, who rather affects clean hard sand-banks, is simply sandy and speckled with grey; the plaice, who goes in by preference for a bed of mixed pebbles, has red and yellow spots scattered up and down irregularly among the brown, to look as much as possible like agates and carnelians: the brill, who hugs a still rougher ledge, has gone so far as to acquire raised lumps or tubercles on his upper surface, which make him seem like a mere bit of the shingle-strewn rock on which he reposes. In short, where the environment is most uniform the colouring follows suit : just in proportion as the environment varies from place to place, the colouring must vary in order to simulate it. There is a deep biological joy in the term 'environment'; it almost rivals the well-known consolatory properties of that sweet word 'Mesopotamia.' 'Surroundings,' perhaps, would equally well express the meaning, but then, as Mr. Wordsworth justly observes, 'the difference to me !'

Between England and the West Indies, about the time

when one begins to recover from the first bout of sea-sickness, we come upon a certain sluggish tract of ocean, uninvaded by either Gulf Stream or arctic current, but slowly stagnating in a sort of endless eddy of its own, and known to sailors and books of physical geography as the Sargasso Sea. The sargasso or floating seaweed from which it takes its poetical name is a pretty yellow rootless alga, swimming in vast quantities on the surface of the water, and covered with tiny bladder-like bodies which at first sight might easily be mistaken for amber berries. If you drop a bucket over the ship's side and pull up a tangled mass of this beautiful seaweed, it will seem at first to be all plant alike ; but, when you come to examine its tangles closely, you will find that it simply swarms with tiny crabs, fishes, and shrimps, all coloured so precisely to shade that they look exactly like the sargasso itself. Here the colour about is less uniform than in the arctic snows, but, so far as the sargasso-haunting animals are concerned, it comes pretty much to the same thing. The floating mass of weed is their whole world, and they have had to accommodate themselves to its tawny hue under pain of death, immediate and violent.

Caterpillars and butterflies often show us a further step in advance in the direction of minute imitiaton of ordinary surroundings. Dr. Weismann has published a very long and learned memoir, fraught with the best German erudition and prolixity, upon this highly interesting and obscure subject. As English readers, however, not unnaturally object to trudging through a stout volume on the larva of the sphinx moth, conceived in the spirit of those patriarchal ages of Hilpa and Shalum, when man lived to nine hundred and ninety-nine years, and devoted a stray century or so without stint to the work of education, I shall not refer them to Dr. Weismann's original treatise, as well translated and still further enlarged by Mr. Raphael Meldola, but will present them instead with a brief *résumé*, boiled down and condensed into a patent royal elixir of learning. Your caterpillar, then, runs many serious risks in early life from the annoying persistence of sundry evil-disposed birds, who insist at inconvenient times in picking him off the leaves of gooseberry bushes and other his chosen places of residence. His infant mortality, indeed, is something simply appalling, and it is only by laying the eggs that produce him in enormous quantities that his fond mother the butterfly ever succeeds in rearing on an average two of her brood to replace the imago generation just departed. Accordingly, the caterpillar has been forced by adverse circumstances to assume the most ridiculous and impossible disguises, appearing now in the shape of a leaf or stem, now as a bundle of dark-green pine needles, and now again as a bud or flower all for the innocent purpose of concealing his whereabouts from the inquisitive gaze of the birds his enemies.

When the caterpillar lives on a plant like a grass, the ribs or veins of which run up and down longitudinally, he is usually striped or streaked with darker lines in the same direction as those on his native foliage. When, on the contrary, he lives upon broader leaves, provided with a midrib and branching veins, his stripes and streaks (not to be out of the fashion) run transversely and obliquely, at exactly the same angle as those of his wonted food-plant. Very often, if you take a green caterpillar of this sort away from his natural surroundings, you will be surprised at the conspicuousness of his pale lilac or mauve markings; surely, you will think to yourself, such very distinct variegation as that must betray him instantly to his watchful enemies. But no; if you replace him gently where you first found him, you will see that the lines exactly harmonise with the joints and shading of his native leaf: they are delicate representations of the soft shadow cast by a rib or vein, and the local colour is precisely what a painter would have had to use in order to produce the corresponding effect. The shadow of yellowish green is, of course, always purplish or lilac. It may at first sight seem surprising that a caterpillar should possess so much artistic sense and dexterity; but then the penalty for bungling or inharmonious work is so very severe as necessarily to stimulate his imitative genius. Birds are for ever hunting him down among the green leaves, and only those caterpillars which effectually deceive them by their admirable imitations can ever hope to survive and become the butterflies who hand on their larval peculiarities to after ages. Need I add that the variations are, of course, unconscious, and that accident in the first place is ultimately answerable for each fresh step in the direction of still closer simulation?

The geometric moths have brown caterpillars, which generally stand erect when at rest on the branches of trees and so resemble small twigs; and, in order that the resemblance may be the more striking, they are often covered with tiny warts which look like buds or knots upon the surface. The larva of that familiar and much-dreaded insect, the death's-head hawk-moth, feeds as a rule on the foliage of the potato, and its very varied colouring, as Sir John Lubbock has pointed out, so beautifully harmonises with the brown of the earth, the yellow and green of the leaves, and the faint purplish blue of the lurid flowers, that it can only be distinguished when the eye happens accidentally to focus itself exactly upon the spot occupied by the unobtrusive caterpillar. Other larvæ which frequent pine trees have their bodies covered with tufts of green hairs that serve to imitate the peculiar pine foliage. One queer little caterpillar, which lives upon the hoary foliage of the sea-buckthorn, has a grey-green body, just like the buckthorn leaves, relieved by a very conspicuous red spot which really represents in size and colour one of the berries that grow around it. Finally the larva of the elephant hawk-moth, which grows to a very large size, has a pair of huge spots that seem like great eyes; and direct experiment establishes the fact that small birds mistake it for a young snake, and stand in terrible awe of it accordingly, though it is in reality a perfectly harmless insect, and also, as I am credibly informed (for I cannot speak upon the point from personal experience), a very tasty and well-flavoured insect, and 'quite good to eat' too, says an eminent authority. One of these big snake-like caterpillars once frightened Mr. Bates himself on the banks of the Amazon.

Now, I know that cantankerous person, the universal objector, has all along been bursting to interrupt me and declare that he himself frequently finds no end of caterpillars, and has not the slightest difficulty at all in distinguishing them with the naked eye from the leaves and plants among which they are lurking. But observe how promptly we crush and demolish this very inconvenient and disconcerting critic. The caterpillars *he* finds are almost all hairy ones, very conspicuous and easy to discover —'woolly bears,' and such like common and unclean creatures—and the reason they take no pains to conceal themselves from his unobservant eyes is simply this: nobody on earth wants to discover them. For either they are protectively encased in horrid hairs, which get down your throat and choke you and bother you (I speak as a bird, from the point of view of a confirmed caterpillar eater), or else they are bitter and nasty to the taste, like the larva of the spurge moth and the machaon butterfly. These are the ordinary brown and red and banded caterpillars that the critical objector finds in hundreds on his peregrinations about his own garden—commonplace things which the

experienced naturalist has long since got utterly tired of.
But has your rash objector ever lighted upon that rare larva
which lives among the periwinkles, and exactly imitates a
periwinkle petal? Has he ever discovered those deceptive
creatures which pretend for all the world to be leaves of
lady's-bedstraw, or dress themselves up as flowers of
buttonweed? Has he ever hit upon those immoral caterpillars which wriggle through life upon the false pretence
that they are only the shadows of projecting ribs on the
under surface of a full-grown lime leaf? No, not he; he
passes them all by without one single glance of recognition;
and when the painstaking naturalist who has hunted them
every one down with lens and butterfly net ventures tentatively to describe their personal appearance, he comes up
smiling with his great russet woolly bear comfortably nest-
ling upon a green cabbage leaf, and asks you in a voice of
triumphant demonstration, where is the trace of conceal-
ment or disguise in that amiable but very inedible insect?
Go to, Sir Critic, I will have none of you; I only use you
for a metaphorical marionette to set up and knock down
again, as Mr. Punch in the street show knocks down the
policeman who comes to arrest him, and the grimy black
personage of sulphurous antecedents who pops up with a
fizz through the floor of his apartment.

Queerer still than the caterpillars which pretend to be
leaves or flowers for the sake of protection are those truly
diabolical and perfidious Brazilian spiders which, as Mr.
Bates observed, are brilliantly coloured with crimson and
purple, but ' double themselves up at the base of leaf-stalks,
so as to resemble flower buds, and thus deceive the insects
upon which they prey.' There is something hideously
wicked and cruel in this lowest depth of imitative infamy.
A flower-bud is something so innocent and childlike; and
to disguise oneself as such for purposes of murder and

rapine argues the final abyss of arachnoid perfidy. It reminds one of that charming and amiable young lady in Mr. Robert Louis Stevenson's 'Dynamiter,' who amused herself in moments of temporary gaiety by blowing up inhabited houses, inmates and all, out of pure lightness of heart and girlish frivolity. An Indian mantis or praying insect, a little less wicked, though no less cruel than the spiders, deceives the flies who come to his arms under the false pretence of being a quiet leaf, upon which they may light in safety for rest and refreshment. Yet another abandoned member of the same family, relying boldly upon the resources of tropical nature, gets itself up as a complete orchid, the head and fangs being moulded in the exact image of the beautiful blossom, and the arms folding treacherously around the unhappy insect which ventures to seek for honey in its deceptive jaws.

Happily, however, the tyrants and murderers do not always have things all their own way. Sometimes the inoffensive prey turn the tables upon their torturers with distinguished success. For example, Mr. Wallace noticed a kind of sand-wasp, in Borneo, much given to devouring crickets ; but there was one species of cricket which exactly reproduced the features of the sand-wasps, and mixed among them on equal terms without fear of detection. Mr. Belt saw a green leaf-like locust in Nicaragua, overrun by foraging ants in search of meat for dinner, but remaining perfectly motionless all the time, and evidently mistaken by the hungry foragers for a real piece of the foliage it mimicked. So thoroughly did this innocent locust understand the necessity for remaining still, and pretending to be a leaf under all advances, that even when Mr. Belt took it up in his hands it never budged an inch, but strenuously preserved its rigid leaf-like attitude. As other insects 'sham dead,' this ingenious creature shammed vegetable.

In order to understand how cases like these begin to arise, we must remember that first of all they start of necessity from very slight and indefinite resemblances, which succeed as it were by accident in occasionally eluding the vigilance of enemies. Thus, there are stick insects which only look like long round cylinders, not obviously stick-shaped, but rudely resembling a bit of wood in outline only. These imperfectly mimetic insects may often obtain a casual immunity from attack by being mistaken for a twig by birds or lizards. There are others, again, in which natural selection has gone a step further, so as to produce upon their bodies bark-like colouring and rough patches which imitate knots, wrinkles, and leaf-buds. In these cases the protection given is far more marked, and the chances of detection are proportionately lessened. But sharp-eyed birds, with senses quickened by hunger, the true mother of invention, must learn at last to pierce such flimsy disguises, and suspect a stick insect in the most innocent-looking and apparently rigid twigs. The final step, therefore, consists in the production of that extraordinary actor, the *Xeroxylus laceratus*, whose formidable name means no more than 'ragged dry-stick,' and which really mimics down to the minutest particular a broken twig, overgrown with mosses, liverworts, and lichens.

Take, on the other hand, the well-known case of that predaceous mantis which exactly imitates the white ants, and, mixing with them like one of their own horde, quietly devours a stray fat termite or so, from time to time, as occasion offers. Here we must suppose that the ancestral mantis happened to be somewhat paler and smaller than most of its fellow-tribesmen, and so at times managed unobserved to mingle with the white ants, especially in the shade or under a dusky sky, much to the advantage of its own appetite. But the termites would soon begin to observe the visits of their suspicious friend, and to note their coincidence with the frequent mysterious disappearance of a fellow-townswoman, evaporated into space, like the missing young women in neat cloth jackets who periodically vanish from the London suburbs. In proportion as their reasonable suspicions increased, the termites would carefully avoid all doubtful looking mantises; but, at the same time, they would only succeed in making the mantises which survived their inquisition grow more and more closely to resemble the termite pattern in all particulars. For any mantis which happened to come a little nearer the white ants in hue or shape would thereby be enabled to make a more secure meal upon his unfortunate victims; and so the very vigilance which the ants exerted against his vile deception would itself react in time against their own kind, by leaving only the most ruthless and indistinguishable of their foes to become the parents of future generations of mantises.

Once more, the beetles and flies of Central America must have learned by experience to get out of the way of the nimble Central American lizards with great agility, cunning, and alertness. But green lizards are less easy to notice beforehand than brown or red ones; and so the lizards of tropical countries are almost always bright green, with complementary shades of yellow, grey, and purple, just to fit them in with the foliage they lurk among. Everybody who has ever hunted the green tree-toads on the leaves of waterside plants on the Riviera must know how difficult it is to discriminate these brilliant leaf-coloured creatures from the almost identical background on which they rest. Now, just in proportion as the beetles and flies grow still more cautious, even the green lizards themselves fail to pick up a satisfactory livelihood; and so at last we get that most remarkable Nicaraguan form, decked all round with leaf-like expansions, and looking so like the foliage on which it rests that no beetle on earth can possibly detect it. The more cunning you get your detectives, the more cunning do the thieves become to outwit them.

Look, again, at the curious life-history of the flies which dwell as unbidden guests or social parasites in the nests and hives of wild honey-bees. These burglarious flies are belted and bearded in the very selfsame pattern as the bumble-bees themselves; but their larvæ live upon the young grubs of the hive, and repay the unconscious hospitality of the busy workers by devouring the future hope of their unwilling hosts. Obviously, any fly which entered a bee-hive could only escape detection and extermination at the hands (or stings) of its outraged inhabitants, provided it so far resembled the real householders as to be mistaken at a first glance by the invaded community for one of its own numerous members. Thus any fly which showed the slightest superficial resemblance to a bee might at first be enabled to rob honey for a time with comparative impunity, and to lay its eggs among the cells of the helpless larvæ. But when once the vile attempt was fairly discovered, the burglars could only escape fatal detection from generation to generation just in proportion as they more and more closely approximated to the shape and colour of the bees themselves. For, as Mr. Belt has well pointed out, while the mimicking species would become naturally more numerous from age to age, the senses of the mimicked species would grow sharper and sharper by constant practice in detecting and punishing the unwelcome intruders.

It is only in external matters, however, that the appearance of such mimetic species can ever be altered. Their underlying points of structure and formative detail always show to the very end (if only one happens to observe them) their proper place in a scientific classification. For instance, these same parasitic flies which so closely resemble bees in their shape and colour have only one pair of wings apiece, like all the rest of the fly order, while the bees of course have the full complement of two pairs, an upper and an under, possessed by them in common with all other well-conducted members of the hymenopterous family. So, too, there is a certain curious American insect, belonging to the very unsavoury tribe which supplies London lodging-houses with one of their most familiar entomological specimens ; and this cleverly disguised little creature is banded and striped in every part exactly like a local hornet, for whom it evidently wishes itself to be mistaken. If you were travelling in the wilder parts of Colorado you would find a close resemblance to Buffalo Bill was no mean personal protection. Hornets, in fact, are insects to which birds and other insectivorous animals prefer to give a very wide berth, and the reason why they should be imitated by a defenceless beetle must be obvious to the intelligent student. But while the vibrating wing-cases of this deceptive masquerader are made to look as thin and hornet-like as possible, in all underlying points of structure any competent naturalist would see at once that the creature must really be classed among the noisome Hemiptera. I seldom trouble the public with a Greek or Latin name, but on this occasion I trust I may be pardoned for not indulging in all the ingenuous bluntness of the vernacular.

Sometimes this effective mimicry of stinging insects seems to be even consciously performed by the tiny actors. Many creatures, which do not themselves possess stings, nevertheless endeavour to frighten their enemies by assuming the characteristic hostile attitudes of wasps or hornets. Everybody in England must be well acquainted with those common British earwig-looking insects, popularly known as the devil's coach-horses, which, when irritated or interfered with, cock up their tails behind them in the most aggressive fashion, exactly reproducing the threatening action of an angry scorpion. Now, as a matter of fact, the devil's coach-horse is quite harmless, but I have often seen, not only little boys and girls, but also chickens, small birds, and shrew-mice, evidently alarmed at his minatory attitude. So, too, the bumble-bee flies, which are inoffensive insects got up in sedulous imitation of various species of wild bee, flit about and buzz angrily in the sunlight, quite after the fashion of the insects they mimic; and when disturbed they pretend to get excited, and seem as if they wished to fly in their assailant's face and roundly sting him. This curious instinct may be put side by side with the parallel instinct of shamming dead, possessed by many beetles and other small defenceless species.

Certain beetles have also been modified so as exactly to imitate wasps; and in these cases the beetle waist, usually so solid, thick, and clumsy, grows as slender and graceful as if the insects had been supplied with corsets by a fashionable West End house. But the greatest refinement of all is perhaps that noticed in certain allied species which mimic bees, and which have acquired useless little tufts of hair on their hind shanks to represent the dilated and tufted pollen-gathering apparatus of the true bees.

I have left to the last the most marvellous cases of mimicry of all—those noticed among South American butterflies by Mr. Bates, who found that certain edible kinds exactly resembled a handsome and conspicuous but bitter-tasted species 'in every shade and stripe of colour.' Several of these South American imitative insects long deceived the very entomologists; and it was only by a close inspection of their structural differences that the utter

distinctness of the mimickers and the mimicked was satisfactorily settled. Scarcely less curious is the case of Mr.
Wallace's Malayan orioles, two species of which exactly
copy two pugnacious honey-suckers in every detail of
plumage and coloration. As the honey-suckers are avoided
by birds of prey, owing to their surprising strength and
pugnacity, the orioles gain immunity from attack by their
close resemblance to the protected species. When Dr.
Sclater, the distinguished ornithologist, was examining
Mr. Forbes's collections from Timorlaut, even his experienced eye was so taken in by another of these deceptive bird-mimicries that he classified two birds of totally
distinct families as two different individuals of the same
species.

Even among plants a few instances of true mimicry
have been observed. In the stony African Karoo, where
every plant is eagerly sought out for food by the scanty
local fauna, there are tubers which exactly resemble the
pebbles around them ; and I have little doubt that our
perfectly harmless English dead-nettle secures itself from
the attacks of browsing animals by its close likeness to the
wholly unrelated, but well-protected, stinging-nettle.

Finally, we must not forget the device of those
animals which not merely assimilate themselves in colour
to the ordinary environment in a general way, but have
also the power of adapting themselves at will to whatever
object they may happen to lie against. Cases like that of
the ptarmigan, which in summer harmonises with the
brown heather and grey rock, while in winter it changes to
the white of the snow-fields, lead us up gradually to such
ultimate results of the masquerading tendency. There is
a tiny crustacean, the chameleon shrimp, which can alter
its hue to that of any material on which it happens to

rest. On a sandy bottom it appears grey or sand-coloured ; when lurking among seaweed it becomes green, or red, or brown, according to the nature of its momentary background. Probably the effect is quite unconscious, or at least involuntary, like blushing with ourselves—and nobody ever blushes on purpose, though they do say a distinguished poet once complained that an eminent actor did not follow his stage directions because he omitted to obey the rubrical remark, ' Here Harold purples with anger.' The change is produced by certain automatic muscles which force up particular pigment cells above the others, green coming to the top on a green surface, red on a ruddy one, and brown or grey where the circumstances demand them. Many kinds of fish similarly alter their colour to suit their background by forcing forward or backward certain special pigment-cells known as chromatophores, whose various combinations produce at will almost any required tone or shade. Almost all reptiles and amphibians possess the power of changing their hue in accordance with their environment in a very high degree ; and among certain tree-toads and frogs it is difficult to say what is the normal colouring, as they vary indefinitely from buff and dove-colour to chocolate-brown, rose, and even lilac.

But of all the particoloured reptiles the chameleon is by far the best known, and on the whole the most remarkable for his inconstancy of coloration. Like a lacertine Vicar of Bray, he varies incontinently from buff to blue, and from blue back to orange again, under stress of circumstances. The mechanism of this curious change is extremely complex. Tiny corpuscles of different pigments are sometimes hidden in the depths of the chameleon's skin, and sometimes spread out on its surface in an interlacing network of brown or purple. In addition to this prime colouring matter, however, the animal also possesses a normal yellow pigment, and a bluish layer in the skin which acts like the iridium glass so largely employed by Dr. Salviati, being seen as straw-coloured with a transmitted light, but assuming a faint lilac tint against an opaque absorbent surface. While sleeping the chameleon becomes almost white in the shade, but if light falls upon him he slowly darkens by an automatic process. The movements of the corpuscles are governed by opposite nerves and muscles, which either cause them to bury themselves under the true skin, or to form an opaque ground behind the blue layer, or to spread out in a ramifying mass on the outer surface, and so produce as desired almost any necessary shade of grey, green, black, or yellow. It is an interesting fact that many chrysalids undergo precisely similar changes of colour in adaptation to the background against which they suspend themselves, being grey on a grey surface, green on a green one, and even half black and half red when hung up against pieces of particoloured paper.

Nothing could more beautifully prove the noble superiority of the human intellect than the fact that while our grouse are russet-brown to suit the bracken and heather, and our caterpillars green to suit the lettuce and the cabbage leaves, our British soldier should be wisely coated in brilliant scarlet to form an effective mark for the rifles of an enemy. Red is the easiest of all colours at which to aim from a great distance; and its selection by authority for the uniform of unfortunate Tommy Atkins reminds me of nothing so much as Mr. McClelland's exquisite suggestion that the peculiar brilliancy of the Indian river carps makes them serve 'as a better mark for kingfishers, terns, and other birds which are destined to keep the number of these fishes in check.' The idea of Providence and the Horse Guards conspiring to render any creature an easier target for the attacks of enemies is worthy of the decadent school

of natural history, and cannot for a moment be dispassion-
ately considered by a judicious critic. Nowadays we all
know that the carp are decked in crimson and blue to
please their partners, and that soldiers are dressed in
brilliant red to please—the æsthetic authorities who command them from a distance.

SEVEN-YEAR SLEEPERS

FOR many generations past that problematical animal, the
toad-in-a-hole (literal, not culinary) has been one of the
most familiar and interesting personages of contemporary
folk-lore and popular natural history. From time to time
he turns up afresh, with his own wonted perennial vigour,
on paper at least, in company with the great sea-serpent,
the big gooseberry, the shower of frogs, the two-headed
calf, and all the other common objects of the country or
the seaside in the silly season. No extraordinary natural
phenomenon on earth was ever better vouched for—in
the fashion rendered familiar to us by the Tichborne
claimant—that is to say, no other could ever get a larger
number of unprejudiced witnesses to swear positively and
unreservedly in its favour. Unfortunately, however, swear-
ing alone no longer settles causes offhand, as if by show of
hands, ' the Ayes have it,' after the fashion prevalent in the
good old days when the whole Hundred used to testify that
of its certain knowledge John Nokes did not commit such
and such a murder ; whereupon John Nokes was forthwith
acquitted accordingly. Nowadays, both justice and science
have become more exacting ; they insist upon the unpleasant and discourteous habit of cross-examining their witnesses
(as if they doubted them, forsooth !), instead of accepting
the witnesses' own simple assertion that it's all right, and
there's no need for making a fuss about it. Did you
yourself see the block of stone in which the toad is said

to have been found, before the toad himself was actually extracted ? Did you examine it all round to make quite sure there was no hole, or crack, or passage in it anywhere ? Did you satisfy yourself after the toad was released from his close quarters that no such hole, or crack, or passage had been dexterously closed up, with intent to deceive, by plaster, cement, or other artificial composition ? Did you ever offer the workmen who found it a nominal reward— say five shillings—for the first perfectly unanswerable specimen of a genuine unadulterated antediluvian toad ? Have you got the toad now present, and can you produce him here in court (on writ of *habeas corpus* or otherwise), together with all the fragments of the stone or tree from which he was extracted ? These are the disagreeable, prying, inquisitorial, I may even say insulting, questions with which a modern man of science is ready to assail the truthful and reputable gentlemen who venture to assert their discovery, in these degenerate days, of the ancient and unsophisticated toad-in-a-hole.

Now, the worst of it is that the gentlemen in question, being unfamiliar with what is technically described as scientific methods of investigation, are very apt to lose their temper when thus cross-questioned, and to reply, after the fashion usually attributed to the female mind, with another question, whether the scientific person wishes to accuse them of downright lying. And as nothing on earth could be further from the scientific person's mind than such an imputation, he is usually fain in the end to give up the social pursuit of postprandial natural history (the subject generally crops up about the same time as the after-dinner coffee), and to let the prehistoric toad go on his own triumphant way, unheeded.

As a matter of fact, nobody ever makes larger allowances for other people, in the estimate of their veracity, than the scientific inquirer. Knowing himself, by painful experience, how extremely difficult a matter it is to make perfectly sure you have observed anything on earth quite correctly, and have eliminated all possible chances of error, he acquires the fixed habit of doubting about one-half of whatever his fellow-creatures tell him in ordinary conversation, without for a single moment venturing to suspect them of deliberate untruthfulness. Children and servants, if they find that anything they have been told is erroneous, immediately jump at the conclusion that the person who told them meant deliberately to deceive them; in their own simple and categorical fashion they answer plumply, ' That's a lie.' But the man of science is only too well acquainted in his own person with the exceeding difficulty of ever getting at the exact truth. He has spent hours of toil, himself, in watching and observing the behaviour of some plant, or animal, or gas, or metal; and after repeated experiments, carefully designed to exclude all possibility of mistake, so far as he can foresee it, he at last believes he has really settled some moot point, and triumphantly publishes his final conclusions in a scientific journal. Ten to one, the very next number of that same journal contains a dozen supercilious letters from a dozen learned and high-salaried professors, each pointing out a dozen distinct and separate precautions which the painstaking observer neglected to take, and any one of which would be quite sufficient to vitiate the whole body of his observations. There might have been germs in the tube in which he boiled the water (germs are very fashionable just at present); or some of the germs might have survived and rather enjoyed the boiling; or they might have adhered to the under surface of the cork; or the mixture might have been tampered with during the experimenter's temporary absence by his son, aged ten years (scientific observers have no right, apparently, to have sons of ten years old, except perhaps for purposes of psychological research) ; and so forth, *ad infinitum*. And the worst of it all is that the unhappy experimenter is bound himself to admit that every one of the objections is perfectly valid, and that he very likely never really saw what with perfect confidence he thought and said he had seen.

This being an unbelieving age, then, when even the book of Deuteronomy is ' critically examined,' let us see how much can really be said for and against our old friend, the toad-in-a-hole ; and first let us begin with the antecedent probability, or otherwise, of any animal being able to live in a more or less torpid condition, without air or food, for any considerable period of time together.

A certain famous historical desert snail was brought from Egypt to England as a conchological specimen in the year 1846. This particular mollusk (the only one of his race, probably, who ever attained to individual distinction), at the time of his arrival in London, was really alive and vigorous ; but as the authorities of the British Museum, to whose tender care he was consigned, were ignorant of this important fact in his economy, he was gummed, mouth downward, on to a piece of cardboard, and duly labelled and dated with scientific accuracy, ' *Helix desertorum*, March 25, 1846.' Being a snail of a retiring and contented disposition, however, accustomed to long droughts and corresponding naps in his native sand-wastes, our mollusk thereupon simply curled himself up into the topmost recesses of his own whorls, and went placidly to sleep in perfect contentment for an unlimited period. Every conchologist takes it for granted, of course, that the shells which he receives from foreign parts have had their inhabitants properly boiled and extracted before being exported ; for it is only the mere outer shell or skeleton of the animal that we preserve in our cabinets, leaving the actual flesh and muscles of the creature himself to wither unobserved upon its native shores. At the British Museum the desert snail might have snoozed away his inglorious existence unsuspected, but for a happy accident which attracted public attention to his remarkable case in a most extraordinary manner. On March 7, 1850, nearly four years later, it was casually observed that the card on which he reposed was slightly discoloured; and this discovery led to the suspicion that perhaps a living animal might be temporarily immured within that papery tomb. The Museum authorities accordingly ordered our friend a warm bath (who shall say hereafter that science is unfeeling!), upon which the grateful snail, waking up at the touch of the familiar moisture, put his head cautiously out of his shell, walked up to the top of the basin, and began to take a cursory survey of British institutions with his four eye-bearing tentacles. So strange a recovery from a long torpid condition, only equalled by that of the Seven Sleepers of Ephesus, deserved an exceptional amount of scientific recognition. The desert snail at once awoke and found himself famous. Nay, he actually sat for his portrait to an eminent zoological artist, Mr. Waterhouse; and a woodcut from the sketch thus procured, with a history of his life and adventures, may be found even unto this day in Dr. Woodward's ' Manual of the Mollusca,' to witness if I lie.

I mention this curious instance first, because it is the best authenticated case on record (so far as my knowledge goes) of any animal existing in a state of suspended animation for any long period of time together. But there are other cases of encysted or immured animals which, though less striking as regards the length of time during which torpidity has been observed, are much more closely analogous to the real or mythical conditions of the toad-in-a-hole. That curious West African mud-fish, the Lepidosiren (familiar to all readers of evolutionary literature as one of the most singular existing links between fish and amphibians), lives among the shallow pools and broads of the Gambia, which are dried up during the greater part of the tropical summer. To provide against this annual contingency, the mud-fish retires into the soft clay at the bottom of the pools, where it forms itself a sort of nest, and there hibernates, or rather æstivates, for months together, in a torpid condition. The surrounding mud then hardens into a dry ball ; and these balls are dug out of the soil of the rice-fields by the natives, with the fish inside them, by which means many specimens of lepidosiren have been sent alive to Europe, embedded in their natural covering. Here the strange fish is chiefly prized as a zoological curiosity for aquariums, because of its possessing gills and lungs together, to fit it for its double existence ; but the unsophisticated West Africans grub it up on their own account as a delicacy, regardless of its claims to scientific consideration as the earliest known ancestor of all existing terrestrial animals. Now, the torpid state of the mud-fish in his hardened ball of clay closely resembles the real or supposed condition of the toad-in-a-hole ; but with one important exception. The mud-fish leaves a small canal or pipe open in his cell at either end to admit the air for breathing, though he breathes (as I shall proceed to explain) in a very slight degree during his æstivation ; whereas every proper toad-in-a-hole ought by all accounts to live entirely without either feeding or breathing in any way. However, this is a mere detail ; and indeed, if toads-in-a-hole do really exist at all, we must in all probability ultimately admit that they breathe to some extent, though perhaps very slightly, during their long immurement.

And this leads us on to consider what in reality hibernation is. Everybody knows nowadays, I suppose, that there is a very close analogy between an animal and a steam-engine. Food is the fuel that makes the animal engine go ; and this food acts almost exactly as coal does in the artificial machine. But coal alone will not drive an engine ; a free draught of open air is also required in order to produce combustion. Just in like manner the food we eat cannot be utilised to drive our muscles and other organs unless it is supplied with oxygen from the air to burn it slowly inside our bodies. This oxygen is taken into the system, in all higher animals, by means of lungs or gills. Now, when we are working at all hard, we require a great deal of oxygen, as most of us have familiarly discovered (especially if we are somewhat stout) in the act of climbing hills or running to catch a train. But when we are doing very little work indeed, as in our sleeping hours, during which muscular movement is suspended, and only the general organic life continues, we breathe much more slowly and at longer intervals. However, there is this important difference (generally speaking) between an animal and a steam-engine. You can let the engine run short of coals and come to a dead standstill, without impairing its future possibilities of similar motion ; you have only to get fresh coals, after weeks or months of inaction, and light up a fresh fire, when your engine will immediately begin to work again, exactly the same as before. But if an animal organism once fairly runs down, either from want of food or any other cause—in short, if it dies—it very seldom comes to life again.

I say ' very seldom ' on purpose, because there are a few cases among the extreme lower animals where a water-haunting creature can be taken out of the water and can be thoroughly dried and desiccated, or even kept for an apparently unlimited period wrapped up in paper or on the slide of a microscope ; and yet, the moment a drop of water is placed on top of it, it begins to move and live again exactly as before. This sort of thorough-going suspended animation is the kind we ought to expect from any well-constituted and proper-minded toad-in-a-hole. Whether anything like it ever really occurs in the higher ranks of animal life, however, is a different question ; but there can be no doubt that to some slight extent a body to all intents and purposes quite dead (physically speaking) by long immersion in water—a drowned man, for example—may really be resuscitated by heat and stimulants, applied immediately, provided no part of the working organism has been seriously injured or decomposed. Such people may be said to be *pro tem.* functionally, though not structurally, dead. The heart has practically ceased to beat, the lungs have ceased to breathe, and physical life in the body is temporarily extinct. The fire, in short, has gone out. But if only it can be lighted again before any serious change in the system takes place, all may still go on precisely as of old.

Many animals, however, find it convenient to assume a state of less complete suspended animation during certain special periods of the year, according to the circumstances of their peculiar climate and mode of life. Among the very highest animals, the most familiar example of this sort of semi-torpidity is to be found among the bears and the dormice. The common European brown bear is a carnivore by descent, who has become a vegetarian in practice, though whether from conscientious scruples or mere practical considerations of expediency, does not appear. He feeds chiefly on roots, berries, fruits, vegetables, and honey, all of which he finds it comparatively difficult to procure during winter weather. Accordingly, as everyone knows, he eats immoderately in the summer season, till he has grown fat enough to supply bear's grease to all Christendom. Then he hunts himself out a hollow tree or rock-shelter, curls himself up quietly to sleep, and snores away the whole livelong winter. During this period of hibernation, the action of the heart is reduced to a minimum, and the bear breathes but very slowly. Still, he does breathe, and his heart does beat ; and in performing those indispensable functions, all his store of accumulated fat is gradually used up, so that he wakes in spring as thin as a lath and as hungry as a hunter. The machine has been working at very low pressure all the winter : but it *has* been working for all that, and the continuity of its action has never once for a moment been interrupted. This is the central principle of all hibernation ; it consists essentially of a very long and profound sleep, during which all muscular motion, except that of the heart and lungs, is completely suspended, while even these last are reduced to the very smallest amount compatible with the final restoration of full animal activity.

Thus, even among warm-blooded animals like the bears and dormice, hibernation actually occurs to a very considerable degree ; but it is far more common and more complete among cold-blooded creatures, whose bodies do not need to be kept heated to the same degree, and with whom, accordingly, hibernation becomes almost a complete torpor, the breathing and the action of the heart being still further reduced to very nearly zero. Mollusks in particular, like oysters and mussels, lead very monotonous and un-eventful lives, only varied as a rule by the welcome change of being cut out of their shells and eaten alive ; and their powers of living without food under adverse circumstances are really very remarkable. Freshwater snails and mussels, in cold weather, bury themselves in the mud of ponds or rivers ; and land-snails hide themselves in the ground or under moss and leaves.   The heart then ceases perceptibly to beat, but respiration continues in a very faint degree. The common garden snail closes the mouth of his shell when he wants to hibernate, with a slimy covering ; but he leaves a very small hole in it somewhere, so as to allow a little air to get in, and keep up his breathing to a slight amount.   My experience has been, however, that a great many snails go to sleep in this way, and never wake up again.   Either they get frozen to death, or else the respiration falls so low that it never picks itself up properly when spring returns.   In warm climates, it is during the summer that mollusks and other mud-haunting creatures go to sleep ; and when they get well plastered round with clay, they almost approach in tenacity of life the mildest recorded specimens of the toad-in-a-hole.

For example, take the following cases, which I extract, with needful simplifications, from Dr. Woodward.

' In June 1850, a living pond mussel, which had been more than a year out of water, was sent to Mr. Gray, from Australia.   The big pond snails of the tropics have been found alive in logs of mahogany imported from Honduras ; and M. Caillaud carried some from Egypt to Paris, packed in sawdust.   Indeed, it isn't easy to ascertain the limit of their endurance ; for Mr. Laidlay, having placed a number in a drawer for this very purpose, found them alive after *five years'* torpidity, although in the warm climate of Calcutta.   The pretty snails called *cyclostomas*, which have a lid to their shells, are well known to survive imprisonments of many months ; but in the ordinary open-mouthed land-snails such cases are even more remarkable. Several of the enormous tropical snails often used to decorate cottage mantelpieces, brought by Lieutenant Greaves from Valparaiso, revived after being packed, some for thirteen, others for twenty months.   In 1849, Mr. Pickering received

G

from Mr. Wollaston a basketful of Madeira snails (of twenty or thirty different kinds), three-fourths of which proved to be alive, after several months' confinement, including a sea voyage. Mr. Wollaston has himself recorded the fact that specimens of two Madeira snails survived a fast and imprisonment in pill-boxes of two years and a half duration, and that large numbers of a small species, brought to England at the same time, were *all* living after being inclosed in a dry bag for a year and a half.'

Whether the snails themselves liked their long deprivation of food and moisture we are not informed; their personal tastes and inclinations were very little consulted in the matter; but as they and their ancestors for many generations must have been accustomed to similar long fasts during tropical droughts, in all likelihood they did not much mind it.

The real question, then, about the historical toad-in-a-hole narrows itself down in the end merely to this—how long is it credible that a cold-blooded creature might sustain life in a torpid or hibernating condition, without food, and with a very small quantity of fresh air, supplied (let us say) from time to time through an almost imperceptible fissure? It is well known that reptiles and amphibians are particularly tenacious of life, and that some turtles in particular will live for months, or even for years, without tasting food. The common Greek tortoise, hawked on barrows about the streets of London and bought by a confiding British public under the mistaken impression that its chief fare consists of slugs and cockroaches (it is really far more likely to feed upon its purchaser's choicest sea-kale and asparagus), buries itself in the ground at the first approach of winter, and snoozes away five months of the year in a most comfortable and dignified torpidity. A snake at the Zoo has even been known to live eighteen months in a voluntary fast, refusing all the most tempting offers of birds and rabbits, merely out of pique at her forcible confinement in a strange cage. As this was a lady snake, however, it is possible that she only went on living out of feminine obstinacy, so that this case really counts for very little.

Toads themselves are well known to possess all the qualities of mind and body which go to make up the career of a successful and enduring anchorite. At the best of times they eat seldom and sparingly, while a forty days' fast, like Dr. Tanner's, would seem to them but an ordinary incident in their everyday existence. In the winter they hibernate by burying themselves in the mud, or by getting down cracks in the ground. It is also undoubtedly true that they creep into holes wherever they can find one, and that in these holes they lie torpid for a considerable period. On the other hand, there is every reason to believe that they cannot live for more than a certain fixed and relatively short time entirely without food or air. Dr. Buckland tried a number of experiments upon toads in this manner—experiments wholly unnecessary, considering the trivial nature of the point at issue—and his conclusion was that no toad could get beyond two years without feeding or breathing. There can be very little doubt that in this conclusion he was practically correct, and that the real fine old crusted antediluvian toad-in-a-hole is really a snare and a delusion.

That, however, does not wholly settle the question about such toads, because, even though they may not be all that their admirers claim for them, they may yet possess a very respectable antiquity of their own, and may be very far from the category of mere vulgar cheats and impostors. Because a toad is not as old as Methuselah, it need not follow that he may not be as old as Old Parr ;

G 2

because he does not date back to the Flood, it need not follow that he cannot remember Queen Elizabeth. There are some toads-in-a-hole, indeed, which, however we may account for the origin of their legend, are on the very face of it utterly incredible. For example, there is the favourite and immensely popular toad who was extracted from a perfectly closed hole in a marble mantelpiece. The implication of the legend clearly is that the toad was coeval with the marble. But marble is limestone, altered in texture by pressure and heat, till it has assumed a crystalline structure. In other words we are asked to believe that that toad lived through an amount of fiery heat sufficient to burn him up into fine powder, and yet remains to tell the tale. Such a toad as this obviously deserves no credit. His discoverers may have believed in him themselves, but they will hardly get other people to do so.

Still, there are a great many ways in which it is quite conceivable that toads might get into holes in rocks or trees so as to give rise to the common stories about them, and might even manage to live there for a considerable time with very small quantities of food or air. It must be remembered that from the very nature of the conditions the hole can never be properly examined and inspected until after it has been split open and the toad has been extracted from it. Now, if you split open a tree or a rock, and find a toad inside it, with a cavity which he exactly fills, it is extremely difficult to say whether there was or was not a fissure before you broke the thing to pieces with your hatchet or pickaxe. A very small fissure indeed would be quite sufficient to account for the whole delusion ; for if the toad could get a little air to breathe slowly during his torpid period, and could find a few dead flies or worms among the water that trickled scantily into his hole, he could manage to drag out a peaceful and monotonous existence almost indefinitely. Here are a few possible cases, any one of which will quite suffice to give rise to at least as good a toad-in-the-hole as ninety-nine out of a hundred published instances.

An adult toad buries himself in the mud by a dry pond, and gets coated with a hard solid coat of sun-baked clay. His nodule is broken open with a spade, and the toad himself is found inside, almost exactly filling the space within the cavity. He has only been there for a few months at the outside ; but the clay is as hard as a stone, and to the bucolic mind looks as if it might have been there ever since the Deluge. Good blue lias clay, which dries as solid as limestone, would perform this trick to perfection ; and the toad might easily be relegated accordingly to the secondary ages of geology. Observe, however, that the actual toads so found are not the geological toads we should naturally expect under such remarkable circumstances, but the common everyday toads of modern England. This shows a want of accurate scientific knowledge on the part of the toads which is truly lamentable. A toad who really wished to qualify himself for the post ought at least to avoid presenting himself before a critical eye in the foolish guise of an embodied anachronism. He reminds one of the Roman mother in a popular burlesque, who suspects her son of smoking, and vehemently declares that she smells tobacco, but, after a moment, recollects the historical proprieties, and mutters to herself, apologetically, ' No, not tobacco ; that's not yet invented.' A would-be silurian or triassic toad ought, in like manner, to remember that in the ages to whose honours he aspires his own amphibian kind was not yet developed. He ought rather to come out in the character of a ceratodus or a labyrinthodon.

Again, another adult toad crawls into the hollow of a tree, and there hibernates. The bark partially closes over the slit by which he entered, but leaves a little crack by

which air can enter freely. The grubs in the bark and other
insects supply him from time to time with a frugal repast.
There is no good reason why, under such circumstances, a
placid and contented toad might not manage to prolong his
existence for several consecutive seasons.

Once more, the spawn of toads is very small, as regards
the size of the individual eggs, compared with the size of
the full-grown animal. Nothing would be easier than
for a piece of spawn or a tiny tadpole to be washed into
some hole in a mine or cave, where there was sufficient
water for its developement, and where the trickling drops
brought down minute objects of food, enough to keep up
its simple existence. A toad brought up under such peculiar
circumstances might pass almost its entire life in a state of
torpidity, and yet might grow and thrive in its own sleepy
vegetative fashion.

In short, while it would be difficult in any given case to
prove to a certainty either that the particular toad-in-a-hole
had or had not access to air and food, the ordinary conditions of toad life are exactly those under which the delusive
appearance of venerable antiquity would be almost certain
frequently to arise. The toad is a nocturnal animal; it
lives through the daytime in dark and damp places; it
shows a decided liking for crannies and crevices; it is
wonderfully tenacious of life; it possesses the power of
hibernation; it can live on extremely small quantities of
food for very long periods of time together; it buries itself
in mud or clay; it passes the early part of its life as a
water-haunting tadpole; and last, not least, it can swell out
its body to nearly double its natural size by inflating itself,
which fully accounts for the stories of toads being taken
out of holes every bit as big as themselves. Considering
all these things, it would be wonderful indeed if toads were
not often found in places and conditions which would

naturally give rise to the familiar myth. Throw in a little allowance for human credulity, human exaggeration, and human love of the marvellous, and you have all the elements of a very excellent toad-in-the-hole in the highest ideal perfection.

At the same time I think it quite possible that some toads, under natural circumstances, do really remain in a torpid or semi-torpid condition for a period far exceeding the twenty-four months allowed as the maximum in Dr. Buckland's unpleasant experiments. If the amount of air supplied through a crack or through the texture of the stone were exactly sufficient for keeping the animal alive in the very slightest fashion—the engine working at the lowest possible pressure, short of absolute cessation—I see no reason on earth why a toad might not remain dormant, in a moist place, with perhaps a very occasional worm or grub for breakfast, for at least as long a time as the desert snail slept comfortably in the British Museum. Altogether, while it is impossible to believe the stories about toads that have been buried in a mine for whole centuries, and still more impossible to believe in their being disentombed from marble mantelpieces or very ancient geological formations it is quite conceivable that some toads-in-a-hole may really be far from mere vulgar impostors, and may have passed the traditional seven years of the Indian philosophers in solitary meditation on the syllable Om, or on the equally significant Ko-ax, Ko-ax of the irreverent Attic dramatist. 'Certainly not a centenarian, but perhaps a good seven-year sleeper for all that,' is the final verdict which the court is disposed to return, after due consideration of all the probabilities *in re* the toad-in-a-hole.

A FOSSIL CONTINENT

IF an intelligent Australian colonist were suddenly to be translated backward from Collins Street, Melbourne, into the flourishing woods of the secondary geological period—say about the precise moment of time when the English chalk downs were slowly accumulating, speck by speck, on the silent floor of some long-forgotten Mediterranean—the intelligent colonist would look around him with a sweet smile of cheerful recognition, and say to himself in some surprise, ' Why, this is just like Australia.'   The animals, the trees, the plants, the insects, would all more or less vividly remind him of those he had left behind him in his happy home of the southern seas and the nineteenth century.   The sun would have moved back on the dial of ages for a few million summers or so, indefinitely (in geology we refuse to be bound by dates), and would have landed him at last, to his immense astonishment, pretty much at the exact point whence he first started.

In other words, with a few needful qualifications, to be made hereafter, Australia is, so to speak, a fossil continent, a country still in its secondary age, a surviving fragment of the primitive world of the chalk period or earlier ages. Isolated from all the remainder of the earth about the beginning of the tertiary epoch, long before the mammoth and the mastodon had yet dreamt of appearing upon the stage of existence, long before the first shadowy ancestor of the horse had turned tail on nature's rough draft of the

still undeveloped and unspecialised lion, long before the
extinct dinotheriums and gigantic Irish elks and colossal
giraffes of late tertiary times had even begun to run their
race on the broad plains of Europe and America, the
Australian continent found itself at an early period of its
development cut off entirely from all social intercourse with
the remainder of our planet, and turned upon itself, like the
German philosopher, to evolve its own plants and animals
out of its own inner consciousness. The natural consequence was that progress in Australia has been absurdly
slow, and that the country as a whole has fallen most woe-
fully behind the times in all matters pertaining to the
existence of life upon its surface. Everybody knows that
Australia as a whole is a very peculiar and original continent ; its peculiarity, however, consists, at bottom, for
the most part in the fact that it still remains at very nearly
the same early point of development which Europe had
attained a couple of million years ago or thereabouts.
' Advance, Australia,' says the national motto ; and, indeed,
it is quite time nowadays that Australia should advance ;
for, so far, she has been left out of the running for some
four mundane ages or so at a rough computation.

Example, says the wisdom of our ancestors, is better
than precept ; so perhaps, if I take a single example to
start with, I shall make the principle I wish to illustrate a
trifle clearer to the European comprehension. In Australia,
when Cook or Van Diemen first visited it, there were no
horses, cows, or sheep ; no rabbits, weasels, or cats ; no
indigenous quadrupeds of any sort except the pouched
mammals or marsupials, familiarly typified to every one of
us by the mamma kangaroo in Regent's Park, who carries
the baby kangaroos about with her, neatly deposited in the
sac or pouch which nature has provided for them instead
of a cradle. To this rough generalisation, to be sure, two

special exceptions must needs be made ; namely, the noble
Australian black-fellow himself, and the dingo or wild dog
whose ancestors no doubt came to the country in the same
ship with him, as the brown rat came to England with
George I. of blessed memory. But of these two solitary
representatives of the later and higher Asiatic fauna 'more
anon ' ; for the present we may regard it as approximately
true that aboriginal and unsophisticated Australia in the
lump was wholly given over, on its first discovery, to
kangaroos, phalangers, dasyures, wombats; and other quaint
marsupial animals, with names as strange and clumsy as
their forms.

Now, who and what are the marsupials as a family,
viewed in the dry light of modern science ? Well, they
are simply one of the very oldest mammalian families, and
therefore, I need hardly say, in the levelling and topsy-
turvy view of evolutionary biology, the least entitled to
consideration or respect from rational observers. For of
course in the kingdom of science the last shall be first, and
the first last ; it is the oldest families that are accounted
the worst, while the best families mean always the newest.
Now, the earliest mammals to appear on earth were
creatures of distinctly marsupial type. As long ago as the
time when the red marl of Devonshire and the blue lias of
Lyme Regis were laid down on the bed of the muddy sea
that once covered the surface of Dorset and the English
Channel, a little creature like the kangaroo rats of Southern
Australia lived among the plains of what is now the south
of England. In the ages succeeding the deposition of the
red marl Europe seems to have been broken up into an
archipelago of coral reefs and atolls ; and the islands of
this ancient oolitic ocean were tenanted by numbers of tiny
ancestral marsupials, some of which approached in appearance the pouched ant-eaters of Western Australia, while

others resembled rather the phalangers and wombats, or turned into excellent imitation carnivores, like our modern friend the Tasmanian devil. Up to the end of the time when the chalk deposits of Surrey, Kent, and Sussex were laid down, indeed, there is no evidence of the existence anywhere in the world of any mammals differing in type from those which now inhabit Australia. In other words, so far as regards mammalian life, the whole of the world had then already reached pretty nearly the same point of evolution that poor Australia still sticks at.

About the beginning of the tertiary period, however, just after the chalk was all deposited, and just before the comparatively modern clays and sandstones of the London basin began to be laid down, an arm of the sea broke up the connection which once subsisted between Australia and the rest of the world, probably by a land bridge, *viâ* Java, Sumatra, the Malay peninsula, and Asia generally. 'But how do you know,' asks the candid inquirer, ' that such a connection ever existed at all ?' Simply thus, most laudable investigator—because there are large land mammals in Australia. Now, large land mammals do not swim across a broad ocean. There are none in New Zealand, none in the Azores, none in Fiji, none in Tahiti, none in Madeira, none in Teneriffe—none, in short, in any oceanic island which never at any time formed part of a great continent. How could there be, indeed ? The mammals must necessarily have got there from somewhere ; and whenever we find islands like Britain, or Japan, or Newfoundland, or Sicily, possessing large and abundant indigenous quadrupeds, of the same general type as adjacent continents, we see at once that the island must formerly have been a mere peninsula, like Italy or Nova Scotia at the present day. The very fact that Australia incloses a large group of biggish quadrupeds, whose congeners once inhabited Europe and America, suffices in itself to prove beyond question that uninterrupted land communication must once have existed between Australia and those distant continents.

In fact, to this day a belt of very deep sea, known as Wallace's Line, from the great naturalist who first pointed out its far-reaching zoological importance, separates what is called by science ' the Australian province ' on the south-west from ' the Indo-Malayan province ' to the north and east of it. This belt of deep sea divides off sharply the plants and animals of the Australian type from those of the common Indian and Burmese pattern. South of Wallace's Line we now find several islands, big and small, including New Guinea, Australia, Tasmania, the Moluccas, Celebes, Timor, Amboyna, and Banda. All these lands, whose precise geographical position on the map must of course be readily remembered, in this age of school boards and universal examination, by every pupil-teacher and every Girton girl, are now divided by minor straits of much shallower water ; but they all stand on a great submarine bank, and obviously formed at one time parts of the same wide Australian continent, because animals of the Austra-lian type are still found in every one of them. No Indian or Malayan animal, however, of the larger sort (other than birds) is to be discovered anywhere south of Wallace's Line. That narrow belt of deep sea, in short, forms an ocean barrier which has subsisted there without alteration ever since the end of the secondary period. From that time to this, as the evidence shows us, there has never been any direct land communication between Australia and any part of the outer world beyond that narrow line of division.

Some years ago, in fact, a clever hoax took the world by surprise for a moment, under the audacious title of ' Captain Lawson's Adventures in New Guinea.' The gallant captain, or his unknown creator in some London lodging, pretended to have explored the Papuan jungles, and there to have met with marvellous escapes from terrible beasts of the common tropical Asiatic pattern—rhinoceroses, tigers, monkeys, and leopards. Everybody believed the new Munchausen at first, except the zoologists. Those canny folks saw through the wicked hoax on the very first blush of it. If there were rhinoceroses in Papua, they must have got there by an overland route. If there had ever been a land connection between New Guinea and the Malay region, then, since Australian animals range into New Guinea, Malayan animals would have ranged into Australia, and we should find Victoria and New South Wales at the present day peopled by tapirs, orang-outangs, wild boars, deer, elephants, and squirrels, like those which now people Borneo, instead of, or side by side with, the kangaroos, wombats, and other marsupials, which, as we know, actually form the sole indigenous mammalian population of Greater Britain beneath the Southern Cross. Of course, in the end, the mysterious and tremendous Captain Lawson proved to be a myth, an airy nothing upon whom imagination had bestowed a local habitation (in New Guinea) and a name (not to be found in the Army List). Wallace's Line was saved from reproach, and the intrusive rhinoceros was banished without appeal from the soil of Papua.

After the deep belt of open sea was thus established between the bigger Australian continent and the Malayan region, however, the mammals of the great mainlands continued to develop on their own account, in accordance with the strictest Darwinian principles, among the wider plains of their own habitats. The competition there was fiercer and more general; the struggle for life was bloodier and more arduous. Hence, while the old-fashioned marsupials continued to survive and to evolve slowly along their own lines in their own restricted southern world, their collateral descendants in Europe and Asia and America or elsewhere went on progressing into far higher, stronger, and better adapted forms—the great central mammalian fauna. In place of the petty phalangers and pouched ant-eaters of the oolitic period, our tertiary strata in the larger continents show us a rapid and extraordinary development of the mammalian race into monstrous creatures, some of them now quite extinct, and some still holding their own undisturbed in India, Africa, and the American prairies. The palæotherium and the deinoceras, the mastodon and the mammoth, the huge giraffes and antelopes of sunnier times, succeed to the ancestral kangaroos and wombats of the secondary strata. Slowly the horses grow more horse-like, the shadowy camel begins to camelise himself, the buffaloes acquire the rudiments of horns, the deer branch out by tentative steps into still more complicated and more complicated antlers. Side by side with this wonderful out-growth of the mammalian type, in the first plasticity of its vigorous youth, the older marsupials die away one by one in the geological record before the faces of their more successful competitors ; the new carnivores devour them wholesale, the new ruminants eat up their pastures, the new rodents outwit them in the modernised forests. At last the pouched creatures all disappear utterly from all the world, save only Australia, with the solitary exception of a single advanced marsupial family, the familiar opossum of plantation melodies. And the history of the opossum himself is so very singular that it almost deserves to receive the polite attention of a separate paragraph for its own proper elucidation.

For the opossums form the only members of the mar-supial class now living outside Australia ; and yet, what is at least equally remarkable, none of the opossums are found *per contra* in Australia itself. They are, in fact, the highest and best product of the old dying marsupial stock, specially evolved in the great continents through the fierce competition of the higher mammals then being developed on every side of them. Therefore, being later in point of time than the separation, they could no more get over to Australia than the elephants and tigers and rhinoceroses could. They are the last bid for life of the marsupial race in its hopeless struggle against its more developed mammalian cousins. In Europe and Asia the opossums lived on lustily, in spite of competition, during the whole of the Eocene period, side by side with hog-like creatures not yet perfectly piggish, with nondescript animals, half horse half tapir, and with hornless forms of deer and antelopes, unprovided, so far, with the first rudiment of budding antlers. But in the succeeding age they seem to disappear from the eastern continent, though in the western, thanks to their hand-like feet, opposable thumb, and tree-haunting life, they still drag out a precarious existence in many forms from Virginia to Chili, and from Brazil to California. It is worth while to notice, too, that whereas the kangaroos and other Australian marsupials are proverbially the very stupidest of mammals, the opossums, on the contrary, are well known to those accurate observers of animal psychology, the plantation negroes, to be the very cleverest, cunningest, and slyest of American quadrupeds. In the fierce struggle for life of the crowded American lowlands, the opossum was absolutely forced to acquire a certain amount of Yankee smartness, or else to be improved off the face of the earth by the keen competition of the pouchless mammals.

Up to the day, then, when Captain Cook and Sir Joseph Banks, landing for the first time on the coast of New South Wales, saw an animal with short front limbs, huge hind legs, a monstrous tail, and a curious habit of hopping along the ground (called by the natives a kangaroo), the opossums of America were the only pouched mammals known to the European world in any part of the explored continents. Australia, severed from all the rest of the earth—*penitus toto orbe divisa*—ever since the end of the secondary period, remained as yet, so to speak, in the secondary age so far as its larger life-elements were concerned, and presented to the first comers a certain vague and indefinite picture of what 'the world before the flood' must have looked like. Only it was a very remote flood; an antediluvian age separated from our own not by thousands, but by millions, of seasons.

To this rough approximate statement, however, sundry needful qualifications must be made at the very outset. No statement is ever quite correct until you have contradicted in minute detail about two-thirds of it.

In the first place there are a good many modern elements in the indigenous population of Australia; but then they are elements of the stray and casual sort one always finds even in remote oceanic islands. They are waifs wafted by accident from other places. For example, the flora is by no means exclusively an ancient flora, for a considerable number of seeds and fruits and spores of ferns always get blown by the wind, or washed by the sea, or carried on the feet or feathers of birds, from one part of the world to another. In all these various ways, no doubt, modern plants from the Asiatic region have invaded Australia at different times, and altered to some extent the character and aspect of its original native vegetation. Nevertheless, even in the matter of its plants and trees, Australia must still be considered a very old-fashioned and stick-in-the-mud continent. The strange puzzle-monkeys, the quaint-jointed casuarinas (like horsetails grown into big willows), and the park-like forests of blue gum-trees, with their smooth stems robbed of their outer bark, impart a marvellously antiquated and unfamiliar tone to the general appearance of Australian woodland. All these types belong by birth to classes long since extinct in the larger continents. The scrub shows no turfy greensward; grasses, which elsewhere carpet the ground, were almost unknown till introduced from Europe; in the wild lands, bushes, and undershrubs of ancient aspect cover the soil, remarkable for their stiff, dry, wiry foliage, their vertically instead of horizontally flattened leaves, and their general dead blue-green or glaucous colour. Altogether, the vegetation itself, though it contains a few more modern forms than the animal world, is still essentially antique in type, a strange survival from the forgotten flora of the chalk age, the oolite, and even the lias.

Again, to winged animals, such as birds and bats and flying insects, the ocean forms far less of a barrier than it does to quadrupeds, to reptiles, and to fresh-water fishes. Hence Australia has, to some extent, been invaded by later types of birds and other flying creatures, who live on there side by side with the ancient animals of the secondary pattern. Warblers, thrushes, flycatchers, shrikes, and crows must all be comparatively recent immigrants from the Asiatic mainland. Even in this respect, however, the Australian life-region still bears an antiquated and undeveloped aspect. Nowhere else in the world do we find those very oldest types of birds represented by the cassowaries, the emus, and the mooruk of New Britain. The extreme term in this exceedingly ancient set of creature is given us by the wingless bird, the apteryx or kiwi of New Zealand, whose feathers nearly resemble hair, and whose grotesque appearance makes it as much a wonder in its own class as the puzzle-monkey and the casuarina are among forest trees. No feathered creatures so closely

H

approach the lizard-tailed birds of the oolite or the toothed birds of the cretaceous period as do these Australian and New Zealand emus and apteryxes. Again, while many characteristic Oriental families are quite absent, like the vultures, woodpeckers, pheasants and bulbuls, the Australian region has many other fairly ancient birds, found nowhere else on the surface of our modern planet. Such are the so-called brush turkeys and mound builders, the only feathered things that never sit upon their own eggs, but allow them to be hatched, after the fashion of reptiles, by the heat of the sand or of fermenting vegetable matter. The piping crows, the honeysuckers, the lyre-birds, and the more-porks are all peculiar to the Australian region. So are the wonderful and æsthetic bower-birds. Brush-tongued lories, black cockatoos, and gorgeously coloured pigeons, though somewhat less antique, perhaps, in type, give a special character to the bird-life of the country. And in New Guinea, an isolated bit of the same old continent, the birds of paradise, found nowhere else in the whole world, seem to recall some forgotten Eden of the remote past, some golden age of Saturnian splendour. Poetry apart, into which I have dropped for a moment like Mr. Silas Wegg, the birds of paradise are, in fact, gorgeously dressed crows, specially adapted to forest life in a rich fruit-bearing tropical country, where food is abundant and enemies unknown.

Last of all, a certain small number of modern mammals have passed over to Australia at various times by pure chance. They fall into two classes—the rats and mice, who doubtless got transported across on floating logs or balks of timber ; and the human importations, including the dog, who came, perhaps on their owners' canoes, perhaps on the wreck and *débris* of inundations. Yet even in these cases again, Australia still maintains its proud pre-eminence as the most antiquated and unprogressive of continents. For the Australian black-fellow must have got there a very long time ago indeed ; he belongs to an extremely ancient human type, and strikingly recalls in his jaws and skull the Neanderthal savage and other early prehistoric races ; while the woolly-headed Tasmanian, a member of a totally distinct human family, and perhaps the very lowest sample of humanity that has survived to modern times, must have crossed over to Tasmania even earlier still, his brethren on the mainland having no doubt been exterminated later on when the stone-age Australian black-fellows first got cast ashore upon the continent inhabited by the yet more barbaric and helpless negrito race. As for the dingo, or Australian wild dog, only half domesticated by the savage natives, he represents a low ancestral dog type, half wolf and half jackal, incapable of the higher canine traits, and with a suspicious, ferocious, glaring eye that betrays at once his uncivilisable tendencies.

Omitting these later importations, however—the modern plants, birds, and human beings—it may be fairly said that Australia is still in its secondary stage, while the rest of the world has reached the tertiary and quaternary periods. Here again, however, a deduction must be made, in order to attain the necessary accuracy. Even in Australia the world never stands still. Though the Australian animals are still at bottom the European and Asiatic animals of the secondary age, they are those animals with a difference. They have undergone an evolution of their own. It has not been the evolution of the great continents ; but it has been evolution all the same ; slower, more local, narrower, more restricted, yet evolution in the truest sense. One might compare the difference to the difference between the civilisation of Europe and the civilisation of Mexico or Peru. The Mexicans, when Cortez blotted out their in-

digenous culture, were still, to be sure, in their stone age ;
but it was a very different stone age from that of the cave-
dwellers or mound builders in Britain.   Even so, though
Australia is still zoologically in the secondary period, it is
a secondary period a good deal altered and adapted in detail
to meet the wants of special situations.

The oldest types of animals in Australia are the
ornithorhynchus and the echidna, the ' beast with a bill,'
and the ' porcupine ant-eater ' of popular natural history.
These curious creatures, genuine living fossils, occupy in
some respects an intermediate place between the mammals
on the one hand and the birds and lizards on the other.
The echidna has no teeth, and a very bird-like skull and
body ; the ornithorhynchus has a bill like a duck's, webbed
feet, and a great many quaint anatomical peculiarities
which closely ally it to the birds and reptiles.   Both, in fact,
are early arrested stages in the development of mammals
from the old common vertebrate ancestor ; and they could
only have struggled on to our own day in a continent free
from the severe competition of the higher types which have
since been evolved in Europe and Asia.   Even in Australia
itself the ornithorhynchus and echidna have had to put up
perforce with the lower places in the hierarchy of nature.
The first is a burrowing and aquatic creature, specialised
in a thousand minute ways for his amphibious life and
queer subterranean habits ; the second is a spiny hedge-
hog-like nocturnal prowler, who buries himself in the earth
during the day, and lives by night on insects which he
licks up greedily with his long ribbon-like tongue.   Apart
from the specialisations brought about by their necessary
adaptation to a particular niche in the economy of life,
these two quaint and very ancient animals probably
preserve for us in their general structure the features of
an extremely early descendant of the common ancestor

from whom mammals, birds, and reptiles alike are originally derived.

The ordinary Australian pouched mammals belong to far less ancient types than ornithorhynchus and echidna, but they too are very old in structure, though they have undergone an extraordinary separate evolution to fit them for the most diverse positions in life. Almost every main form of higher mammal (except the biggest ones) has, as it were, its analogue or representative among the marsupial fauna of the Australasian region fitted to fill the same niche in nature. For instance, in the blue gum forests of New South Wales a small animal inhabits the trees, in form and aspect exactly like a flying squirrel. Nobody who was not a structural and anatomical naturalist would ever for a moment dream of doubting its close affinity to the flying squirrels of the American woodlands. It has just the same general outline, just the same bushy tail, just the same rough arrangement of colours, and just the same expanded parachute-like membrane stretching between the fore and hind limbs. Why should this be so? Clearly because both animals have independently adapted themselves to the same mode of life under the same general circumstances. Natural selection, acting upon unlike original types, but in like conditions, has produced in the end very similar results in both cases. Still, when we come to examine the more intimate underlying structure of the two animals, a profound fundamental difference at once exhibits itself. The one is distinctly a true squirrel, a rodent of the rodents, externally adapted to an arboreal existence ; the other is equally a true phalanger, a marsupial of the marsupials, which has independently undergone on his own account very much the same adaptation, for very much the same reasons. Just so a dolphin looks externally very like a fish, in head and tail and form and movement ; its flippers closely resemble fins ; and nothing about it seems to differ very markedly from the outer aspect of a shark or a codfish. But in reality it has no gills and no swim-bladder ; it lays no eggs ; it does not own one truly fish-like organ. It breathes air, it possesses lungs, it has warm blood, it suckles its young ; in heart and brain and nerves and organisation it is a thoroughgoing mammal, with an acquired resemblance to the fishy form, due entirely to mere similarity in place of residence.

Running hastily through the chief marsupial developments, one may say that the wombats are pouched animals who take the place of rabbits or marmots in Europe, and resemble them both in burrowing habits and more or less in shape, which closely approaches the familiar and ungraceful guinea-pig outline. The vulpine phalanger does duty for a fox ; the fat and sleepy little dormouse phalanger takes the place of a European dormouse. Both are so ridiculously like the analogous animals of the larger continents that the colonists always call them, in perfect good faith, by the familiar names of the old-country creatures. The koala poses as a small bear ; the cuscus answers to the racoons of America. The pouched badgers explain themselves at once by their very name, like the Plyants, the Pinchwifes, the Brainsicks, and the Carelesses of the Restoration comedy. The ' native rabbit ' of Swan River is a rabbit-like bandicoot ; the pouched ant-eater similarly takes the place of the true ant-eaters of other continents. By way of carnivores, the Tasmanian devil is a fierce and savage marsupial analogue of the American wolverine ; a smaller species of the same type usurps the name and place of the marten ; and the dog-headed Thylacinus is in form and figure precisely like a wolf or a jackal. The pouched weasels are very weasel-like ; the kangaroo rats and kangaroo mice run the true rats and mice a close race in every particular. And it is worth notice, in this connection, that the one marsupial family which could compete with higher American life, the opossums, are really, so to speak, the monkey development of the marsupial race. They have opposable thumbs, which make their feet almost into hands; they have prehensile tails, by which they hang from branches in true monkey fashion; they lead an arboreal omnivorous existence; they feed off fruits, birds' eggs, insects, and roots; and altogether they are just active, cunning, intelligent, tree-haunting marsupial spider-monkeys.

Australia has also one still more ancient denizen than any of these, a living fossil of the very oldest sort, a creature of wholly immemorial and primitive antiquity. The story of its discovery teems with the strangest romance of natural history. To those who could appreciate the facts of the case it was just as curious and just as interesting as though we were now to discover somewhere in an unknown island or an African oasis some surviving mammoth, some belated megatherium, or some gigantic and misshapen liassic saurian. Imagine the extinct animals of the Crystal Palace grounds suddenly appearing to our dazzled eyes in a tropical ramble, and you can faintly conceive the delight and astonishment of naturalists at large when the barramunda first 'swam into their ken' in the rivers of Queensland. To be sure, in size and shape this 'extinct fish,' still living and grunting quietly in our midst, is comparatively insignificant beside the 'dragons of the prime' immortalised in a famous stanza by Tennyson: but, to the true enthusiast, size is nothing; and the barramunda is just as much a marvel and a monster as the Atlantosaurus himself would have been if he had suddenly walked upon the stage of time, dragging fifty feet of lizard-like tail in a train behind him. And this is the plain story of that marvellous discovery of a 'missing link' in our own pedigree.

In the oldest secondary rocks of Britain and elsewhere there occur in abundance the teeth of a genus of ganoid fishes known as the Ceratodi. (I apologise for ganoid, though it is not a swear-word). These teeth reappear from time to time in several subsequent formations, but at last slowly die out altogether; and of course all naturalists naturally concluded that the creature to which they belonged had died out also, and was long since numbered with the dodo and the mastodon. The idea that a Ceratodus could still be living, far less that it formed an important link in the development of all the higher animals, could never for a moment have occurred to anybody. As well expect to find a palæolithic man quietly chipping flints on a Pacific atoll, or to discover the ancestor of all horses on the isolated and crag-encircled summit of Roraima, as to unearth a real live Ceratodus from a modern estuary. In 1870, however, Mr. Krefft took away the breath of scientific Europe by informing it that he had found the extinct ganoid swimming about as large as life, and six feet long, without the faintest consciousness of its own scientific importance, in a river in Queensland at the present day. The unsophisticated aborigines knew it as barramunda; the almost equally ignorant white settlers called it with irreverent and unfilial contempt the flat-head. On further examination, however, the despised barramunda proved to be a connecting link of primary rank between the oldest surviving group of fishes and the lowest air-breathing animals like the frogs and salamanders. Though a true fish, it leaves its native streams at night, and sets out on a foraging expedition after vegetable food in the neighbouring woodlands. There it browses on myrtle leaves and grasses, and otherwise behaves itself in a manner wholly unbecoming its piscine antecedents and aquatic education. To fit it for this strange amphibious life, the barramunda has both lungs and gills; it can breathe either air or water at will, or, if it chooses, the two together. Though covered with scales, and most fish-like in outline, it presents points of anatomical resemblance both to salamanders and lizards; and, as a connecting bond between the North American mud-fish on the one hand and the wonderful lepidosiren on the other, it forms a true member of the long series by which the higher animals generally trace their descent from a remote race of marine ancestors. It is very interesting, therefore, to find that this living fossil link between fish and reptiles should have survived only in the fossil continent, Australia. Everywhere else it has long since been beaten out of the field by its own more developed amphibian descendants; in Australia alone it still drags on a lonely existence as the last relic of an otherwise long-forgotten and extinct family.

A VERY OLD MASTER

THE work of art which lies before me is old, unquestionably old; a good deal older, in fact, than Archbishop Ussher (who invented all out of his own archiepiscopal head the date commonly assigned for the creation of the world) would by any means have been ready to admit. It is a bas-relief by an old master, considerably more antique in origin than the most archaic gem or intaglio in the Museo Borbonico at Naples, the mildly decorous Louvre in Paris, or the eminently respectable British Museum, which is the glory of our own smoky London in the spectacled eyes of German professors, all put together. When Assyrian sculptors carved in fresh white alabaster the flowing curls of Sennacherib's hair, just like a modern coachman's wig, this work of primæval art was already hoary with the rime of ages. When Memphian artists were busy in the morning twilight of time with the towering coiffure of Ramses or Sesostris, this far more ancient relic of plastic handicraft was lying, already fossil and forgotten, beneath the concreted floor of a cave in the Dordogne. If we were to divide the period for which we possess authentic records of man's abode upon this oblate spheroid into ten epochs— an epoch being a good high-sounding word which doesn't commit one to any definite chronology in particular—then it is probable that all known art, from the Egyptian onward, would fall into the tenth of the epochs thus loosely demarcated, while my old French bas-relief would fall into the first. To put the date quite succinctly, I should say it was most likely about 244,000 years before the creation of Adam according to Ussher.

The work of the old master is lightly incised on reindeer horn, and represents two horses, of a very early and heavy type, following one another, with heads stretched forward, as if sniffing the air suspiciously in search of enemies. The horses would certainly excite unfavourable comment at Newmarket. Their ' points ' are undoubtedly coarse and clumsy : their heads are big, thick, stupid, and ungainly ; their manes are bushy and ill-defined ; their legs are distinctly feeble and spindle-shaped ; their tails more closely resemble the tail of the domestic pig than that of the noble animal beloved with a love passing the love of women by the English aristocracy. Nevertheless there is little (if any) reason to doubt that my very old master did, on the whole, accurately represent the ancestral steed of his own exceedingly remote period. There were once horses even as is the horse of the pre-historic Dordonian artist. Such clumsy, big-headed brutes, dun in hue and striped down the back like modern donkeys, did actually once roam over the low plains where Paris now stands, and browse off lush grass and tall water-plants around the quays of Bordeaux and Lyons. Not only do the bones of the contemporary horses, dug up in caves, prove this, but quite recently the Russian traveller Prjevalsky (whose name is so much easier to spell than to pronounce) has discovered a similar living horse, which drags on an obscure existence somewhere in the high table-lands of Central Asia. Prjevalsky's horse (you see, as I have only to write the word, without uttering it, I don't mind how often or how intrepidly I use it) is so singularly like the clumsy brutes that sat, or rather stood, for their portraits to my old master that we can't do better than begin by describing him *in propria persona.*

The horse family of the present day is divided, like most other families, into two factions, which may be described for variety's sake as those of the true horses and the donkeys, these latter including also the zebras, quaggas, and various other unfamiliar creatures whose names, in very choice Latin, are only known to the more diligent visitors at the Sunday Zoo. Now everybody must have noticed that the chief broad distinction between these two great groups consists in the feathering of the tail. The domestic donkey, with his near congeners, the zebra and co. have smooth short-haired tails, ending in a single bunch or fly-whisk of long hairs collected together in a tufted bundle at the extreme tip. The horse, on the other hand, besides having horny patches or callosities on both fore and hind legs, while the donkeys have them on the fore legs only, has a hairy tail, in which the long hairs are almost equally distributed from top to bottom, thus giving it its peculiarly bushy and brushy appearance. But Prjevalsky's horse, as one would naturally expect from an early intermediate form, stands halfway in this respect between the two groups, and acts the thankless part of a family mediator; for it has most of its long tail-hairs collected in a final flourish, like the donkey, but several of them spring from the middle distance, as in the genuine Arab, though never from the very top, thus showing an approach to the true horsey habit without actually attaining that final pinnacle of equine glory. So far as one can make out from the somewhat rude handicraft of my prehistoric Phidias the horse of the quaternary epoch had much the same caudal peculiarity; his tail was bushy, but only in the lower half. He was still in the intermediate stage between horse and donkey, a natural mule still struggling up aspiringly toward perfect horsehood. In all other matters the two creatures—the cave man's horse and Prjevalsky's—closely agree. Both display large heads, thick necks, coarse manes, and a general disregard of ' points ' which would strike disgust and dismay into the stout breasts of Messrs. Tattersall. In fact over a T.Y.C. it may be confidently asserted, in the pure Saxon of the sporting papers, that Prjevalsky's and the cave man's lot wouldn't be in it. Nevertheless a candid critic would be forced to admit that, in spite of clumsiness, they both mean staying.

So much for the two sitters ; now let us turn to the artist who sketched them. Who was he, and when did he live ? Well, his name, like that of many other old masters, is quite unknown to us ; but what does that matter so long as his work itself lives and survives ? Like the Comtists he has managed to obtain objective immortality. The work, after all, is for the most part all we ever have to go upon. ' I have my own theory about the authorship of the Iliad and Odyssey,' said Lewis Carroll (of ' Alice in Wonderland ') once in Christ Church common room : ' it is that they weren't really written by Homer, but by another person of the same name.' There you have the Iliad in a nutshell as regards the authenticity of great works. All we know about the supposed Homer (if anything) is that he was the reputed author of the two unapproachable Greek epics ; and all we know directly about my old master, viewed personally, is that he once carved with a rude flint flake on a fragment of reindeer horn these two clumsy prehistoric horses. Yet by putting two and two together we can make, not four, as might be naturally expected, but a fairly connected history of the old master himself and what Mr. Herbert Spencer would no doubt playfully term ' his environment.'

The work of art was dug up from under the firm concreted floor of a cave in the Dordogne. That cave was once nhabited by the nameless artist himself, his wife, and family. It had been previously tenanted by various other early families, as well as by bears, who seem to have lived there in the intervals between the different human occupiers. Probably the bears ejected the men, and the men in turn ejected the bears, by the summary process of eating one another up. In any case the freehold of the cave was at last settled upon our early French artist. But the date of his occupancy is by no means recent; for since he lived there the long cold spell known as the Great Ice Age, or Glacial Epoch, has swept over the whole of Northern Europe, and swept before it the shivering descendants of my poor prehistoric old master. Now, how long ago was the Great Ice Age? As a rule, if you ask a geologist for a definite date, you will find him very chary of giving you a distinct answer. He knows that the chalk is older than the London clay, and the oolite than the chalk, and the red marl than the oolite; and he knows also that each of them took a very long time indeed to lay down, but exactly how long he has no notion. If you say to him, 'Is it a million years since the chalk was deposited?' he will answer, like the old lady of Prague, whose ideas were excessively vague, 'Perhaps.' If you suggest five millions, he will answer oracularly once more, 'Perhaps'; and if you go on to twenty millions, 'Perhaps,' with a broad smile, is still the only confession of faith that torture will wring out of him. But in the matter of the Glacial Epoch, a comparatively late and almost historical event, geologists have broken through their usual reserve on this chronological question and condescended to give us a numerical determination. And here is how Dr. Croll gets at it.

Every now and again, geological evidence goes to show us, a long cold spell occurs in the northern or southern hemisphere. During these long cold spells the ice cap at the poles increases largely, till it spreads over a great part of what are now the temperate regions of the globe, and makes ice a mere drug in the market as far south as Covent Garden or the Halles at Paris. During the greatest extension of this ice sheet in the last glacial epoch, in fact, all England except a small south-western corner (about Torquay and Bournemouth) was completely covered by one enormous mass of glaciers, as is still the case with almost the whole of Greenland. The ice sheet, grinding slowly over the hills and rocks, smoothed and polished and striated their surfaces in many places till they resembled the *roches moutonnées* similarly ground down in our own day by the moving ice rivers of Chamouni and Grindelwald. Now, since these great glaciations have occurred at various intervals in the world's past history, they must depend upon some frequently recurring cause. Such a cause, therefore, Dr. Croll began ingeniously to hunt about for.

He found it at last in the eccentricity of the earth's orbit. This world of ours, though usually steady enough in its movements, is at times decidedly eccentric. Not that I mean to impute to our old and exceedingly respectable planet any occasional aberrations of intellect, or still less of morals (such as might be expected from Mars and Venus) ; the word is here to be accepted strictly in its scientific or Pickwickian sense as implying merely an irregularity of movement, a slight wobbling out of the established path, a deviation from exact circularity. Owing to a combination of astronomical revolutions, the precession of the equinoxes and the motion of the aphelion (I am not going to explain them here ; the names alone will be quite sufficient for most people ; they will take the

rest on trust)—owing to the combination of these profoundly interesting causes, I say, there occur certain
periods in the world's life when for a very long time together (10,500 years, to be quite precise) the northern
hemisphere is warmer than the southern, or *vice versa*.
Now, Dr. Croll has calculated that about 250,000 years ago
this eccentricity of the earth's orbit was at its highest, so
that a cycle of recurring cold and warm epochs in either
hemisphere alternately then set in ; and such cold spells it
was that produced the Great Ice Age in Northern Europe.
They went on till about 80,000 years ago, when they
stopped short for the present, leaving the climate of
Britain and the neighbouring continent with its existing
inconvenient Laodicean temperature. And, as there are
good reasons for believing that my old master and his
contemporaries lived just before the greatest cold of the
Glacial Epoch, and that his immediate descendants, with
the animals on which they feasted, were driven out of
Europe, or out of existence, by the slow approach of the
enormous ice sheet, we may, I think, fairly conclude that
his date was somewhere about B.C. 248,000. In any case
we must at least admit, with Mr. Andrew Lang, the
laureate of the twenty-five thousandth century, that

> He lived in the long long agoes ;
> 'Twas the manner of primitive man.

The old master, then, carved his bas-relief in pre-
Glacial Europe, just at the moment before the temporary
extinction of his race in France by the coming on of the
Great Ice Age. We can infer this fact from the character
of the fauna by which he was surrounded, a fauna in
which species of cold and warm climates are at times
quite capriciously intermingled. We get the reindeer and
the mammoth side by side with the hippopotamus and the

hyena; we find the chilly cave bear and the Norway lemming, the musk sheep and the Arctic fox in the same deposits with the lion and the lynx, the leopard and the rhinoceros. The fact is, as Mr. Alfred Russel Wallace has pointed out, we live to-day in a zoologically impoverished world, from which all the largest, fiercest, and most remarkable animals have lately been weeded out. And it was in all probability the coming on of the Ice Age that did the weeding. Our Zoo can boast no mammoth and no mastodon. The sabre-toothed lion has gone the way of all flesh; the deinotherium and the colossal ruminants of the Pliocene Age no longer browse beside the banks of Seine. But our old master saw the last of some at least among those gigantic quadrupeds; it was his hand or that of one among his fellows that scratched the famous mammoth etching on the ivory of La Madelaine and carved the figure of the extinct cave bear on the reindeer-horn ornaments of Laugerie Basse. Probably, therefore, he lived in the period immediately preceding the Great Ice Age, or else perhaps in one of the warm interglacial spells with which the long secular winter of the northern hemisphere was then from time to time agreeably diversified.

And what did the old master himself look like? Well, painters have always been fond of reproducing their own lineaments. Have we not the familiar young Raffael, painted by himself, and the Rembrandt, and the Titian, and the Rubens, and a hundred other self-drawn portraits, all flattering and all famous? Even so primitive man has drawn himself many times over, not indeed on this particular piece of reindeer horn, but on several other media to be seen elsewhere, in the original or in good copies. One of the best portraits is that discovered in the old cave at Laugerie Basse by M. Elie Massénat, where a

I

very early pre-Glacial man is represented in the act of hunting an aurochs, at which he is casting a flint-tipped javelin. In this, as in all other pictures of the same epoch, I regret to say that the ancient hunter is represented in the costume of Adam before the fall. Our old master's studies, in fact, are all in the nude. Primitive man was evidently unacquainted as yet with the use of clothing, though primitive woman, while still unclad, had already learnt how to heighten her natural charms by the simple addition of a necklace and bracelets. Indeed, though dresses were still wholly unknown, rouge was even then extremely fashionable among French ladies, and lumps of the ruddle with which primitive woman made herself beautiful for ever are now to be discovered in the corner of the cave where she had her little prehistoric boudoir. To return to our hunter, however, who for aught we know to the contrary may be our old master himself in person, he is a rather crouching and semi-erect savage, with an arched back, recalling somewhat that of the gorilla, a round head, long neck, pointed beard, and weak, shambling, ill-developed legs. I fear we must admit that pre-Glacial man cut, on the whole, a very sorry and awkward figure.

Was he black? That we don't certainly know, but all analogy would lead one to answer positively, Yes. White men seem, on the whole, to be a very recent and novel improvement on the original evolutionary pattern. At any rate he was distinctly hairy, like the Ainos, or aborigines of Japan, in our own day, of whom Miss Isabella Bird has drawn so startling and sensational a picture. Several of the pre-Glacial sketches show us lank and gawky savages with the body covered with long scratches, answering exactly to the scratches which represent the hanging hair of the mammoth, and suggesting that man then still retained his old original hairy covering. The few skulls and other fragments of skeletons now preserved to us also indicate that our old master and his contemporaries much resembled in shape and build the Australian black fellows, though their foreheads were lower and more receding, while their front teeth still projected in huge fangs, faintly recalling the immense canines of the male gorilla. Quite apart from any theoretical considerations as to our probable descent (or ascent) from Mr. Darwin's hypothetical ' hairy arboreal quadrumanous ancestor,' whose existence may or may not be really true, there can be no doubt that the actual historical remains set before us pre-Glacial man as evidently approaching in several important respects the higher monkeys.

It is interesting to note too that while the Men of the Time still retained (to be frankly evolutionary) many traces of the old monkey-like progenitor, the horses which our old master has so cleverly delineated for us on his scrap of horn similarly retained many traces of the earlier united horse-and-donkey ancestor. Professor Huxley has admirably reconstructed for us the pedigree of the horse, beginning with a little creature from the Eocene beds of New Mexico, with five toes to each hind foot, and ending with the modern horse, whose hoof is now practically reduced to a single and solid-nailed toe. Intermediate stages show us an Upper Eocene animal as big as a fox, with four toes on his front feet and three behind ; a Miocene kind as big as a sheep, with only three toes on the front foot, the two outer of which are smaller than the big middle one ; and finally a Pliocene form, as big as a donkey, with one stout middle toe, the real hoof, flanked by two smaller ones, too short by far to reach the ground. In our own horse these lateral toes have become reduced to what are known by veterinaries as splint bones, combined with the canon in a single solidly morticed piece. But in the pre-

Glacial horses the splint bones still generally remained quite distinct, thus pointing back to the still earlier period when they existed as two separate and independent side toes in the ancestral quadruped. In a few cave specimens, however, the splints are found united with the canons in a single piece, while conversely horses are sometimes, though very rarely, born at the present day with three-toed feet, exactly resembling those of their half-forgotten ancestor, the Pliocene hipparion.

The reason why we know so much about the horses of the cave period is, I am bound to admit, simply and solely because the man of the period ate them. Hippophagy has always been popular in France; it was practised by pre-Glacial man in the caves of Périgord, and revived with immense enthusiasm by the gourmets of the Boulevards after the siege of Paris and the hunger of the Commune. The cave men hunted and killed the wild horse of their own times, and one of the best of their remaining works of art represents a naked hunter attacking two horses, while a huge snake winds itself unperceived behind close to his heel. In this rough prehistoric sketch one seems to catch some faint antique foreshadowing of the rude humour of the 'Petit Journal pour Rire.' Some archæologists even believe that the horse was domesticated by the cave men as a source of food, and argue that the familiarity with its form shown in the drawings could only have been acquired by people who knew the animal in its domesticated state; they declare that the cave man was obviously horsey. But all the indications seem to me to show that tame animals were quite unknown in the age of the cave men. The mammoth certainly was never domesticated; yet there is a famous sketch of the huge beast upon a piece of his own ivory, discovered in the cave of La Madelaine by Messrs. Lartet and Christy, and engraved a hundred times in works on archæology, which forms one of the finest existing relics of pre-Glacial art. In another sketch, less well known, but not unworthy of admiration, the early artist has given us with a few rapid but admirable strokes his own reminiscence of the effect produced upon him by the sudden onslaught of the hairy brute, tusks erect and mouth wide open, a perfect glimpse of elephantine fury. It forms a capital example of early impressionism, respectfully recommended to the favourable attention of Mr. J. M. Whistler.

The reindeer, however, formed the favourite food and favourite model of the pre-Glacial artists. Perhaps it was a better sitter than the mammoth; certainly it is much more frequently represented on these early prehistoric bas-reliefs. The high-water mark of palæolithic art is undoubtedly to be found in the reindeer of the cave of Thayngen, in Switzerland, a capital and spirited representation of a buck grazing, in which the perspective of the two horns is better managed than a Chinese artist would manage it at the present day. Another drawing of two reindeer fighting, scratched on a fragment of schistose rock and unearthed in one of the caves of Périgord, though far inferior to the Swiss specimen in spirit and execution, is yet not without real merit. The perspective, however, displays one marked infantile trait, for the head and legs of one deer are seen distinctly through the body of another. Cave bears, fish, musk sheep, foxes, and many other extinct or existing animals are also found among the archaic sculptures. Probably all these creatures were used as food; and it is even doubtful whether the artistic troglodytes were not also confirmed cannibals. To quote Mr. Andrew Lang once more on primitive man, ' he lived in a cave by the seas; he lived upon oysters and foes. The oysters are quite undoubted, and the foes may be inferred with considerable certainty.

I have spoken of our old master more than once under this rather question-begging style and title of primitive man. In reality, however, the very facts which I have here been detailing serve themselves to show how extremely far our hero was from being truly primitive. You can't speak of a distinguished artist, who draws the portraits of extinct animals with grace and accuracy, as in any proper sense primordial. Grant that our good troglodytes were indeed light-hearted cannibals; nevertheless they could design far better than the modern Esquimaux or Polynesians, and carve far better than the civilised being who is now calmly discoursing about their personal peculiarities in his own study. Between the cave men of the pre-Glacial age and the hypothetical hairy quadrumanous ancestor aforesaid there must have intervened innumerable generations of gradually improving intermediate forms. The old master, when he first makes his bow to us, naked and not ashamed, in his Swiss or French grotto, flint scalpel in hand and necklet of bear's teeth dropping loosely on his hairy bosom, is nevertheless in all essentials a completely evolved human being, with a whole past of slowly acquired culture lying dimly and mysteriously behind him. Already he had invented the bow with its flint-tipped arrow, the neatly chipped javelin-head, the bone harpoon, the barbed fish-hook, the axe, the lance, the dagger, and the needle. Already he had learnt how to decorate his implements with artistic skill, and to carve the handles of his knives with the figures of animals. I have no doubt that he even knew how to brew and to distil; and he was probably acquainted with the noble art of cookery as applied to the persons of his human fellow creatures. Such a personage cannot reasonably be called primitive; cannibalism, as somebody has rightly remarked, is the first step on the road to civilisation.

No, if we want to get at genuine, unadulterated primitive man we must go much further back in time than the mere trifle of 250,000 years with which Dr. Croll and the cosmic astronomers so generously provide us for pre-Glacial humanity. We must turn away to the immeasurably earlier fire-split flints which the Abbé Bourgeois—undaunted mortal !—ventured to discover among the Miocene strata of the *calcaire de Beauce*. Those flints, if of human origin at all, were fashioned by some naked and still more hairy creature who might fairly claim to be considered as genuinely primitive. So rude are they that, though evidently artificial, one distinguished archæologist will not admit they can be in any way human ; he will have it that they were really the handiwork of the great European anthropoid ape of that early period. This, however, is nothing more than very delicate hair-splitting; for what does it matter whether you call the animal that fashioned these exceedingly rough and fire-marked implements a man-like ape or an ape-like human being ? The fact remains quite unaltered, whichever name you choose to give to it. When you have got to a monkey who can light a fire and proceed to manufacture himself a convenient implement, you may be sure that man, noble man, with all his glorious and admirable faculties—cannibal or otherwise—is lurking somewhere very close just round the corner. The more we examine the work of our old master, in fact, the more does the conviction force itself upon us that he was very far indeed from being primitive—that we must push back the early history of our race not for 250,000 winters alone, but perhaps for two or three million years into the dim past of Tertiary ages.

But if pre-Glacial man is thus separated from the origin of the race by a very long interval indeed, it is none the less true that he is separated from our own time by

the intervention of a vast blank space, the space occupied
by the coming on and passing away of the Glacial Epoch.
A great gap cuts him off from what we may consider as the
relatively modern age of the mound-builders, whose grassy
barrows still cap the summits of our southern chalk downs.
When the great ice sheet drove away palæolithic man—the
man of the caves and the unwrought flint axes—from
Northern Europe, he was still nothing more than a naked
savage in the hunting stage, divinely gifted for art, indeed,
but armed only with roughly chipped stone implements,
and wholly ignorant of taming animals or of the very
rudiments of agriculture.   He knew nothing of the use of
metals—*aurum irrepertum spernere fortior*—and he had
not even learnt how to grind and polish his rude stone
tomahawks to a finished edge.   He couldn't make himself
a bowl of sun-baked pottery, and, if he had discovered the
almost universal art of manufacturing an intoxicating liquor
from grain or berries (for, as Byron, with too great anthropo-
logical truth, justly remarks, ' man, being reasonable, *must*
get drunk '), he at least drank his aboriginal beer or toddy
from the capacious horn of a slaughtered aurochs.   That
was the kind of human being who alone inhabited France
and England during the later pre-Glacial period.

A hundred and seventy thousand years elapse (as the
play-bills put it), and then the curtain rises afresh upon
neolithic Europe.   Man meanwhile, loitering somewhere
behind the scenes in Asia or Africa (as yet imperfectly explored from this point of view), had acquired the important
arts of sharpening his tomahawks and producing hand-
made pottery for his kitchen utensils.   When the great ice
sheet cleared away he followed the returning summer into
Northern Europe, another man, physically, intellectually,
and morally, with all the slow accumulations of nearly two
thousand centuries (how easily one writes the words ! how

hard to realise them !) upon his maturer shoulders. Then comes the age of what older antiquaries used to regard as primitive antiquity—the age of the English barrows, of the Danish kitchen middens, of the Swiss lake dwellings. The men who lived in it had domesticated the dog, the cow, the sheep, the goat, and the invaluable pig ; they had begun to sow small ancestral wheat and undeveloped barley ; they had learnt to weave flax and wear decent clothing : in a word, they had passed from the savage hunting condition to the stage of barbaric herdsmen and agriculturists. That is a comparatively modern period, and yet I suppose we must conclude with Dr. James Geikie that it isn't to be measured by mere calculations of ten or twenty centuries, but of ten or twenty thousand years. The perspective of the past is opening up rapidly before us ; what looked quite close yesterday is shown to-day to lie away off somewhere in the dim distance. Like our palæolithic artists, we fail to get the reindeer fairly behind the ox in the foreground, as we ought to do if we saw the whole scene properly foreshortened.

On the table where I write there lie two paper-weights, preserving from the fate of the sibylline leaves the sheets of foolscap to which this essay is now being committed. One of them is a very rude flint hatchet, produced by merely chipping off flakes from its side by dexterous blows, and utterly unpolished or unground in any way. It belongs to the age of the very old master (or possibly even to a slightly earlier epoch), and it was sent me from Ightham, in Kent, by that indefatigable unearther of prehistoric memorials, Mr. Benjamin Harrison. That flint, which now serves me in the office of a paper-weight, is far ruder, simpler, and more ineffective than any weapon or implement at present in use among the lowest savages. Yet with it, I doubt not, some naked black fellow by the banks of the Thames has hunted the mammoth among unbroken forest two hundred thousand years ago and more ; with it he has faced the angry cave bear and the original and only genuine British lion (for everybody knows that the existing mongrel heraldic beast is nothing better than a bastard modification of the leopard of the Plantagenets). Nay, I have very little doubt in my own mind that with it some æsthetic ancestor has brained and cut up for his use his next-door neighbour in the nearest cavern, and then carved upon his well-picked bones an interesting sketch of the entire performance. The Du Mauriers of that remote age, in fact, habitually drew their society pictures upon the personal remains of the mammoth or the man whom they wished to caricature in deathless bone-cuts. The other paper-weight is a polished neolithic tomahawk, belonging to the period of the mound-builders, who succeeded the Glacial Epoch, and it measures the distance between the two levels of civilisation with great accuracy. It is the military weapon of a trained barbaric warrior as opposed to the universal implement and utensil of a rude, solitary, savage hunter. Yet how curious it is that even in the midst of this ' so-called nineteenth century,' which perpetually pro-claims itself an age of progress, men should still prefer to believe themselves inferior to their original ancestors, instead of being superior to them ! The idea that man has risen is considered base, degrading, and positively wicked ; the idea that he has fallen is considered to be immensely inspiring, ennobling, and beautiful. For myself, I have somehow always preferred the boast of the Homeric Glaucus that we indeed maintain ourselves to be much better men than ever were our fathers.

BRITISH AND FOREIGN

STRICTLY speaking, there is nothing really and truly British; everybody and everything is a naturalised alien. Viewed as Britons, we all of us, human and animal, differ from one another simply in the length of time we and our ancestors have continuously inhabited this favoured and foggy isle of Britain. Look, for example, at the men and women of us. Some of us, no doubt, are more or less remotely of Norman blood, and came over, like that noble family the Slys, with Richard Conqueror. Others of us, perhaps, are in the main Scandinavian, and date back a couple of generations earlier, to the bare-legged followers of Canute and Guthrum. Yet others, once more, are true Saxon Englishmen, descendants of Hengest, if there ever was a Hengest, or of Horsa, if a genuine Horsa ever actually existed. None of these, it is quite clear, have any just right or title to be considered in the last resort as true-born Britons; they are all of them just as much foreigners at bottom as the Spitalfields Huguenots or the Pembrokeshire Flemings, the Italian organ-boy and the Hindoo prince disguised as a crossing-sweeper. But surely the Welshman and the Highland Scot at least are undeniable Britishers, sprung from the soil and to the manner born ! Not a bit of it ; inexorable modern science, diving back remorselessly into the remoter past, traces the Cymry across the face of Germany, and fixes in shadowy hypothetical numbers the exact date, to a few centuries, of the first prehistoric Gaelic invasion. Even the still earlier brown Euskarians and yellow Mongolians, who held the land before the advent of the ancient Britons, were themselves immigrants ; the very Autochthones in person turn out, on close inspection, to be vagabonds and wanderers and foreign colonists. In short, man as a whole is not an indigenous animal at all in the British Isles. Be he who he may, when we push his pedigree back to its prime original, we find him always arriving in the end by the Dover steamer or the Harwich packet. Five years, in fact, are quite sufficient to give him a legal title to letters of naturalisation, unless indeed he be a German grand-duke, in which case he can always become an Englishman offhand by Act of Parliament.

It is just the same with all the other animals and plants that now inhabit these isles of Britain. If there be any-thing at all with a claim to be considered really indigenous, it is the Scotch ptarmigan and the Alpine hare, the northern holygrass and the mountain flowers of the Highland sum-mits. All the rest are sojourners and wayfarers, brought across as casuals, like the gipsies and the Oriental plane, at various times to the United Kingdom, some of them recently, some of them long ago, but not one of them (it seems), except the oyster, a true native. The common brown rat, for instance, as everybody knows, came over, not, it is true, with William the Conqueror, but with the Hanoverian dynasty and King George I. of blessed memory. The familiar cockroach, or 'black beetle,' of our lower regions, is an Oriental importation of the last century. The hum of the mosquito is now just beginning to be heard in the land, especially in some big London hotels. The Colorado beetle is hourly expected by Cunard steamer. The Canadian roadside erigeron is well established already in the remoter suburbs ; the phylloxera battens on our hothouse vines ; the American river-weed stops the navigation on our principal canals. The Ganges and the Mississippi have long since flooded the tawny Thames, as Juvenal's cynical friend declared the Syrian Orontes had flooded the Tiber. And what has thus been going on slowly within the memory of the last few generations has been going on constantly from time immemorial, and peopling Britain in all its parts with its now existing fauna and flora.

But if all the plants and animals in our islands are thus ultimately imported, the question naturally arises, What was there in Great Britain and Ireland before any of their present inhabitants came to inherit them? The answer is, succinctly, Nothing. Or if this be a little too extreme, then let us imitate the modesty of Mr. Gilbert's hero and modify the statement into Hardly anything. In England, as in Northern Europe generally, modern history begins, not with the reign of Queen Elizabeth, but with the passing away of the Glacial Epoch. During that great age of universal ice our Britain, from end to end, was covered at various times by sea and by glaciers; it resembled on the whole the cheerful aspect of Spitzbergen or Nova Zembla at the present day. A few reindeer wandered now and then over its frozen shores; a scanty vegetation of the correlative reindeer-moss grew with difficulty under the sheets and drifts of endless snow; a stray walrus or an occasional seal basked in the chilly sunshine on the ice-bound coast. But during the greatest extension of the North-European ice-sheet it is probable that life in London was completely extinct; the metropolitan area did not even vegetate. Snow and snow and snow and snow was then the short sum-total of British scenery. Murray's Guides were rendered quite unnecessary, and penny ices were a drug in the market. England was given up to one unchanging universal winter.

Slowly, however, times altered, as they are much given
to doing; and a new era dawned upon Britain.   The thermometer rose rapidly, or at least it would have risen, with
effusion, if it had yet been invented.   The land emerged
from the sea, and southern plants and animals began to
invade the area that was afterwards to be England, across
the broad belt which then connected us with the Continental
system.   But in those days communications were slow and
land transit difficult.   You had to foot it.   The European fauna and flora moved but gradually and tentatively
north-westward, and before any large part of it could settle in
England our island was finally cut off from the mainland
by the long and gradual wearing away of the cliffs at Dover
and Calais.   That accounts for the comparative poverty of
animal and vegetable life in England, and still more for its
extreme paucity and meagreness in Ireland and the Highlands.   It has been erroneously asserted, for example, that
St. Patrick expelled snakes and lizards, frogs and toads, from
the soil of Erin.   This detail, as the French newspapers
politely phrase it, is inexact.   St. Patrick did not expel the
reptiles, because there were never any reptiles in Ireland
(except dynamiters) for him to expel.   The creatures never
got so far on their long and toilsome north-westward march
before St. George's Channel intervened to prevent their
passage across to Dublin.   It is really, therefore, to St.
George, rather than to St. Patrick, that the absence of
toads and snakes from the soil of Ireland is ultimately due.
The doubtful Cappadocian prelate is well known to have
been always death on dragons and serpents.

As long ago as the sixteenth century, indeed, Verstegan
the antiquary clearly saw that the existence of badgers and
foxes in England implied the former presence of a belt of
land joining the British Islands to the Continent of Europe;
for, as he acutely observed, nobody (before fox-hunting, at

least) would ever have taken the trouble to bring them over. Still more does the presence in our islands of the red deer, and formerly of the wild white cattle, the wolf, the bear, and the wild boar, to say nothing of the beaver, the otter, the squirrel, and the weasel, prove that England was once conterminous with France or Belgium. At the very best of times, however, before Sir Ewen Cameron of Lochiel had killed positively the last 'last wolf' in Britain (several other 'last wolves' having previously been des- patched by various earlier intrepid exterminators), our English fauna was far from a rich one, especially as regards the larger quadrupeds. In bats, birds, and insects we have always done better, because to such creatures a belt of sea is not by any means an insuperable barrier; whereas in reptiles and amphibians, on the contrary, we have always been weak, seeing that most reptiles are bad swimmers, and very few can rival the late lamented Captain Webb in his feat of crossing the Channel, as Leander and Lord Byron did the Hellespont.

Only one good-sized animal, so far as known, is now peculiar to the British Isles, and that is our familiar friend the red grouse of the Scotch moors. I doubt, how- ever, whether even he is really indigenous in the strictest sense of the word: that is to say, whether he was evolved in and for these islands exclusively, as the moa and the ap- teryx were evolved for New Zealand, and the extinct dodo for Mauritius alone. It is far more probable that the red grouse is the original variety of the willow grouse of Scandinavia, which has retained throughout the year its old plumage, while its more northern cousins among the fiords and fjelds have taken, under stress of weather, to donning a complete white dress in winter, and a grey or speckled tourist suit for the summer season.

Even since the insulation of Britain a great many new

plants and animals have been added to our population,
both by human design and in several other casual fashions.
The fallow deer is said to have been introduced by the
Romans, and domesticated ever since in the successive
parks of Celt and Saxon, Dane and Norman.   The edible
snail, still scattered thinly over our southern downs, and
abundant at Box Hill and a few other spots in Surrey or
Sussex, was brought over, they tell us, by the same luxurious Italian epicures, and is even now confined, imaginative naturalists declare, to the immediate neighbourhood
of Roman stations.   The mediæval monks, in like manner,
introduced the carp for their Friday dinners.   One of our
commonest river mussels at the present day did not exist
in England at all a century ago, but was ferried hither
from the Volga, clinging to the bottoms of vessels from the
Black Sea, and has now spread itself through all our brooks
and streams to the very heart and centre of England.
Thus, from day to day, as in society at large, new introduc-
tions constantly take place, and old friends die out for ever.
The brown rat replaces the old English black rat ; strange
weeds kill off the weeds of ancient days ; fresh flies and
grubs and beetles crop up, and disturb the primitive
entomological balance.   The bustard is gone from Salisbury Plain ; the fenland butterflies have disappeared with
the drainage of the fens.   In their place the red-legged
partridge invades Norfolk ; the American black bass is
making himself quite at home, with Yankee assurance, in
our sluggish rivers ; and the spoonbill is nesting of its
own accord among the warmer corners of the Sussex downs.

In the plant world, substitution often takes place far
more rapidly.   I doubt whether the stinging nettle, which
renders picnicking a nuisance in England, is truly indigenous ; certainly the two worst kinds, the smaller nettle
and the Roman nettle, are quite recent denizens, never

straying, even at the present day, far from the precincts of
farmyards and villages. The shepherd's-purse and many
other common garden weeds of cultivation are of Eastern
origin, and came to us at first with the seed-corn and the
peas from the Mediterranean region. Corn-cockles and
corn-flowers are equally foreign and equally artificial ; even
the scarlet poppy, seldom found except in wheat-fields or
around waste places in villages, has probably followed the
course of tillage from some remote and ancient Eastern
origin. There is a pretty blue veronica which was unknown
in England some thirty years since, but which then began
to spread in gardens, and is now one of the commonest and
most troublesome weeds throughout the whole country.
Other familiar wild plants have first been brought over as
garden flowers. There is the wall-flower, for instance, now
escaped from cultivation in every part of Britain, and mant-
ling with its yellow bunches both old churches and houses
and also the crannies of the limestone cliffs around half
the shores of England. The common stock has similarly
overrun the sea-front of the Isle of Wight ; the monkey-
plant, originally a Chilian flower, has run wild in many
boggy spots in England and Wales ; and a North American
balsam, seldom cultivated even in cottage gardens, has
managed to establish itself in profuse abundance along the
banks of the Wey about Guildford and Godalming. One
little garden linaria, at first employed as an ornament for
hanging-baskets, has become so common on old walls and
banks as to be now considered a mere weed, and exterminated accordingly by fashionable gardeners. Such are the
unaccountable reverses of fortune, that one age will pay
fifty guineas a bulb for a plant which the next age grubs
up unanimously as a vulgar intruder. White of Selborne
noticed with delight in his own kitchen that rare insect,
the Oriental cockroach, lately imported ; and Mr. Brewer

K

observed with joy in his garden at Reigate the blue Bux-
baum speedwell, which is now the acknowledged and hated
pest of the Surrey agriculturist.

The history of some of these waifs and strays which go
to make up the wider population of Britain is indeed sufficiently remarkable. Like all islands, England has a fragmentary fauna and flora, whose members have often drifted
towards it in the most wonderful and varied manner.
Sometimes they bear witness to ancient land connections,
as in the case of the spotted Portuguese slug which Professor Allman found calmly disporting itself on the basking
cliffs in the Killarney district. In former days, when Spain
and Ireland joined hands in the middle of the Bay of
Biscay, the ancestors of this placid Lusitanian mollusk
must have ranged (good word to apply to slugs) from the
groves of Cintra to the Cove of Cork. But, as time rolled
on, the cruel crawling sea rolled on also, and cut away all
the western world from the foot of the Asturias to
Macgillicuddy's Reeks. So the spotted slug continued to
survive in two distinct and divided bodies, a large one in
South-western Europe, and a small isolated colony, all
alone by itself, around the Kerry mountains and the Lakes
of Killarney. At other times pure accident accounts for
the presence of a particular species in the mainlands of
Britain. For example, the Bermuda grass-lily, a common
American plant, is known in a wild state nowhere in Europe
save at a place called Woodford, in county Galway. Nobody
ever planted it there ; it has simply sprung up from some
single seed, carried over, perhaps, on the feet of a bird, or
cast ashore by the Gulf Stream on the hospitable coast of
Western Ireland. Yet there it has flourished and thriven
ever since, a naturalised British subject of undoubted
origin, without ever spreading to north or south above a
few miles from its adopted habitat.

There are several of these unconscious American importations in various parts of Britain, some of them, no doubt,
brought over with seed-corn or among the straw of packing-
cases, but others unconnected in any way with human
agency, and owing their presence here to natural causes.
That pretty little Yankee weed, the claytonia, now common
in parts of Lancashire and Oxfordshire, first made its
appearance amongst us, I believe, by its seeds being
accidentally included with the sawdust in which Wenham
Lake ice is packed for transport. The Canadian river-weed
is known first to have escaped from the botanical gardens
at Cambridge, whence it spread rapidly through the congenial dykes and sluices of the fen country, and so into
the entire navigable network of the Midland counties. But
there are other aliens of older settlement amongst us, aliens
of American origin which nevertheless arrived in Britain,
in all probability, long before Columbus ever set foot on the
low basking sandbank of Cat Island. Such is the jointed
pond-sedge of the Hebrides, a water-weed found abundantly
in the lakes and tarns of the Isle of Skye, Mull and Coll,
and the west coast of Ireland, but occurring nowhere else
throughout the whole expanse of Europe or Asia. How
did it get there ? Clearly its seeds were either washed by
the waves or carried by birds, and thus deposited on the
nearest European shores to America. But if Mr. Alfred
Russel Wallace had been alive in pre-Columban days
(which, as Euclid remarks, is absurd), he would readily
have inferred, from the frequent occurrence of such unknown plants along the western verge of Britain, that a
great continent lay unexplored to the westward, and would
promptly have proceeded to discover and annex it. As Mr.
Wallace was not yet born, however, Columbus took a mean
advantage over him, and discovered it first by mere right
of primogeniture.

In other cases, the circumstances under which a particular plant appears in England are often very suspicious. Take the instance of the belladonna, or deadly nightshade, an extremely rare British species, found only in the immediate neighbourhood of old castles and monastic buildings. Belladonna, of course, is a deadly poison, and was much used in the half-magical, half-criminal sorceries of the Middle Ages. Did you wish to remove a troublesome rival or an elder brother, you treated him to a dose of deadly nightshade. Yet why should it, in company with many other poisonous exotics, be found so frequently around the ruins of monasteries? Did the holy fathers—but no, the thought is too irreverent. Let us keep our illusions, and forget the friar and the apothecary in 'Romeo and Juliet.'

Belladonna has never fairly taken root in English soil. It remains, like the Roman snail and the Portuguese slug, a mere casual straggler about its ancient haunts. But there are other plants which have fairly established their claim to be considered as native-born Britons, though they came to us at first as aliens and colonists from foreign parts. Such, to take a single case, is the history of the common alexanders, now a familiar weed around villages and farmyards, but only introduced into England as a pot-herb about the eighth or ninth century. It was long grown in cottage gardens for table purposes, but has for ages been superseded in that way by celery. Nevertheless it continues to grow all about our lanes and hedges, side by side with another quaintly-named plant, bishop-weed or gout-weed, whose very titles in themselves bear curious witness to its original uses in this isle of Britain. I don't know why, but it is an historical fact that the early prelates of the English Church, saintly or otherwise, were peculiarly liable to that very episcopal disease, the gout. Whether their frequent fasting produced this effect; whether, as they themselves piously alleged, it was due to constant kneeling on the cold stones of churches; or whether, as their enemies rather insinuated, it was due in greater measure to the excellent wines presented to them by their Italian *confrères*, is a minute question to be decided by Mr. Freeman, not by the present humble inquirer. But the fact remains that bishops and gout got indelibly associated in the public mind; that the episcopal toes were looked upon as especially subject to that insidious disease up to the very end of the last century; and that they do say the bishops even now—but I refrain from the commission of *scandalum magnatum*. Anyhow, this particular weed was held to be a specific for the bishop's evil; and, being introduced and cultivated for the purpose, it came to be known indifferently to herbalists as bishop-weed and gout-weed. It has now long since ceased to be a recognised member of the British Pharmacopœia, but, having overrun our lanes and thickets in its flush period, it remains to this day a visible botanical and etymological memento of the past twinges of episcopal remorse.

Taken as a whole, one may fairly say that the total population of the British Isles consists mainly of three great elements. The first and oldest—the only one with any real claim to be considered as truly native—is the cold Northern, Alpine and Arctic element, comprising such animals as the white hare of Scotland, the ptarmigan, the pine marten, and the capercailzie—the last once extinct, and now reintroduced into the Highlands as a game bird. This very ancient fauna and flora, left behind soon after the Glacial Epoch, and perhaps in part a relic of the type which still struggled on in favoured spots during that terrible period of universal ice and snow, now survives for the most part only in the extreme north and on the highest

and chilliest mountain-tops, where it has gradually been
driven, like tourists in August, by the increasing warmth
and sultriness of the southern lowlands. The summits of
the principal Scotch hills are occupied by many Arctic
plants, now slowly dying out, but lingering yet as last
relics of that old native British flora. The Alpine milk
vetch thus loiters among the rocks of Braemar and Clova ;
the Arctic brook-saxifrage flowers but sparingly near the
summit of Ben Lawers, Ben Nevis, and Lochnagar ; its
still more northern ally, the drooping saxifrage, is now extinct in all Britain, save on a single snowy Scotch height,
where it now rarely blossoms, and will soon become
altogether obsolete. There are other northern plants of
this first and oldest British type, like the Ural oxytrope,
the cloudberry, and the white dryas, which remain as yet
even in the moors of Yorkshire, or over considerable tracts
in the Scotch Highlands ; there are others restricted to a
single spot among the Welsh hills, an isolated skerry
among the outer Hebrides, or a solitary summit in the
Lake District. But wherever they linger, these true-born
Britons of the old rock are now but strangers and outcasts
in the land ; the intrusive foreigner has driven them to die
on the cold mountain-tops, as the Celt drove the Mongolian
to the hills, and the Saxon, in turn, has driven the Celt to
the Highlands and the islands. Yet as late as the twelfth
century itself, even the true reindeer, the Arctic monarch
of the Glacial Epoch, was still hunted by Norwegian jarls
of Orkney on the mainland of Caithness and Sutherland-
shire.

Second in age is the warm western and south-western
type, the type represented by the Portuguese slug, the
arbutus trees and Mediterranean heaths of the Killarney
district, the flora of Cornwall and the Scilly Isles, and the
peculiar wild flowers of South Wales, Devonshire, and the

west country generally. This class belongs by origin to the submerged land of Lyonesse, the warm champaign country that once spread westward over the Bay of Biscay, and derived from the Gulf Stream the genial climate still preserved by its last remnants at Tresco and St. Mary's. The animals belonging to this secondary stratum of our British population are few and rare, but of its plants there are not a few, some of them extending over the whole western shores of England, Wales, Scotland, and Ireland, wherever they are washed by the Gulf Stream, and others now confined to particular spots, often with the oddest apparent capriciousness. Thus, two or three southern types of clover are peculiar to the Lizard Point, in Cornwall; a little Spanish and Italian restharrow has got stranded in the Channel Islands and on the Mull of Galloway; the spotted rock-rose of the Mediterranean grows only in Kerry, Galway, and Anglesea; while other plants of the same warm habit are confined to such spots as Torquay, Babbicombe, Dawlish, Cork, Swansea, Axminster, and the Scilly Isles. Of course, all peninsulas and islands are warmer in temperature than inland places, and so these relics of the lost Lyonesse have survived here and there in Cornwall, Carnarvonshire, Kerry, and other very projecting headlands long after they have died out altogether from the main central mass of Britain. Southwestern Ireland in particular is almost Portuguese in the general aspect of its fauna and flora.

Third and latest of all in time, though almost contemporary with the southern type, is the central European or Germanic element in our population. Sad as it is to confess it, the truth must nevertheless be told, that our beasts and birds, our plants and flowers, are for the most part of purely Teutonic origin. Even as the rude and hard-headed Anglo-Saxon has driven the gentle, poetical, and imaginative Celt ever westward before him into the hills and the sea, so the rude and vigorous Germanic beasts and weeds have driven the gentler and softer southern types into Wales and Cornwall, Galloway and Connemara. It is to the central European population that we owe or owed the red deer, the wild boar, the bear, the wolf, the beaver, the fox, the badger, the otter, and the squirrel. It is to the central European flora that we owe the larger part of the most familiar plants in all eastern and south-eastern England. They crossed in bands over the old land belt before Britain was finally insulated, and they have gone on steadily ever since, with true Teutonic persistence, overrunning the land and pushing slowly west-ward, like all other German bands before or since, to the detriment and discomfort of the previous inhabitants. Let us humbly remember that we are all of us at bottom foreigners alike, but that it is the Teutonic English, the people from the old Low Dutch fatherland by the Elbe, who have finally given to this isle its name of England, and to every one of us, Celt or Teuton, their own Teutonic name of Englishmen. We are at best, as an irate Teuton once remarked, ' nozzing but segond-hand Chermans.' In the words of a distinguished modern philologist of our own blood, ' English is Dutch, spoken with a Welsh accent.'

THUNDERBOLTS

THE subject of thunderbolts is a very fascinating one, and all the more so because there are no such things in existence at all as thunderbolts of any sort. Like the snakes of Iceland, their whole history might, from the positive point of view at least, be summed up in the simple statement of their utter nonentity. But does that do away in the least, I should like to know, with their intrinsic interest and importance? Not a bit of it. It only adds to the mystery and charm of the whole subject. Does anyone feel as keenly interested in any real living cobra or anaconda as in the non-existent great sea-serpent? Are ghosts and vampires less attractive objects of popular study than cats and donkeys? Can the present King of Abyssinia, interviewed by our own correspondent, equal the romantic charm of Prester John, or the butcher in the next street rival the personality of Sir Roger Charles Doughty Tichborne, Baronet? No, the real fact is this: if there *were* thunderbolts, the question of their nature and action would be a wholly dull, scientific, and priggish one; it is their unreality alone that invests them with all the ˈmysterious weirdness of pure fiction. Lightning, now, is a common thing that one reads about wearily in the books on electricity; a mere ordinary matter of positive and negative, density and potential, to be measured in ohms (whatever they may be), and partially imitated with Leyden jars and red sealing-wax apparatus. Why, did not Benjamin Franklin, a fat old

gentleman in ill-fitting small clothes, bring it down from
the clouds with a simple door-key, somewhere near Philadelphia ? and does not Mr. Robert Scott (of the Meteorological Office) calmly predict its probable occurrence within
the next twenty-four hours in his daily report, as published
regularly in the morning papers ? This is lightning, mere
vulgar lightning, a simple result of electrical conditions
in the upper atmosphere, inconveniently connected with
algebraical formulas in x, y, z, with horrid symbols interspersed in Greek letters. But the real thunderbolts of
Jove, the weapons that the angry Zeus, or Thor, or Indra
hurls down upon the head of the trembling malefactor—
how infinitely grander, more fearsome, and more mysterious !

And yet even nowadays, I believe, there are a large
number of well-informed people, who have passed the sixth
standard, taken prizes at the Oxford Local, and attended
the dullest lectures of the Society for University Extension,
but who nevertheless in some vague and dim corner of their
consciousness retain somehow a lingering faith in the
existence of thunderbolts. They have not yet grasped in
its entirety the simple truth that lightning is the reality of
which thunderbolts are the mythical, or fanciful, or verbal
representation. We all of us know now that lightning is
a mere flash of electric light and heat ; that it has no solid
existence or core of any sort ; in short, that it is dynamical
rather than material, a state or movement rather than a
body or thing. To be sure, local newspapers still talk
with much show of learning about ' the electric fluid '
which did such remarkable damage last week upon the
slated steeple of Peddlington Torpida Church ; but the
well-crammed schoolboy of the present day has long since
learned that the electric fluid is an exploded fallacy, and
that the lightning which pulled the ten slates off the

steeple in question was nothing more in its real nature than a very big immaterial spark. However, the word thunderbolt has survived to us from the days when people still believed that the thing which did the damage during a thunderstorm was really and truly a gigantic white-hot bolt or arrow ; and, as there is a natural tendency in human nature to fit an existence to every word, people even now continue to imagine that there must be actually something or other somewhere called a thunderbolt. They don't figure this thing to themselves as being identical with the lightning ; on the contrary, they seem to regard it as something infinitely rarer, more terrible, and more mystic ; but they firmly hold that thunderbolts do exist in real life, and even sometimes assert that they themselves have positively seen them.

But, if seeing is believing, it is equally true, as all who have looked into the phenomena of spiritualism and 'psychical research' (modern English for ghost-hunting) know too well, that believing is seeing also. The origin of the faith in thunderbolts must be looked for (like the origin of the faith in ghosts and 'psychical phenomena') far back in the history of our race. The noble savage, at that early period when wild in woods he ran, naturally noticed the existence of thunder and lightning, because thunder and lightning are things that forcibly obtrude themselves upon the attention of the observer, however little he may by nature be scientifically inclined. Indeed, the noble savage, sleeping naked on the bare ground, in tropical countries where thunder occurs almost every night on an average, was sure to be pretty often awaked from his peaceful slumbers by the torrents of rain that habitually accompany thunderstorms in the happy realms of ever-lasting dog-days. Primitive man was thereupon compelled to do a little philosophising on his own account as to the cause and origin of the rumbling and flashing which he saw so constantly around him. Naturally enough, he concluded that the sound must be the voice of somebody ; and that the fiery shaft, whose effects he sometimes noted upon trees, animals, and his fellow-man, must be the somebody's arrow. It is immaterial from this point of view whether, as the scientific anthropologists hold, he was led to his conception of these supernatural personages from his prior belief in ghosts and spirits, or whether, as Professor Max Müller will have it, he felt a deep yearning in his primitive savage breast toward the Infinite and the Unknowable (which he would doubtless have spelt, like the Professor, with a capital initial, had he been acquainted with the intricacies of the yet uninvented alphabet) ; but this much at least is pretty certain, that he looked upon the thunder and the lightning as in some sense the voice and the arrows of an aërial god.

Now, this idea about the arrows is itself very significant of the mental attitude of primitive man, and of the way that mental attitude has coloured all subsequent thinking and superstition upon this very subject. Curiously enough, to the present day the conception of the thunderbolt is essentially one of a *bolt*—that is to say, an arrow, or at least an arrowhead. All existing thunderbolts (and there are plenty of them lying about casually in country houses and local museums) are more or less arrow-like in shape and appearance ; some of them, indeed, as we shall see by-and-by, are the actual stone arrowheads of primitive man himself in person. Of course the noble savage was himself in the constant habit of shooting at animals and enemies with a bow and arrow. When, then, he tried to figure to himself the angry god, seated in the storm-clouds, who spoke with such a loud rumbling voice, and killed those who displeased him with his fiery darts, he naturally thought of him as using in his cloudy home the familiar bow and arrow of this nether planet. To us nowadays, if we were to begin forming the idea for ourselves all over again *de novo*, it would be far more natural to think of the thunder as the noise of a big gun, of the lightning as the flash of the powder, and of the supposed 'bolt' as a shell or bullet. There is really a ridiculous resemblance between a thunderstorm and a discharge of artillery. But the old conception derived from so many generations of primitive men has held its own against such mere modern devices as gunpowder and rifle balls; and none of the objects commonly shown as thunderbolts are ever round: they are distinguished, whatever their origin, by the common peculiarity that they more or less closely resemble a dart or arrowhead.

Let us begin, then, by clearly disembarrassing our minds of any lingering belief in the existence of thunderbolts. There are absolutely no such things known to science. The two real phenomena that underlie the fable are simply thunder and lightning. A thunderstorm is merely a series of electrical discharges between one cloud and another, or between clouds and the earth; and these discharges manifest themselves to our senses under two forms—to the eye as lightning, to the ear as thunder. All that passes in each case is a huge spark—a commotion, not a material object. It is in principle just like the spark from an electrical machine; but while the most powerful machine of human construction will only send a spark for three feet, the enormous electrical apparatus provided for us by nature will send one for four, five, or even ten miles. Though lightning when it touches the earth always seems to us to come from the clouds to the ground, it is by no means certain that the real course may not at least occasionally be in the opposite direction. All we know is that sometimes there is an instantaneous discharge between one cloud and another, and sometimes an instantaneous discharge between a cloud and the earth.

But this idea of a mere passage of highly concentrated energy from one point to another was far too abstract, of course, for primitive man, and is far too abstract even now for nine out of ten of our fellow-creatures. Those who don't still believe in the bodily thunderbolt, a fearsome aërial weapon which buries itself deep in the bosom of the earth, look upon lightning as at least an embodiment of the electric fluid, a long spout or line of molten fire, which is usually conceived of as striking the ground and then proceeding to hide itself under the roots of a tree or beneath the foundations of a tottering house. Primitive man naturally took to the grosser and more material conception. He figured to himself the thunderbolt as a barbed arrowhead; and the forked zigzag character of the visible flash, as it darts rapidly from point to point, seemed almost inevitably to suggest to him the barbs, as one sees them represented on all the Greek and Roman gems, in the red right hand of the angry Jupiter.

The thunderbolt being thus an accepted fact, it followed naturally that whenever any dart-like object of unknown origin was dug up out of the ground, it was at once set down as being a thunderbolt; and, on the other hand, the frequent occurrence of such dart-like objects, precisely where one might expect to find them in accordance with the theory, necessarily strengthened the belief itself. So commonly are thunderbolts picked up to the present day that to disbelieve in them seems to many country people a piece of ridiculous and stubborn scepticism. Why, they've ploughed up dozens of them themselves in their time, and just about the very place where the thunderbolt struck the old elm-tree two years ago, too.

The most favourite form of thunderbolt is the polished stone hatchet or ' celt ' of the newer stone age men. I have never heard the very rude chipped and unpolished axes of the older drift men or cave men described as thunderbolts : they are too rough and shapeless ever to attract attention from any except professed archæologists. Indeed, the wicked have been known to scoff at them freely as mere accidental lumps of broken flint, and to deride the notion of their being due in any way to deliberate human handicraft. These are the sort of people who would regard a grand piano as a fortuitous concourse of atoms. But the shapely stone hatchet of the later neolithic farmer and herdsman is usually a beautifully polished wedge-shaped piece of solid greenstone ; and its edge has been ground to such a delicate smoothness that it seems rather like a bit of nature's exquisite workmanship than a simple relic of prehistoric man. There is something very fascinating about the naïf belief that the neolithic axe is a genuine unadulterated thunderbolt. You dig it up in the ground exactly where you would expect a thunderbolt (if there were such things) to be. It is heavy, smooth, well shaped, and neatly pointed at one end. If it could really descend in a red-hot state from the depths of the sky, launched forth like a cannon-ball by some fierce discharge of heavenly artillery, it would certainly prove a very formidable weapon indeed ; and one could easily imagine it scoring the bark of some aged oak, or tearing off the tiles from a projecting turret, exactly as the lightning is so well known to do in this prosaic workaday world of ours. In short, there is really nothing on earth against the theory of the stone axe being a true thunderbolt, except the fact that it unfortunately happens to be a neolithic hatchet.

But the course of reasoning by which we discover the true nature of the stone axe is not one that would in any case appeal strongly to the fancy or the intelligence of the British farmer. It is no use telling him that whenever one opens a barrow of the stone age one is pretty sure to find a neolithic axe and a few broken pieces of pottery beside the mouldering skeleton of the old nameless chief who lies there buried. The British farmer will doubtless stolidly retort that thunderbolts often strike the tops of hills, which are just the places where barrows and tumuli (tumps, he calls them) most do congregate ; and that as to the skeleton, isn't it just as likely that the man was killed by the thunderbolt as that the thunderbolt was made by a man ? Ay, and a sight likelier, too.

All the world over, this simple and easy belief, that the buried stone axe is a thunderbolt, exists among Europeans and savages alike. In the West of England, the labourers will tell you that the thunder-axes they dig up fell from the sky. In Brittany, says Mr. Tylor, the old man who mends umbrellas at Carnac, beside the mysterious stone avenues of that great French Stonehenge, inquires on his rounds for *pierres de tonnerre*, which of course are found with suspicious frequency in the immediate neighbourhood of prehistoric remains. In the Chinese Encyclopædia we are told that the ' lightning stones ' have sometimes the shape of a hatchet, sometimes that of a knife, and some-times that of a mallet. And then, by a curious misappre-hension, the sapient author of that work goes on to observe that these lightning stones are used by the wandering Mongols instead of copper and steel. It never seems to have struck his celestial intelligence that the Mongols made the lightning stones instead of digging them up out of the earth. So deeply had the idea of the thunderbolt buried itself in the recesses of his soul, that though a neighbouring people were still actually manufacturing stone axes almost under his very eyes, he reversed mentally the entire process, and supposed they dug up the thunder-bolts which he saw them using, and employed them as common hatchets. This is one of the finest instances on record of the popular figure which grammarians call the *hysteron proteron*, and ordinary folk describe as putting the cart before the horse. Just so, while in some parts of Brazil the Indians are still laboriously polishing their stone hatchets, in other parts the planters are digging up the precisely similar stone hatchets of earlier generations, and religiously preserving them in their houses as undoubted thunderbolts. I have myself had pressed upon my attention as genuine lightning stones, in the West Indies, the exquisitely polished greenstone tomahawks of the old Carib marauders. But then, in this matter, I am pretty much in the position of that philosophic sceptic who, when he was asked by a lady whether he believed in ghosts, answered wisely, ' No, madam, I have seen by far too many of them.'

One of the finest accounts ever given of the nature of thunderbolts is that mentioned by Adrianus Tollius in his edition of ' Boethius on Gems.' He gives illustrations of some neolithic axes and hammers, and then proceeds to state that in the opinion of philosophers they are generated in the sky by a fulgureous exhalation (whatever that may look like) conglobed in a cloud by a circumfixed humour, and baked hard, as it were, by intense heat. The weapon, it seems, then becomes pointed by the damp mixed with it flying from the dry part, and leaving the other end denser ; while the exhalations press it so hard that it breaks out through the cloud, and makes thunder and lightning. A very lucid explanation certainly, but rendered a little difficult of apprehension by the effort necessary for realising in a mental picture the conglobation of a fulgureous ex-halation by a circumfixed humour.

L

One would like to see a drawing of the process, though the sketch would probably much resemble the picture of a muchness, so admirably described by the mock turtle. The excellent Tollius himself, however, while demurring on the whole to this hypothesis of the philosophers, bases his objection mainly on the ground that, if this were so, then it is odd the thunderbolts are not round, but wedge-shaped, and that they have holes in them, and those holes not equal throughout, but widest at the ends. As a matter of fact, Tollius has here hit the right nail on the head quite accidentally ; for the holes are really there, of course, to receive the haft of the axe or hammer. But if they were truly thunderbolts, and if the bolts were shafted, then the holes would have been lengthwise, as in an arrowhead, not crosswise, as in an axe or hammer. Which is a complete *reductio ad absurdum* of the philosophic opinion.

Some of the ceauniæ, says Pliny, are like hatchets. He would have been nearer the mark if he had said 'are hatchets' outright. But this *aperçu*, which was to Pliny merely a stray suggestion, became to the northern peoples a firm article of belief, and caused them to represent to themselves their god Thor or Thunor as armed, not with a bolt, but with an axe or hammer. Etymologically Thor, Thunor, and thunder are the self-same word ; but while the southern races looked upon Zeus or Indra as wielding his forked darts in his red right hand, the northern races looked upon the Thunder-god as hurling down an angry hammer from his seat in the clouds. There can be but little doubt that the very notion of Thor's hammer itself was derived from the shape of the supposed thunderbolt, which the Scandinavians and Teutons rightly saw at once to be an axe or mallet, not an arrow-head. The 'fiery axe' of Thunor is a common metaphor in Anglo-Saxon poetry. Thus, Thor's hammer is itself merely the picture which our northern ancestors formed to themselves, by compounding the idea of thunder and lightning with the idea of the polished stone hatchets they dug up among the fields and meadows.

Flint arrowheads of the stone age are less often taken for thunderbolts, no doubt because they are so much smaller that they look quite too insignificant for the weapons of an angry god. They are more frequently described as fairy-darts or fairy-bolts. Still, I have known even arrow-heads regarded as thunderbolts, and preserved superstitiously under that belief. In Finland, stone arrows are universally so viewed ; and the rainbow is looked upon as the bow of Tiermes, the thunder-god, who shoots with it the guilty sorcerers.

But why should thunderbolts, whether stone axes or flint arrowheads, be preserved, not merely as curiosities, but from motives of superstition ? The reason is a simple one. Everybody knows that in all magical ceremonies it is necessary to have something belonging to the person you wish to conjure against, in order to make your spells effectual. A bone, be it but a joint of the little finger, is sufficient to raise the ghost to which it once belonged ; cuttings of hair or clippings of nails are enough to put their owner magically in your power ; and that is the reason why, if you are a prudent person, you will always burn all such off-castings of your body, lest haply an enemy should get hold of them, and cast the evil eye upon you with their potent aid. In the same way, if you can lay hands upon anything that once belonged to an elf, such as a fairy-bolt or flint arrowhead, you can get its former possessor to do anything you wish by simply rubbing it and calling upon him to appear. This is the secret of half the charms and amulets in existence, most of which are either real old arrowheads, or carnelians cut in the same

shape, which has now mostly degenerated from the barb
to the conventional heart, and been mistakenly associated
with the idea of love. This is the secret, too, of all the
rings, lamps, gems, and boxes, possession of which gives
a man power over fairies, spirits, gnomes, and genii. All
magic proceeds upon the prime belief that you must
possess something belonging to the person you wish to
control, constrain, or injure. And, failing anything else,
you must at least have a wax image of him, which you
call by his name, and use as his substitute in your incantations.

On this primitive principle, possession of a thunderbolt
gives you some sort of hold, as it were, over the thunder-
god himself in person. If you keep a thunderbolt in your
house it will never be struck by lightning. In Shetland,
stone axes are religiously preserved in every cottage as a
cheap and simple substitute for lightning-rods. In Cornwall, the stone hatchets and arrowheads not only guard
the house from thunder, but also act as magical barometers,
changing colour with the changes of the weather, as if
in sympathy with the temper of the thunder-god. In
Germany, the house where a thunderbolt is kept is safe
from the storm; and the bolt itself begins to sweat on the
approach of lightning-clouds. Nay, so potent is the protection afforded by a thunderbolt that where the lightning
has once struck it never strikes again; the bolt already
buried in the soil seems to preserve the surrounding place
from the anger of the deity. Old and pagan in their
nature as are these beliefs, they yet survive so thoroughly
into Christian times that I have seen a stone hatchet built
into the steeple of a church to protect it from lightning.
Indeed, steeples have always of course attracted the
electric discharge to a singular degree by their height and
tapering form, especially before the introduction of light-

ning-rods; and it was a sore trial of faith to mediæval reasoners to understand why heaven should hurl its angry darts so often against the towers of its very own churches. In the Abruzzi the flint axe has actually been Christianised into St. Paul's arrows—*saetti de San Paolo.* Families hand down the miraculous stones from father to son as a precious legacy; and mothers hang them on their children's necks side by side with medals of saints and madonnas, which themselves are hardly so highly prized as the stones that fall from heaven.

Another and very different form of thunderbolt is the belemnite, a common English fossil often preserved in houses in the west country with the same superstitious reverence as the neolithic hatchets. The very form of the belemnite at once suggests the notion of a dart or lance-head, which has gained for it its scientific name. At the present day, when all our girls go to Girton and enter for the classical tripos, I need hardly translate the word belemnite ' for the benefit of the ladies,' as people used to do in the dark and unemancipated eighteenth century; but as our boys have left off learning Greek just as their sisters are beginning to act the ' Antigone ' at private theatricals, I may perhaps be pardoned if I explain, ' for the benefit of the gentlemen,' that the word is practically equivalent to javelin-fossil. The belemnites are the internal shells of a sort of cuttle-fish which swam about in enormous numbers in the seas whose sediment forms our modern lias, oolite, and gault. A great many different species are known and have acquired charming names in very doubtful Attic at the hands of profoundly learned geological investigators, but almost all are equally good representatives of the mythical thunderbolt. The finest specimens are long, thick, cylindrical, and gradually tapering, with a hole at one end as if on purpose to receive the shaft. Sometimes they have petrified into iron pyrites or copper compounds, shining like gold, and then they make very noble thunderbolts indeed, heavy as lead, and capable of doing profound mischief if properly directed. At other times they have crystallised in transparent spar, and then they form very beautiful objects, as smooth and polished as the best lapidary could possibly make them. Belemnites are generally found in immense numbers together, especially in the marlstone quarries of the Midlands, and in the lias cliffs of Dorsetshire. Yet the quarrymen who find them never seem to have their faith shaken in the least by the enormous quantities of thunderbolts that would appear to have struck a single spot with such extraordinary frequency This little fact also tells rather hardly against the theory that the lightning never falls twice upon the same place.

Only the largest and heaviest belemnites are known as thunder stones; the smaller ones are more commonly described as agate pencils. In Shakespeare's country their connection with thunder is well known, so that in all probability a belemnite is the original of the beautiful lines in ' Cymbeline ':—

> Fear no more the lightning flash,
> Nor the all-dreaded thunder stone,

where the distinction between the lightning and the thunderbolt is particularly well indicated. In every part of Europe belemnites and stone hatchets are alike regarded as thunderbolts; so that we have the curious result that people confuse under a single name a natural fossil of immense antiquity and a human product of comparatively recent but still prehistoric date. Indeed, I have had two thunderbolts shown me at once, one of which was a large belemnite, and the other a modern Indian tomahawk. Curiously enough, English sailors still call the nearest surviving relatives of the belemnites, the squids or cala-maries of the Atlantic, by the appropriate name of sea-arrows.

Many other natural or artificial objects have added their tittle to the belief in thunderbolts. In the Hima-layas, for example, where awful thunderstorms are always occurring as common objects of the country, the torrents which follow them tear out of the loose soil fossil bones and tusks and teeth, which are universally looked upon as lightning-stones. The nodules of pyrites, often picked up on beaches, with their false appearance of having been melted by intense heat, pass muster easily with children and sailor folk for the genuine thunderbolts. But the grand upholder of the belief, the one true undeniable reality which has kept alive the thunderbolt even in a wicked and sceptical age, is, beyond all question, the occasional falling of meteoric stones. Your meteor is an incontrovertible fact; there is no getting over him; in the British Museum itself you will find him duly classified and labelled and catalogued. Here, surely, we have the ultimate substratum of the thunderbolt myth. To be sure, meteors have no kind of natural connection with thunderstorms; they may fall anywhere and at any time; but to object thus is to be hypercritical. A stone that falls from heaven, no matter how or when, is quite good enough to be considered as a thunderbolt.

Meteors, indeed, might very easily be confounded with lightning, especially by people who already have the full-blown conception of a thunderbolt floating about vaguely in their brains. The meteor leaps upon the earth suddenly with a rushing noise; it is usually red-hot when it falls, by friction against the air; it is mostly composed of native iron and other heavy metallic bodies; and it does its best to bury itself in the ground in the most orthodox and respectable manner. The man who sees this parlous monster come whizzing through the clouds from planetary space, making a fiery track like a great dragon as it moves rapidly across the sky, and finally ploughing its way into the earth in his own back garden, may well be excused for regarding it as a fine specimen of the true antique thunderbolt. The same virtues which belong to the buried stone are in some other places claimed for meteoric iron, small pieces of which are worn as charms, specially useful in protecting the wearer against thunder, lightning, and evil incantations. In many cases miraculous images have been hewn out of the stones that have fallen from heaven ; and in others the meteorite itself is carefully preserved or worshipped as the actual representative of god or goddess, saint or madonna. The image that fell down from Jupiter may itself have been a mass of meteoric iron.

Both meteorites and stone hatchets, as well as all other forms of thunderbolt, are in excellent repute as amulets, not only against lightning, but against the evil eye generally. In Italy they protect the owner from thunder, epidemics, and cattle disease, the last two of which are well known to be caused by witchcraft ; while Prospero in the 'Tempest' is a surviving proof how thunderstorms, too, can be magically produced. The tongues of sheepbells ought to be made of meteoric iron or of elf-bolts, in order to insure the animals against foot-and-mouth disease or death by storm. Built into walls or placed on the threshold of stables, thunderbolts are capital preventives of fire or other damage, though not perhaps in this respect quite equal to a rusty horseshoe from a prehistoric battlefield. Thrown into a well they purify the water ; and boiled in the drink of diseased sheep they render a cure positively certain. In Cornwall thunderbolts are a sovereign remedy for rheumatism ; and in the popular pharma-

copœia of Ireland they have been employed with success
for ophthalmia, pleurisy, and many other painful diseases.
If finely powdered and swallowed piecemeal, they render
the person who swallows them invulnerable for the rest of
his lifetime. But they cannot conscientiously be recommended for dyspepsia and other forms of indigestion.

As if on purpose to confuse our already very vague ideas
about thunderbolts, there is one special kind of lightning
which really seems intentionally to simulate a meteorite,
and that is the kind known as fireballs or (more scientifically) globular lightning. A fireball generally appears as
a sphere of light, sometimes only as big as a Dutch cheese,
sometimes as large as three feet in diameter. It moves
along very slowly and demurely through the air, remaining
visible for a whole minute or two together ; and in the end it
generally bursts up with great violence, as if it were a
London railway station being experimented upon by Irish
patriots. At Milan one day a fireball of this description
walked down one of the streets so slowly that a small
crowd walked after it admiringly, to see where it was going.
It made straight for a church steeple, after the common but
sacrilegious fashion of all lightning, struck the gilded cross
on the topmost pinnacle, and then immediately vanished,
like a Virgilian apparition, into thin air.

A few years ago, too, Dr. Tripe was watching a very
severe thunderstorm, when he saw a fire-ball come quietly
gliding up to him, apparently rising from the earth rather
than falling towards it. Instead of running away, like a
practical man, the intrepid doctor held his ground quietly
and observed the fiery monster with scientific nonchalance.
After continuing its course for some time in a peaceful and
regular fashion, however, without attempting to assault
him, it finally darted off at a tangent in another direction,
and turned apparently into forked lightning. A fire-ball,

noticed among the Glendowan Mountains in Donegal, behaved even more eccentrically, as might be expected from its Irish antecedents. It first skirted the earth in a leisurely way for several hundred yards like a cannon-ball ; then it struck the ground, ricochetted, and once more bounded along for another short spell ; after which it disappeared in the boggy soil, as if it were completely finished and done for. But in another moment it rose again, nothing daunted, with Celtic irrepressibility, several yards away, pursued its ghostly course across a running stream (which shows, at least, there could have been no witchcraft in it), and finally ran to earth for good in the opposite bank, leaving a round hole in the sloping peat at the spot where it buried itself. Where it first struck, it cut up the peat as if with a knife, and made a broad deep trench which remained afterwards as a witness of its eccentric conduct. If the person who observed it had been of a superstitious turn of mind we should have had here one of the finest and most terrifying ghost stories on the entire record, which would have made an exceptionally splendid show in the ' Transactions of the Society for Psychical Research.' Unfortunately, however, he was only a man of science, ungifted with the precious dower of poetical imagination ; so he stupidly called it a remarkable fire-ball, measured the ground carefully like a common engineer, and sent an account of the phenomenon to that far more prosaic periodical, the ' Quarterly Journal of the Meteorological Society.' Another splendid apparition thrown away recklessly, for ever !

There is a curious form of electrical discharge, somewhat similar to the fire-ball but on a smaller scale, which may be regarded as the exact opposite of the thunderbolt, inasmuch as it is always quite harmless. This is St. Elmo's fire, a brush of lambent light, which plays around the masts of ships and the tops of trees, when clouds are low and tension great. It is, in fact, the equivalent in nature of the brush discharge from an electric machine. The Greeks and Romans looked upon this lambent display as a sign of the presence of Castor and Pollux, ' fratres Helenæ, lucida sidera,' and held that its appearance was an omen of safety, as everybody who has read the ' Lays of Ancient Rome ' must surely remember. The modern name, St. Elmo's fire, is itself a curiously twisted and perversely Christianised reminiscence of the great twin brethren ; for St. Elmo is merely a corruption of Helena, made masculine and canonised by the grateful sailors. It was as Helen's brothers that they best knew the Dioscuri in the good old days of the upper empire ; and when the new religion forbade them any longer to worship those vain heathen deities, they managed to hand over the flames at the masthead to an imaginary St. Elmo, whose protection stood them in just as good stead as that of the original alternate immortals.

Finally, the effects of lightning itself are sometimes such as to produce upon the mind of an impartial but unscientific beholder the firm idea that a bodily thunderbolt must necessarily have descended from heaven. In sand or rock, where lightning has struck, it often forms long hollow tubes, known to the calmly discriminating geological intelligence as fulgurites, and looking for all the world like gigantic drills such as quarrymen make for putting in a blast. They are produced, of course, by the melting of the rock under the terrific heat of the electric spark ; and they grow narrower and narrower as they descend till they finally disappear. But to a casual observer, they irresistibly suggest the notion that a material weapon has struck the ground, and buried itself at the bottom of the hole. The summit of Little Ararat, that weather-beaten and many-fabled peak (where an enterprising journalist not long ago discovered the remains of Noah's Ark), has been riddled through and through by frequent lightnings, till the rock is now a mere honeycombed mass of drills and tubes, like an old target at the end of a long day's constant rifle practice.   Pieces of the red trachyte from the summit, a foot long, have been brought to Europe, perforated all over with these natural bullet marks, each of them lined with black glass, due to the fusion of the rock by the passage of the spark.   Specimens of such thunder-drilled rock may be seen in most geological museums.   On some which Humboldt collected from a peak in Mexico, the fused slag from the wall of the tube has overflowed on to the surrounding surface, thus conclusively proving (if proof were necessary) that the holes are due to melting heat alone, and not to the passage of any solid thunderbolt.

But it was the introduction and general employment of lightning-rods that dealt a final deathblow to the thunderbolt theory. A lightning-conductor consists essentially of a long piece of metal, pointed at the end whose business it is, not so much (as most people imagine) to carry off the flash of lightning harmlessly, should it happen to strike the house to which the conductor is attached, but rather to prevent the occurrence of a flash at all, by gradually and gently drawing off the electricity as fast as it gathers before it has had time to collect in sufficient force for a destructive discharge.   It resembles in effect an overflow pipe which drains off the surplus water of a pond as soon as it runs in, in such a manner as to prevent the possibility of an inundation, which might occur if the water were allowed to collect in force behind a dam or embankment.   It is a flood-gate, not a moat : it carries away the electricity of the air quietly to the ground, without allowing it to gather in sufficient amount to produce a flash of lightning.   It might thus be better called a lightning-preventer than a lightning-conductor : it conducts electricity, but it prevents lightning. At first, all lightning-rods used to be made with knobs on the top, and then the electricity used to collect at the surface until the electric force was sufficient to cause a spark. In those happy days, you had the pleasure of seeing that the lightning was actually being drawn off from your neighbourhood piecemeal. Knobs, it was held, must be the best things, because you could incontestably see the sparks striking them with your own eyes. But as time went on, electricians discovered that if you fixed a fine metal point to the conductor of an electric machine it was impossible to get up any appreciable charge because the electricity kept always leaking out by means of the point. Then it was seen that if you made your lightning-rods pointed at the end, you would be able in the same way to dissipate your electricity before it ever had time to come to a head in the shape of lightning. From that moment the thunderbolt was safely dead and buried. It was urged, indeed, that the attempt thus to rob Heaven of its thunders was wicked and impious ; but the common-sense of mankind refused to believe that absolute omnipotence could be sensibly defied by twenty yards of cylindrical iron tubing. Thenceforth the thunderbolt ceased to exist, save in poetry, country houses, and the most rural circles ; even the electric fluid was generally relegated to the provincial press, where it still keeps company harmoniously with caloric, the devouring element, nature's abhorrence of a vacuum, and many other like philosophical fossils : while lightning itself, shorn of its former glories, could no longer wage impious war against cathedral towers, but was compelled to restrict itself to blasting a solitary rider now and again in the open fields, or drilling more holes in the already crumbling summit of Mount Ararat. Yet it will be a thousand years more, in all probability, before the last thunderbolt ceases to be shown as a curiosity here and there to marvelling visitors, and takes its proper place in some village museum as a belemnite, a meteoric stone, or a polished axe-head of our neolithic ancestors. Even then, no doubt, the original bolt will still survive as a recognised property in the stock-in-trade of every well-equipped poet.

HONEY-DEW

PLACE, the garden. Time, summer. Dramatis personæ, a couple of small brown garden-ants, and a lazy clustering colony of wee green 'plant-lice,' or 'blight,' or aphides. The exact scene is usually on the young and succulent branches of a luxuriant rose-bush, into whose soft shoots the aphides have deeply buried their long trunk-like snouts, in search of the sap off which they live so contentedly through their brief lifetime. To them, enter the two small brown ants, their lawful possessors; for ants, too, though absolutely unrecognised by English law (' de minimis non curat lex,' says the legal aphorism), are nevertheless in their own commonwealth duly seised of many and various goods and chattels ; and these same aphides, as everybody has heard, stand to them in pretty much the same position as cows stand to human herdsmen. Throw in for sole spectator a loitering naturalist, and you get the entire *mise-en-scène* of a quaint little drama that works itself out a dozen times among the wilted rose-trees beneath the latticed cottage windows every summer morning.

It is a delightful sight to watch the two little lilliputian proprietors approaching and milking these their wee green motionless cattle. First of all, the ants quickly scent their way with protruded antennæ (for they are as good as blind, poor things !) up the prickly stem of the rose-bush, guided, no doubt, by the faint perfume exhaled from the nectar above them. Smelling their road cautiously to the ends of the branches, they soon reach their own particular aphides, whose bodies they proceed gently to stroke with their outstretched feelers, and then stand by quietly for a moment in happy anticipation of the coming dinner. Presently, the obedient aphis, conscious of its lawful master's friendly presence, begins slowly to emit from two long horn-like tubes near the centre of its back a couple of limpid drops of a sticky pale yellow fluid. Honey-dew our English rustics still call it, because, when the aphides are not milked often enough by ants, they discharge it awkwardly of their own accord, and then it falls as a sweet clammy dew upon the grass beneath them. The ant, approaching the two tubes with cautious tenderness, removes the sweet drops without injuring in any way his little *protégé*, and then passes on to the next in order of his tiny cattle, leaving the aphis apparently as much relieved by the process as a cow with a full hanging udder is relieved by the timely attention of the human milkmaid.

Evidently, this is a case of mutual accommodation in the political economy of the ants and aphides : a free inter-change of services between the ant as consumer and the aphis as producer. Why the aphides should have acquired the curious necessity for getting rid of this sweet, sticky, and nutritious secretion nobody knows with certainty ; but it is at least quite clear that the liquid is a considerable nuisance to them in their very sedentary and monotonous existence—a waste product of which they are anxious to disembarrass themselves as easily as possible—and that while they themselves stand to the ants in the relation of purveyors of food supply, the ants in return stand to them in the relation of scavengers, or contractors for the removal of useless accumulations.

Everybody knows the aphides well by sight, in one of their forms at least, the familiar rose aphis ; but probably few people ever look at them closely and critically enough to observe how very beautiful and wonderful is the organisation of their tiny limbs in all its exquisite detail. If you pick off one good-sized wingless insect, however, from a blighted rose-leaf, and put him on a glass slide under a low power of the microscope, you will most likely be quite surprised to find what a lovely little creature it is that you have been poisoning wholesale all your life long with diluted tobacco-juice. His body is so transparent that you can see through it by transmitted light : a dainty glass globe, you would say, of emerald green, set upon six tapering, jointed, hairy legs, and provided in front with two large black eyes of many facets, and a pair of long and very flexible antennæ, easily moved in any direction, but usually bent backward when the creature is at rest so as to reach nearly to his tail as he stands at ease upon his native rose-leaf. There are, however, two other features about him which specially attract attention, as being very characteristic of the aphides and their allies among all other insects. In the first place, his mouth is provided with a very long snout or proboscis, classically described as a rostrum, with which he pierces the outer skin of the rose-shoot where he lives, and sucks up incessantly its sweet juices. This organ is common to the aphis with all the other bugs and plant-lice. In the second place, he has half-way down his back (or a little more) a pair of very peculiar hollow organs, the honey tubes, from which exudes that singular secretion, the honey-dew. These tubes are not found in quite all species of aphides, but they are very common among the class, and they form by far the most conspicuous and interesting organs in all those aphides which do possess them.

M

The life-history of the rose-aphis, small and familiar a is the insect itself, forms one of the most marvellous and extraordinary chapters in all the fairy tales of modern science. Nobody need wonder why the blight attacks his roses so persistently when once he has learnt the unusual provision for exceptional fertility in the reproduction of these insect plagues. The whole story is too long to give at full length, but here is a brief recapitulation of a year's generations of common aphides.

In the spring, the eggs of last year's crop, which have been laid by the mothers in nooks and crannies out of reach of the frost, are quickened into life by the first return of warm weather, and hatch out their brood of insects. All this brood consists of imperfect females, without a single male among them; and they all fasten at once upon the young buds of their native bush, where they pass a sluggish and uneventful existence in sucking up the juice from the veins on the one hand, and secreting honey-dew upon the other. Four times they moult their skins, these moults being in some respects analogous to the metamorphosis of the cater-pillar into chrysalis and butterfly. After the fourth moult, the young aphides attain maturity; and then they give origin, parthenogenetically, to a second brood, also of im-perfect females, all produced without any fathers. This second brood brings forth in like manner a third generation, asexual, as before; and the same process is repeated with-out intermission as long as the warm weather lasts. In each case, the young simply bud out from the ovaries of the mothers, exactly as new crops of leaves bud out from the rose-branch on which they grow. Eleven generations have thus been observed to follow one another rapidly in a single summer; and indeed, by keeping the aphides in a warm room, one may even make them continue their re-production in this purely vegetative fashion for as many as

four years running.   But as soon as the cold weather begins
to set in, perfect male and female insects are produced by,
the last swarm of parthenogenetic mothers ; and these true
females, after being fertilised, lay the eggs which remain
through the winter, and from which the next summer's
broods have to begin afresh the wonderful cycle.   Thus,
only one generation of aphides, out of ten or eleven, consists of true males and females : all the rest are false
females, producing young by a process of budding.

Setting aside for the present certain special modifications of this strange cycle which have been lately described
by M. Jules Lichtenstein, let us consider for a moment
what can be the origin and meaning of such an unusual
and curious mode of reproduction.

The aphides are on the whole the most purely inactive
and vegetative of all insects, unless indeed we except a few
very debased and degraded parasites.   They fasten themselves early in life on to a particular shoot of a particular
plant ; they drink in its juices, digest them, grow, and
undergo their incomplete metamorphoses ; they produce
new generations with extraordinary rapidity : and they
vegetate, in fact, almost as much as the plant itself upon
which they are living.   Their existence is duller than that
of the very dullest cathedral city.   They are thus essentially degenerate creatures : they have found the conditions
of life too easy for them, and they have reverted to something so low and simple that they are almost plant-like in
some of their habits and peculiarities.

The ancestors of the aphides were free winged insects ;
and, in certain stages of their existence, most living species
of aphides possess at least some winged members.   On
the rose-bush, you can generally pick off a few such larger
winged forms, side by side with the wee green wingless
insects.   But creatures which have taken to passing most

M 2

of their life upon a single spot on a single plant hardly
need the luxury of wings; and so, in nine cases out of ten,
natural selection has dispensed with those needless encum-
brances. Even the legs are comparatively little wanted by
our modern aphides, which only require them to walk away
in a stately sleepy manner when rudely disturbed by man,
lady-birds, or other enemies; and indeed the legs are now
very weak and feeble, and incapable of walking for more
than a short distance at a time under exceptional provoca-
tion. The eyes remain, it is true; but only the big ones:
the little ocelli at the top of the head, found amongst so
many of their allies, are quite wanting in all the aphides.
In short, the plant-lice have degenerated into mere mouths
and sacks for sucking and storing food from the tissues of
plants, provided with large honey-tubes for getting rid of
the waste sugar.

Now, the greater the amount of food any animal gets,
and the less the amount of expenditure it performs in
muscular action, the greater will be the surplus it has left
over for the purposes of reproduction. Eggs or young, in
fact, represent the amount thus left over after all the wants
of the body have been provided for. But in the rose-aphis
the wants of the body, when once the insect has reached
its full growth, are absolutely nothing; and it therefore
then begins to bud out new generations in rapid succession
as fast as ever it can produce them. This is strictly
analogous to what we see every day taking place in all the
plants around us. New leaves are produced one after
another, as fast as material can be supplied for their nutrition,
and each of these new leaves is known to be a separate
individual, just as much as the individual aphis. At last,
however, a time comes when the reproductive power of the
plant begins to fail, and then it produces flowers, that is to
say stamens (male) and pistils (female), whose union results

in fertilisation and the subsequent outgrowth of fruit and seeds. Thus a year's cycle of the plant-lice exactly answers to the life-history of an ordinary annual. The eggs correspond to the seeds; the various generations of aphides budding out from one another by parthenogenesis correspond to the leaves budded out by one another throughout the summer; and the final brood of perfect males and females answers to the flower with its stamen and pistils, producing the seeds, as they produce the eggs, for setting up afresh the next year's cycle.

This consideration, I fancy, suggests to us the most probable explanation of the honey-tubes and honey-dew. Creatures that eat so much and reproduce so fast as the aphides are rapidly sucking up juices all the time from the plant on which they fasten, and converting most of the nutriment so absorbed into material for fresh generations. That is how they swarm so fast over all our shrubs and flowers. But if there is any one kind of material in their food in excess of their needs, they would naturally have to secrete it by a special organ developed or enlarged for the purpose. I don't mean that the organ would or could be developed all at once, by a sudden effort, but that as the habit of fixing themselves upon plants and sucking their juices grew from generation to generation with these descendants of originally winged insects, an organ for permitting the waste product to exude must necessarily have grown side by side with it. Sugar seems to have been such a waste product, contained in the juices of the plant to an extent beyond what the aphides could assimilate or use up in the production of new broods; and this sugar is therefore secreted by special organs, the honey-tubes. One can readily imagine that it may at first have escaped in small quantities, and that two pores on their last segment but two may have been gradually specialised into regular

secreting organs, perhaps under the peculiar agency of the
ants, who have regularly appropriated so many kinds of
aphides as miniature milch cows.

So completely have some species of ants come to
recognise their own proprietary interest in the persons of
the aphides, that they provide them with fences and cow-
sheds on the most approved human pattern. Sometimes
they build up covered galleries to protect their tiny cattle ;
and these galleries lead from the nest to the place where
the aphides are fixed, and completely enclose the little
creatures from all chance of harm. If intruders try to
attack the farmyard, the ants drive them away by biting
and lacerating them. Sir John Lubbock, who has paid
great attention to the mutual relations of ants and aphides,
has even shown that various kinds of ants domesticate
various species of aphis. The common brown garden-ant,
one of the darkest skinned among our English races,
'devotes itself principally to aphides which frequent twigs
and leaves' ; especially, so far as I have myself observed,
the bright green aphis of the rose, and the closely allied
little black aphis of the broad bean. On the other hand a
nearly related reddish ant pays attention chiefly to those
aphides which live on the bark of trees, while the yellow
meadow-ants, a far more subterranean species, keep flocks
and herds of the like-minded aphides which feed upon the
roots of herbs and grasses.

Sir John Lubbock, indeed, even suggests—and how the
suggestion would have charmed 'Civilisation' Buckle !—
that to this difference of food and habit the distinctive
colours of the various species may very probably be due.
The ground which he adduces for this ingenious idea is a
capital example of the excellent use to which out-of-the-
way evidence may be cleverly put by a competent evolutionary thinker. 'The Baltic amber,' he says, 'contains

among the remains of many other insects a species of ant
intermediate between our small brown garden-ants and the
little yellow meadow-ants. This is possibly the stock from
which these and other allied species are descended. One
is tempted to suggest that the brown species which live so
much in the open air, and climb up trees and bushes, have
retained and even deepened their dark colour ; while others,
such as the yellow meadow-ant, which lives almost entirely
below ground, have become much paler.' He might have
added, as confirmatory evidence, the fact that the perfect
winged males and females of the yellow species, which fly
about freely during the brief honeymoon in the open air, are
even darker in hue than the brown garden-ant. But how
the light colour of the neuter workers gets transmitted
through these dusky parents from one generation to another
is part of that most insoluble crux of all evolutionary
reasoning—the transmission of special qualities to neuters
by parents who have never possessed them.

This last-mentioned yellow meadow-ant has carried the
system of domestication further in all probability than any
other species among its congeners. Not only do the yellow
ants collect the root-feeding aphides in their own nests,
and tend them as carefully as their own young, but they
also gather and guard the eggs of the aphides, which, till
they come to maturity, are of course quite useless. Sir
John Lubbock found that his yellow ants carried the winter
eggs of a species of aphis into their nest, and there took
great care of them. In the spring, the eggs hatched out ;
and the ants actually carried the young aphides out of the
nest again, and placed them on the leaves of a daisy
growing in the immediate neighbourhood. They then built
up a wall of earth over and round them. The aphides
went on in their usual lazy fashion throughout the summer,
and in October they laid another lot of eggs, precisely like

those of the preceding autumn. This case, as the practised observer himself remarks, is an instance of prudence unexampled, perhaps, in the animal kingdom, outside man. ' The eggs are laid early in October on the food-plant of the insect. They are of no direct use to the ants; yet they are not left where they are laid, exposed to the severity of the weather and to innumerable dangers, but brought into their nests by the ants, and tended by them with the utmost care through the long winter months until the following March, when the young ones are brought out again and placed on the young shoots of the daisy.' Mr. White of Stonehouse has also noted an exactly similar instance of formican providence.

The connection between so many ants and so many species of the aphides being so close and intimate, it does not seem extravagant to suppose that the honey-tubes in their existing advanced form at least may be due to the deliberate selective action of these tiny insect-breeders. Indeed, when we consider that there are certain species of beetles which have never been found anywhere except in ants' nests, it appears highly probable that these domesticated forms have been produced by the ants themselves, exactly as the dog, the sheep, and the cow, in their existing types, have been produced by deliberate human selection. If this be so, then there is nothing very out-of-the-way in the idea that the ants have also produced the honey-tubes of aphides by their long selective action. It must be remembered that ants, in point of antiquity, date back, under one form or another, no doubt to a very remote period of geological time. Their immense variety of genera and species (over a thousand distinct kinds are known) show them to be a very ancient family, or else they would not have had time to be specially modified in such a wonderful multiformity of ways. Even as long ago as the time when the tertiary deposits of Œningen and Radoboj were laid down, Dr. Heer of Zurich has shown that at least eighty-three distinct species of ants already existed; and the number that have left no trace behind is most probably far greater. Some of the beetles and woodlice which ants domesticate in their nests have been kept underground so long that they have become quite blind—that is to say, have ceased altogether to produce eyes, which would be of no use to them in their subterranean galleries; and one such blind beetle, known as Claviger, has even lost the power of feeding itself, and has to be fed by its masters from their own mandibles. Dr. Taschenberg enumerates 300 species of true ants'-nest insects, mostly beetles, in Germany alone; and M. André gives a list of 584 kinds, habitually found in association with ants in one country or another. Compared with these singular results of formican selection, the mere production or further development of the honey-tubes appears to be a very small matter.

But what good do the aphides themselves derive from the power of secreting honey-dew? For we know now that no animal or plant is ever provided with any organ or part merely for the benefit of another creature: the advantage must at least be mutual. Well, in the first place, it is likely that, in any case, the amount of sugary matter in the food of the aphides is quite in excess of their needs; they assimilate the nitrogenous material of the sap, and secrete its saccharine material as honey-dew. That, however, would hardly account for the development of special secretory ducts, like the honey-tubes, in which you can actually see the little drops of honey rolling, under the microscope. But the ants are useful allies to the aphides, in guarding them from another very dangerous type of insect. They are subject to the attacks of an ichneumon fly, which lays its eggs in them, meaning its larvæ to feed upon their living bodies; and the ants watch over the aphides with the greatest vigilance, driving off the ichneumons whenever they approach their little *protégés*.

Many other insects besides ants, however, are fond of the sweet secretions of the aphides, and it is probable that the honey-dew thus acts to some extent as a preservative of the species, by diverting possible foes from the insects themselves, to the sugary liquid which they distil from their food-plants. Having more than enough and to spare for all their own needs, and the needs of their offspring, the plant-lice can afford to employ a little of their nutriment as a bribe to secure them from the attacks of possible enemies. Such compensatory bribes are common enough in the economy of nature. Thus our common English vetch secretes a little honey on the stipules or wing-like leaflets on the stem, and so distracts thieving ants from committing their depredations upon the nectaries in the flowers, which are intended for the attraction of the fertilising bees; and a South American acacia, as Mr. Belt has shown, bears hollow thorns and produces honey from a gland in each leaflet, in order to allure myriads of small ants which nest in the thorns, eat the honey, and repay the plant by driving away their leaf-cutting congeners. Indeed, as they sting violently, and issue forth in enormous swarms whenever the plant is attacked, they are even able to frighten off browsing cattle from their own peculiar acacia.

Aphides, then, are essentially degraded insects, which have become almost vegetative in their habits, and even in their mode of reproduction, but which still retain a few marks of their original descent from higher and more locomotive ancestors. Their wings, especially, are useful to the perfect forms in finding one another, and to the imperfect ones in migrating from one plant to its nearest neighbours, where they soon become the parents of fresh hordes in rapid succession. Hence various kinds of aphides are among the most dreaded plagues of agriculturists. The 'fly,' which Kentish farmers know so well on hops, is an aphis specialised for that particular bine ; and, when once it appears in the gardens, it spreads with startling rapidity from one end of the long rows to the other. The phylloxera which has spoilt the French vineyards is a root-feeding form that attacks the vine, and kills or maims the plant terribly, by sucking the vital juices on their way up into the fresh-forming foliage. The 'American blight' on apple trees is yet another member of the same family, a wee creeping cottony creature that hides among the fissures of the bark, and drives its very long beak far down into the green sappy layer underlying the dead outer covering. In fact, almost all the best-known 'blights' and bladder-forming insects are aphides of one kind or another, affecting leaves, or stalks, or roots, or branches.

It is one of the most remarkable examples of the limitation of human powers that while we can easily exterminate large animals like the wolf and the bear in England, or the puma and the wolverine in the settled States of America, we should be so comparatively weak against the Colorado beetle or the fourteen-year locust, and so absolutely powerless against the hop-fly, the turnip-fly, and the phylloxera. The smaller and the more insignificant our enemy, viewed individually, the more difficult is he to cope with in the mass. All the elephants in the world could have been hunted down and annihilated, in all probability, with far less labour than has been expended upon one single little all but microscopic parasite in France alone. The enormous rapidity of reproduction in the family of aphides is the true cause of our helplessness before them. It has been calculated that a single aphis may during its own lifetime become the progenitor of 5,904,900,000 descendants.

Each imperfect female produces about ninety young ones, and lives long enough to see its children's children to the fifth generation. Now, ninety multiplied by ninety four times over gives the number above stated. Of course, this makes no allowance for casualties which must be pretty frequent : but even so, the sum-total of aphides produced within a small garden in a single summer must be something very extraordinary.

It is curious, too, that aphides on the whole seem to escape the notice of insect-eating birds very tolerably. I cannot, in fact, discover that birds ever eat them, their chief real enemy being the little lizard-like larva of the lady-bird, which devours them everywhere greedily in immense numbers. Indeed, aphides form almost the sole food of the entire lady-bird tribe in their earlier stages of existence ; and there is no better way of getting rid of blight on roses and other garden plants than to bring in a good boxful of these active and voracious little grubs from the fields and hedges. They will pounce upon the aphides forthwith as a cat pounces upon the mice in a well-stocked barn or farmyard. The two-spotted lady-bird in particular is the determined exterminator of the destructive hop-fly, and is much beloved accordingly by Kentish farmers. No doubt, one reason why birds do not readily see the aphis of the rose and most other species is because of their prevailing green tint, and the close way in which they stick to the leaves or shoots on whose juices they are preying. But in the case of many black and violet species, this protection of imitative colour is wanting, and yet the birds do not seem to care for the very conspicuous little insects on the broad bean, for example, whose dusky hue makes them quite noticeable in large masses. Here there may very likely be some special protection of nauseous taste in the aphides themselves (I will confess that I have not ventured to try the experiment in person), as in many other instances we know that conspicuously-coloured insects advertise their nastiness, as it were, to the birds by their own integuments, and so escape being eaten in mistake for any of their less protected relatives.

On the other hand, it seems pretty clear that certain plants have efficiently armed themselves against the aphides, in turn, by secreting bitter or otherwise unpleasant juices. So far as I can discover, the little plunderers seldom touch the pungent 'nasturtiums' or tropæolums of our flower-gardens, even when these grow side by side with other plants on which the aphides are swarming. Often, indeed, I find winged forms upon the leaf-stem of a nasturtium, having come there evidently in hopes of starting a new colony ; but usually in a dead or dying condition—the pungent juice seems to have poisoned them. So, too, spinach and lettuce may be covered with blight, while the bitter spurges, the woolly-leaved arabis, and the strong-scented thyme close by are utterly untouched. Plants seem to have acquired all these devices, such as close networks of hair upon the leaves, strong essences, bitter or pungent juices, and poisonous principles, mainly as deterrents for insect enemies, of which caterpillars and plant-lice are by far the most destructive. It would be unpardonable, of course, to write about honeydew without mentioning tobacco ; and I may add parenthetically that aphides are determined anti-tobacconists, nicotine, in fact, being a deadly poison to them. Smoking with tobacco, or sprinkling with tobacco-water, are familiar modes of getting rid of the unwelcome intruders in gardens. Doubtless this peculiar property of the tobacco plant has been developed as a prophylactic against insect enemies : and if so, we may perhaps owe the weed itself, as a smokable leaf, to the little aphides. Granting this hypo-

thetical connection, the name of honey-dew would indeed
be a peculiarly appropriate one.   I may mention in passing
that tobacco is quite fatal to almost all insects, a fact which
I present gratuitously to the blowers of counterblasts, who
are at liberty to make whatever use they choose of it.
Quassia and aloes are also well-known preventives of fly or
blight in gardens.

The most complete life-history yet given of any member
of the aphis family is that which M. Jules Lichtenstein
has worked out with so much care in the case of the
phylloxera of the oak-tree.   In April, the winter eggs of
this species, laid in the bark of an oak, each hatch out a
wingless imperfect female, which M. Lichtenstein calls the
foundress.   After moulting four times, the foundress
produces, by parthenogenesis, a number of false eggs, which
it fastens to the leaf-stalks and under side of the foliage.
These false eggs hatch out a larval form, wingless, but
bigger than any of the subsequent generations; and the
larvæ so produced themselves once more give origin to
more larvæ, which acquire wings, and fly away from the
oak on which they were born to another of a different
species in the same neighbourhood.   There these larvæ of
the second crop once more lay false eggs, from which the
third larval generation is developed.   This brood is again
wingless, and it proceeds at once to bud out several generations more, by internal gemmation, as long as the warm
weather lasts.   According to M. Lichtenstein, all previous
observations have been made only on aphides of this third
type; and he maintains that every species in the whole
family really undergoes an analogous alternation of generations.   At last, when the cold weather begins to set in,
a fourth larval form appears, which soon obtains wings,
and flies back to the same kind of oak on which the found-
resses were first hatched out, all the intervening generations

having passed their lives in sucking the juices of the other oak to which the second larval form migrated. The fourth type here produce perfect male and female insects, which are wingless, and have no sucking apparatus. The females, after being impregnated, lay a single egg each, which they hide in the bark, where it remains during the winter, till in spring it once more hatches out into a foundress, and the whole cycle begins over again. Whether all the aphides do or do not pass through corresponding stages is not yet quite certain. But Kentish farmers believe that the hop-fly migrates to hop-bines from plum-trees in the neighbourhood; and M. Lichtenstein considers that such migrations from one plant to another are quite normal in the family. We know, indeed, that many great plagues of our crops are thus propagated, sometimes among closely related plants, but sometimes also among the most widely separated species. For example, turnip-fly (which is not an aphis, but a small beetle) always begins its ravages (as Miss Ormerod has abundantly shown) upon a plot of charlock, and then spreads from patches of that weed to the neighbouring turnips, which are slightly diverse members of the same genus. But, on the other hand, it has long been well known that rust in wheat is specially connected with the presence of the barberry bush; and it has recently been proved that the fungus which produces the disease passes its early stages on the barberry leaves, and only migrates in later generations to the growing wheat. This last case brings even more prominently into light than ever the essential resemblance of the aphides to plant-parasites.

THE MILK IN THE COCO-NUT

FOR many centuries the occult problem how to account for the milk in the coco-nut has awakened the profoundest interest alike of ingenuous infancy and of maturer scientific age. Though it cannot be truthfully affirmed of it, as of the cosmogony or creation of the world, in the ' Vicar of Wakefield,' that it ' has puzzled the philosophers of all ages ' (for Sanchoniathon was certainly ignorant of the very existence of that delicious juice, and Manetho doubtless went to his grave without ever having tasted it fresh from the nut under a tropical verandah), yet it may be safely asserted that for the last three hundred years the philosopher who has not at some time or other of his life meditated upon that abstruse question is unworthy of such an exalted name. The cosmogony and the milk in the coco-nut are, however, a great deal closer together in thought than Sanchoniathon or Manetho, or the rogue who quoted them so glibly, is ever at all likely, in his wildest moments, to have imagined.

The coco-nut, in fact, is a subject well deserving of the most sympathetic treatment at the gentle hands of grateful humanity. No other plant is useful to us in so many diverse and remarkable manners. It has been truly said of that friend of man, the domestic pig, that he is all good, from the end of his snout to the tip of his tail ; but even the pig, though he furnishes us with so many necessaries or luxuries—from tooth-brushes to sausages, from ham to lard, from pepsine wine to pork pies—does not nearly approach, in the multiplicity and variety of his virtues, the all-sufficing and world-supplying coco-nut. A Chinese proverb says that there are as many useful properties in the coco-nut palm as there are days in the year ; and a Polynesian saying tells us that the man who plants a coco-nut plants meat and drink, hearth and home, vessels and clothing, for himself and his children after him. Like the great Mr. Whiteley, the invaluable palm-tree might modestly advertise itself as a universal provider. The solid part of the nut supplies food almost alone to thousands of people daily, and the milk serves them for drink, thus acting as an efficient filter to the water absorbed by the roots in the most polluted or malarious regions. If you tap the flower stalk you get a sweet juice, which can be boiled down into the peculiar sugar called (in the charming dialect of commerce) jaggery ; or it can be fermented into a very nasty spirit known as palm-wine, toddy, or arrack ; or it can be mixed with bitter herbs and roots to make that delectable compound ' native beer.' If you squeeze the dry nut you get coco-nut oil, which is as good as lard for frying when fresh, and is ' an excellent substitute for butter at breakfast,' on tropical tables. Under the mysterious name of copra (which most of us have seen with awe described in the market reports as ' firm ' or ' weak,' ' receding ' or ' steady ') it forms the main or only export of many Oceanic islands, and is largely imported into this realm of England, where the thicker portion is called stearine, and used for making sundry candles with fanciful names, while the clear oil is employed for burning in ordinary lamps. In the process of purification, it yields glycerine ; and it enters largely into the manufacture of most better-class soaps. The fibre that surrounds the nut makes up the other

N

mysterious article of commerce known as coir, which is twisted into stout ropes, or woven into coco-nut matting and ordinary door-mats. Brushes and brooms are also made of it, and it is used, not always in the most honest fashion, in place of real horse-hair in stuffing cushions. The shell, cut in half, supplies good cups, and is artistically carved by the Polynesians, Japanese, Hindoos, and other benighted heathen, who have not yet learnt the true methods of civilised machine-made shoddy manufacture. The leaves serve as excellent thatch; on the flat blades, prepared like papyrus, the most famous Buddhist manuscripts are written; the long mid-ribs or branches (strictly speaking, the leaf-stalks) answer admirably for rafters, posts, or fencing; the fibrous sheath at the base is a remarkable natural imitation of cloth, employed for strainers, wrappers, and native hats; while the trunk, or stem, passes in carpentry under the name of porcupine wood, and produces beautiful effects as a wonderfully coloured cabinet-makers' material. These are only a few selected instances out of the innumerable uses of the coco-nut palm.

Apart even from the manifold merits of the tree that bears it, the milk itself has many and great claims to our respect and esteem, as everybody who has ever drunk it in its native surroundings will enthusiastically admit. In England, to be sure, the white milk in the dry nuts is a very poor stuff, sickly, and strong-flavoured, and rather indigestible. But in the tropics, coco-nut milk, or, as we oftener call it there, coco-nut water, is a very different and vastly superior sort of beverage. At eleven o'clock every morning, when you are hot and tired with the day's work, your black servant, clad from head to foot in his cool clean white linen suit, brings you in a tall soda glass full of a clear, light, crystal liquid, temptingly displayed against the

yellow background of a chased Benares brass-work tray.
The lump of ice bobs enticingly up and down in the centre
of the tumbler, or clinks musically against the edge of the
glass as he carries it along. You take the cool cup thank-
fully and swallow it down at one long draught ; fresh as a
May morning, pure as an English hillside spring, delicate
as—well, as coco-nut water. None but itself can be its
parallel. It is certainly the most delicious, dainty, transparent, crystal drink ever invented. How did it get there,
and what is it for ?

In the early green stage at which coco-nuts are generally picked for household use in the tropics the shell hasn't
yet solidified into a hard stony coat, but still remains quite
soft enough to be readily cut through with a sharp table
knife—just like young walnuts picked for pickling. If you
cut one across while it's in this unsophisticated state, it is
easy enough to see the arrangement of the interior, and
the part borne by the milk in the development and growth
of the mature nut. The ordinary tropical way of opening
coco-nuts for table, indeed, is by cutting off the top of the
shell and rind in successive slices, at the end where the
three pores are situated, until you reach the level of the
water, which fills up the whole interior. The nutty part
around the inside of the shell is then extremely soft and
jelly-like, so that it can be readily eaten with a spoon ; but
as a matter of fact very few people ever do eat the flesh at
all. After their first few months in the tropics, they lose
the taste for this comparatively indigestible part, and confine themselves entirely (like patients at a German spa) to
drinking the water. A young coco-nut is thus seen to
consist, first of a green outer skin, then of a fibrous coat,
which afterwards becomes the hair, and next of a harder
shell which finally gets quite woody ; while inside all comes
the actual seed or unripe nut itself. The office of the coco-

nut water is the deposition of the nutty part around the side of the shell ; it is, so to speak, the mother liquid, from which the harder eatable portion is afterwards derived. This state is not uncommon in embryo seeds. In a very young pea, for example, the inside is quite watery, and only the outer skin is at all solid, as we have all observed when green peas first come into season. But the special peculiarity of the coco-nut consists in the fact that this liquid condition of the interior continues even after the nut is ripe, and that is the really curious point about the milk in the coco-nut which does actually need accounting for.

In order to understand it one ought to examine a coco-nut in the act of budding, and to do this it is by no means necessary to visit the West Indies or the Pacific Islands ; all you need to do is to ask a Covent Garden fruit salesman to get you a few 'growers.' On the voyage to England, a certain number of precocious coco-nuts, stimulated by the congenial warmth and damp of most shipholds, usually begin to sprout before their time ; and these waste nuts are sold by the dealers at a low rate to East-end children and inquiring botanists. An examination of a 'grower' very soon convinces one what is the use of the milk in the coco-nut.

It must be duly borne in mind, to begin with, that the prime end and object of the nut is not to be eaten raw by the ingenious monkey, or to be converted by lordly man into coco-nut biscuits, or coco-nut pudding, but simply and solely to reproduce the coco-nut palm in sufficient numbers to future generations. For this purpose the nut has slowly acquired by natural selection a number of protective defences against its numerous enemies, which serve to guard it admirably in the native state from almost all possible animal depredators. First of all, the actual nut or seed itself consists of a tiny embryo plant, placed just

inside the softest of the three pores or pits at the end of
the shell, and surrounded by a vast quantity of nutritious
pulp, destined to feed and support it during its earliest unprotected days, if not otherwise diverted by man or monkey.
But as whatever feeds a young plant will also feed an
animal, and as many animals betray a felonious desire to
appropriate to their own wicked ends the food-stuffs laid
up by the palm for the use of its own seedling, the coco-
nut has been compelled to inclose this particularly large
and rich kernel in a very solid and defensive shell.   And,
once more, since the palm grows at a very great height
from the ground—I have seen them up to ninety feet in
favourable circumstances—this shell stands a very good
chance of getting broken in tumbling to the earth, so that
it has been necessary to surround it with a mass of soft
and yielding fibrous material, which breaks its fall, and
acts as a buffer to it when it comes in contact with the
soil beneath.   So many protections has the coco-nut gradually devised for itself by the continuous survival of the
best adapted amid numberless and endless spontaneous
variations of all its kind in past time.

Now, when the coco-nut has actually reached the
ground at last, and proceeds to sprout in the spot where
chance (perhaps in the bodily shape of a disappointed monkey) has chosen to cast it, these numerous safeguards and
solid envelopes naturally begin to prove decided nuisances
to the embryo within.   It starts under the great disadvantage of being hermetically sealed within a solid wooden
shell, so that no water can possibly get at it to aid it as
most other seeds are aided in the process of germination.
Fancy yourself a seed-pea, anxious to sprout, but coated
all round with a hard covering of impermeable sealing-
wax, and you will be in a position faintly to appreciate
the unfortunate predicament of a grower coco-nut.   Natural

selection, however—that *deus ex machina* of modern science, which can perform such endless wonders, if only you give it time enough to work in and variations enough to work upon—natural selection has come to the rescue of the unhappy plant by leaving it a little hole at the top of the shell, out of which it can push its feathery green head without difficulty. Everybody knows that if you look at the sharp end of a coco-nut you will see three little brown pits or depressions on its surface. Most people also know that two of these are firmly stopped up (for a reason to which I shall presently recur), but that the third one is only closed by a slight film or very thin shell, which can be easily bored through with a pocket knife, so as to let the milk run off before cracking the shell. So much we have all learnt during our ardent pursuit of natural knowledge on half-holidays in early life. But we probably then failed to observe that just opposite this soft hole lies a small roundish knob, imbedded in the pulp or eatable portion, which knob is in fact the embryo palm or seedling, for whose ultimate benefit the whole arrangement (in brown and green) has been invented. That is very much the way with man : he notices what concerns his own appetite, and omits all the really important parts of the whole subject. *We* think the use of the hole is to let out the milk ; but the nut knows that its real object is to let out the seedling. The knob grows out at last into the young plantlet, and it is by means of the soft hole that it makes its escape through the shell to the air and the sunshine which it seeks without.

This brings us really down at last to the true *raison d'être* for the milk in the coco-nut. As the seed or kernel cannot easily get at much water from outside, it has a good supply of water laid up for it ready beforehand within its own encircling shell. The mother liquid from which the pulp or nutty part has been deposited remains in the centre, as the milk, till the tiny embryo begins to sprout. As soon as it does so, the little knob which was at first so very small enlarges rapidly and absorbs the water, till it grows out into a big spongy cellular mass, which at last almost fills up the entire shell. At the same time, its other end pushes its way out through the soft hole, and then gives birth to a growing bud at the top—the future stem and leaves—and to a number of long threads beneath —the future roots. Meanwhile, the spongy mass inside begins gradually to absorb all the nutty part, using up its oils and starches for the purpose of feeding the young plant above, until it is of an age to expand its leaves to the open tropical sunlight and shift for itself in the struggle for life. It seems at first sight very hard to understand how any tissue so solid as the pulp of coco-nut can be thus softened and absorbed without any visible cause; but in the subtle chemistry of living vegetation such a transformation is comparatively simple and easy to perform. Nature sometimes works much greater miracles than this in the same way : for example, what is called vegetable ivory, a substance so solid that it can be carved or turned only with great difficulty, is really the kernel of another palm-nut, allied to the coco-palm, and its very stony particles are all similarly absorbed during germination by the dissolving power of the young seedling.

Why, however, has the coco-nut three pores at the top instead of one, and why are two out of the three so carefully and firmly sealed up ? The explanation of this strange peculiarity is only to be found in the ancestral history of the coco-nut kind. Most nuts, indeed, start in their earlier stage as if they meant to produce two or more seeds each ; but as they ripen, all the seeds except one become abortive. The almond, for example, has in the flower two seeds or kernels to each nut ; but in the ripe state there is generally only one, though occasionally we find an almond with two—a philipœna, as we commonly call it—just to keep in memory the original arrangement of its earlier ancestors. The reason for this is that plants whose fruits have no special protection for their seeds are obliged to produce a great many of them at once, in order that one seed in a thousand may finally survive the onslaughts of their Argus-eyed enemies; but when they learn to protect themselves by hard coverings from birds and beasts, they can dispense with some of these supernumerary seeds, and put more nutriment into each one of those that they still retain. Compare, for example, the innumerable small round seedlets of the poppyhead with the solitary large and richly stored seed of the walnut, or the tiny black specks of mustard and cress with the single compact and well-filled seed of the filbert and the acorn. To the very end, however, most nuts begin in the flower as if they meant to produce a whole capsuleful of small unstored and unprotected seeds, like their original ancestors; it is only at the last moment that they recollect themselves, suppress all their ovules except one, and store that one with all the best and oiliest food-stuffs at their disposal. The nuts, in fact, have learned by long experience that it is better to be the only son and heir of a wealthy house, set up in life with a good capital to begin upon, than to be one of a poor family of thirteen needy and unprovided children.

Now, the coco-nuts are descended from a great tribe—the palms and lilies—which have as their main distinguishing peculiarity the arrangement of parts in their flowers and fruits by threes each. For example, in the most typical flowers of this great group, there are three green outer calyx-pieces, three bright-coloured petals, three long outer stamens, three short inner stamens, three valves to the capsule, and three seeds or three rows of seeds in each fruit. Many palms still keep pretty well to this primitive arrangement, but a few of them which have specially protected or highly developed fruits or nuts have lost in their later stages the threefold disposition in the fruit, and possess only one seed, often a very large one. There is no better and more typical nut in the whole world than a coco-nut —that is to say, from our present point of view at least, though the fear of that awful person, the botanical Smelfungus, compels me to add that this is not quite technically true. Smelfungus, indeed, would insist upon it that the coco-nut is not a nut at all, and would thrill us with the delightful information, innocently conveyed in that delicious dialect of which he is so great a master, that it is really ' a drupaceous fruit with a fibrous mesocarp.' Still, in spite of Smelfungus with his nice hair-splitting distinctions, it remains true that humanity at large will still call a nut a nut, and that the coco-nut is the highest known development of the peculiar nutty tactics. It has the largest and most richly stored seed of any known plant ; and this seed is surrounded by one of the hardest and most unmanageable of any known shells. Hence the coco-nut has readily been able to dispense with the three kernels which each nut used in its earlier and less developed days to produce. But though the palm has thus taken to reducing the number of its seeds in each fruit to the lowest possible point consistent with its continued existence at all, it still goes on retaining many signs of its ancient threefold arrangement. The ancestral and most deeply ingrained habits persist in the earlier stages ; it is only in the mature form that the later acquired habits begin fully to predominate. Even so our own boys pass through an essentially savage childhood of ogres and fairies, bows and arrows, sugar-plums and barbaric nursery tales, as well as a romantic boyhood of mediæval chivalry and adventure, before they steady down into that crowning glory of our race, the solid, sober, matter-of-fact, commercial British Philistine. Hence the coco-nut in its unstripped state is roughly triangular in form, its angles answering to the separate three fruits of simpler palms ; and it has three pits or weak places in the shell, through which the embryos of the three original kernels used to force their way out. But as only one of them is now needed, that one alone is left soft ; the other two, which would be merely a source of weakness to the plant if unprotected, are covered in the existing nut by harder shell. Doubtless they serve in part to deceive the too inquisitive monkey or other enemy, who probably concludes that if one of the pits is hard and impermeable, the other two are so likewise.

Though I have now, I hope, satisfactorily accounted for the milk in the coco-nut, and incidentally for some other matters in its economy as well, I am loth to leave the young seedling whom I have brought so far on his way to the tender mercies of the winds and storms and tropical animals, some of whom are extremely fond of his juicy and delicate shoots. Indeed, the growing point or bud of most palms is a very pleasant succulent vegetable, and one kind —the West Indian mountain cabbage—deserves a better and more justly descriptive name, for it is really much more like seakale or asparagus. I shall try to follow our young seedling on in life, therefore, so as to give, while I am about it, a fairly comprehensive and complete biography of a single flourishing coco-nut palm.

Beginning, then, with the fall of the nut from the parent-tree, the troubles of the future palm confront it at once in the shape of the nut-eating crab. This evil-disposed crustacean is common around the sea-coast of the eastern tropical islands, which is also the region mainly affected by the coco-nut palm; for coco-nuts are essentially shore-loving trees, and thrive best in the immediate neighbourhood of the sea.   Among the fallen nuts, the clumsy-looking thief of a crab (his appropriate Latin name is *Birgus latro*) makes great and dreaded havoc. To assist him in his unlawful object he has developed a pair of front legs, with specially strong and heavy claws, supplemented by a last or tail-end pair armed only with very narrow and slender pincers.   He subsists entirely upon a coco-nut diet.   Setting to work upon a big fallen nut—with the husk on, coco-nuts measure in the raw state about twelve inches the long way—he tears off all the coarse fibre bit by bit, and gets down at last to the hard shell.   Then he hammers away with his heavy claw on the softest eye-hole till he has pounded an opening right through it.   This done he twists round his body so as to turn his back upon the coco-nut he is operating upon (crabs are never famous either for good manners or gracefulness) and proceeds awkwardly but effectually to extract all the white kernel or pulp through the breach with his narrow pair of hind pincers.   Like man, too, the robber-crab knows the value of the outer husk as well as of the eatable nut itself, for he collects the fibre in surprising quantities to line his burrow, and lies upon it, the clumsy sybarite, for a luxurious couch.   Alas, however, for the helplessness of crabs, and the rapacity and cunning of all-appropriating man!   The spoil-sport Malay digs up the nest for the sake of the fibre it contains, which spares him the trouble of picking junk on his own account, and then he eats the industrious crab who has laid it all up, while he melts down the great lump of fat under the robber's capacious tail, and sometimes gets from it as much as a good quart of what may be practically considered as limpid coco-nut oil.   *Sic vos non vobis* is certainly the melancholy refrain of all natural history.

The coco-nut palm intends the oil for the nourishment of its own seedling ; the crab feloniously appropriates it and stores it up under his capacious tail for future personal use ; the Malay steals it again from the thief for his own purposes ; and ten to one the Dutch or English merchant beguiles it from him with sized calico or poisoned rum, and transmits it to Europe, where it serves to lighten our nights and assist at our matutinal tub, to point a moral and adorn the present tale.

If, however, our coco-nut is lucky enough to escape the robber-crabs, the pigs, and the monkeys, as well as to avoid falling into the hands of man, and being converted into the copra of commerce, or sold from a costermonger's barrow in the chilly streets of ungenial London at a penny a slice, it may very probably succeed in germinating after the fashion I have already described, and pushing up its head through the surrounding foliage to the sunlight above. As a rule, the coco-nut has been dropped by its mother tree on the sandy soil of a sea-beach ; and this is the spot it best loves, and where it grows to the stateliest height. Sometimes, however, it falls into the sea itself, and then the loose husk buoys it up, so that it floats away bravely till it is cast by the waves upon some distant coral reef or desert island.   It is this power of floating and surviving a long voyage that has dispersed the coco-nut so widely among oceanic islands, where so few plants are generally to be found.   Indeed, on many atolls or isolated reefs (for example, on Keeling Island) it is the only tree or shrub that grows in any quantity, and on it the pigs, the poultry, the ducks, and the land crabs of the place entirely subsist. In any case, wherever it happens to strike, the young coco-nut sends up at first a fine rosette of big spreading leaves, not raised as afterwards on a tall stem, but springing direct from the ground in a wide circle, something like a very big

and graceful fern.   In this early stage nothing can be more
beautiful or more essentially tropical in appearance than a
plantation of young coco-nuts.   Their long feathery leaves
spreading out in great clumps from the buried stock, and
waving with lithe motion before the strong sea-breeze of
the Indies, are the very embodiment of those deceptive
ideal tropics which, alas, are to be found in actual reality
nowhere on earth save in the artificial palm-houses at Kew,
and the Casino Gardens at too entrancing Monte Carlo.

For the first two or three years the young palms must
be well watered, and the soil around them opened ; after
which the tall graceful stem begins to rise rapidly into the
open air.   In this condition it may be literally said to make
the tropics—those fallacious tropics, I mean, of painters
and poets, of Enoch Arden and of Locksley Hall.   You
may observe that whenever an artist wants to make a
tropical picture, he puts a group of coco-nut palms in the
foreground, as much as to say, ' You see there's no deception ; these are the genuine unadulterated tropics.'   But
as to painting the tropics without the palms, he might just
as well think of painting the desert without the camels.
At eight or ten years old the tree flowers, bearing blossoms
of the ordinary palm type, degraded likenesses of the lilies
and yuccas, greenish and inconspicuous, but visited by insects for the sake of their pollen.   The flower, however, is
fertilised by the wind, which carries the pollen grains from
one bunch of blossoms to another.   Then the nuts gradually
swell out to an enormous size, and ripen very slowly, even
under the brilliant tropical sun.   (I will admit that the tropics
are hot, though in other respects I hold them to be arrant
impostors, like that precocious American youth who
announced on his tenth birthday that in his opinion life
wasn't all that it was cracked up to be.)   But the worst
thing about the coco-nut palm, the missionaries always

say, is the fatal fact that, when once fairly started, it goes
on bearing fruit uninterruptedly for forty years. This is
very immoral and wrong of the ill-conditioned tree, because
it encourages the idyllic Polynesian to lie under the palms
all day long, cooling his limbs in the sea occasionally,
sporting with Amaryllis in the shade, or with the tangles
·of Neæra's hair, and waiting for the nuts to drop down in
due time, when he ought (according to European notions)
to be killing himself with hard work under a blazing sky,
raising cotton, sugar, indigo, and coffee, for the immediate
benefit of the white merchant, and the ultimate advantage
of the British public. It doesn't enforce habits of steady
industry and perseverance, the good missionaries say; it
doesn't induce the native to feel that burning desire for
Manchester piece-goods and the other blessings of civilisation which ought properly to accompany the propagation of
the missionary in foreign parts. You stick your nut in
the sand ; you sit by a few years and watch it growing ;
you pick up the ripe fruits as they fall from the tree ; and you
sell them at last for illimitable red cloth to the Manchester
piece-goods merchant. Nothing could be more simple or
more satisfactory. And yet it is difficult to see the precise
moral distinction between the owner of a coco-nut grove in
the South Sea Islands and the owner of a coal-mine or a
big estate in commercial England. Each lounges deco-
rously through life after his own fashion ; only the one
lounges in a Russia leather chair at a club in Pall Mall,
while the other lounges in a nice soft dust-heap beside a
rolling surf in Tahiti or the Hawaiian Archipelago.

Curiously enough, at a little distance from the sandy
levels or alluvial flats of the sea-shore, the sea-loving coco-
nut will not bring its nuts to perfection. It will grow,
indeed, but it will not thrive or fruit in due season. On
the coast-line of Southern India, immense groves of coco-

nuts fringe the shore for miles and miles together ; and in some parts, as in Travancore, they form the chief agricultural staple of the whole country. ' The State has hence facetiously been called Coconutcore,' says its historian ; which charmingly illustrates the true Anglo-Indian notion of what constitutes facetiousness, and ought to strike the last nail into the coffin of a competitive examination system. A good tree in full bearing should produce 120 coco-nuts in a season ; so that a very small grove is quite sufficient to maintain a respectable family in decency and comfort. Ah, what a mistake the English climate made when it left off its primitive warmth of the tertiary period, and got chilled by the ice and snow of the Glacial Epoch down to its present misty and dreary wheat-growing condition !   If it were not for that, those odious habits of steady industry and perseverance might never have been developed in ourselves at all, and we might be lazily picking copra off our own coco-palms, to this day, to export in return for the piece-goods of some Arctic Manchester situated somewhere about the north of Spitzbergen or the New Siberian Islands.

Even as things stand at the present day, however, it is wonderful how much use we modern Englishmen now make in our own houses of this far Eastern nut, whose very name still bears upon its face the impress of its originally savage origin. From morning to night we never leave off being indebted to it. We wash with it as old brown Windsor or glycerine soap the moment we leave our beds. We walk across our passages on the mats made from its fibre. We sweep our rooms with its brushes, and wipe our feet on it as we enter our doors. As rope, it ties up our trunks and packages ; in the hands of the housemaid it scrubs our floors ; or else, woven into coarse cloth, it acts as a covering for bales and furniture sent by rail or steamboat. The confectioner undermines our digestion in early life with coco-nut candy ; the cook tempts us later on with coco-nut cake ; and Messrs. Huntley and Palmer cordially invite us to complete the ruin with coco-nut biscuits. We anoint our chapped hands with one of its preparations after washing ; and grease the wheels of our carriages with another to make them run smoothly. Finally, we use the oil to burn in our reading lamps, and light ourselves at last to bed with stearine candles. Altogether, an amateur census of a single small English cottage results in the startling discovery that it contains twenty-seven distinct articles which owe their origin in one way or another to the coco-nut palm. And yet we affect in our black ingratitude to despise the question of the milk in the coconut.

FOOD AND FEEDING

WHEN a man and a bear meet together casually in an American forest, it makes a great deal of difference, to the two parties concerned at least, whether the bear eats the man or the man eats the bear. We haven't the slightest difficulty in deciding afterwards which of the two, in each particular case, has been the eater, and which the eaten. Here, we say, is the grizzly that eat the man; or, here is the man that smoked and dined off the hams of the grizzly. Basing our opinion upon such familiar and well-known instances, we are apt to take it for granted far too readily that between eating and being eaten, between the active and the passive voice of the verb *edo*, there exists necessarily a profound and impassable native antithesis. To swallow an oyster is, in our own personal histories, so very different a thing from being swallowed by a shark that we can hardly realise at first the underlying fundamental identity of eating with mere coalescence. And yet, at the very outset of the art of feeding, when the nascent animal first began to indulge in this very essential animal practice, one may fairly say that no practical difference as yet existed between the creature that ate and the creature that was eaten. After the man and the bear had finished their little meal, if one may be frankly metaphorical, it was impossible to decide whether the remaining being was the man or the bear, or which of the two had swallowed the

o

other. The dinner having been purely mutual, the resulting animal represented both the litigants equally; just as,
in cannibal New Zealand, the chief who ate up his brother
chief was held naturally to inherit the goods and chattels
of the vanquished and absorbed rival, whom he had thus
literally and physically incorporated.

A jelly-speck, floating about at his ease in a drop of
stagnant water under the field of a microscope, collides
accidentally with another jelly-speck who happens to be
travelling in the opposite direction across the same miniature ocean. What thereupon occurs? One jelly-speck
rolls itself gradually into the other, so that, instead of two,
there is now one; and the united body proceeds to float
away quite unconcernedly, without waiting to trouble itself
for a second with the profound metaphysical question,
which half of it is the original personality, and which half
the devoured and digested. In these minute and very
simple animals there is absolutely no division of labour
between part and part; every bit of the jelly-like mass is
alike head and foot and mouth and stomach. The jelly-
speck has no permanent limbs, but it keeps putting forth
vague arms and legs every now and then from one side or
the other; and with these temporary and ever-dissolving
members it crawls along merrily through its tiny drop of
stagnant water. If two of the legs or arms happen to
knock up casually against one another, they coalesce at
once, just like two drops of water on a window-pane, or
two strings of treacle slowly spreading along the surface of
a plate. When the jelly-speck meets any edible thing—
a bit of dead plant, a wee creature like itself, a microscopic
egg—it proceeds to fold its own substance slimily around
it, making, as it were, a temporary mouth for the purpose
of swallowing it, and a temporary stomach for the purpose
of quietly digesting and assimilating it afterwards. Thus

what at one moment is a foot may at the next moment become a mouth, and at the moment after that again a rudimentary stomach. The animal has no skin and no body, no outside and no inside, no distinction of parts or members, no individuality, no identity. Roll it up into one with another of its kind, and it couldn't tell you itself a minute afterwards which of the two it had really been a minute before. The question of personal identity is here considerably mixed.

But as soon as we get to rather larger creatures of the same type, the antithesis between the eater and the eaten begins to assume a more definite character. The big jelly-bag approaches a good many smaller jelly-bags, microscopic plants, and other appropriate food-stuffs, and, surrounding them rapidly with its crawling arms, envelopes them in its own substance, which closes behind them and gradually digests them. Everybody knows, by name at least, that revolutionary and evolutionary hero, the amœba—the terror of theologians, the pet of professors, and the insufferable bore of the general reader. Well, this parlous and subversive little animal consists of a comparatively large mass of soft jelly, pushing forth slender lobes, like threads or fingers, from its own substance, and gliding about, by means of these tiny legs, over water-plants and other submerged surfaces. But though it can literally turn itself inside out, like a glove, it still has some faint beginnings of a mouth and stomach, for it generally takes in food and absorbs water through a particular part of its surface, where the slimy mass of its body is thinnest. Thus the amœba may be said really to eat and drink, though quite devoid of any special organs for eating or drinking.

The particular point to which I wish to draw attention here, however, is this: that even the very simplest and

most primitive animals do discriminate somehow between
what is eatable and what isn't. The amœba has no eyes,
no nose, no mouth, no tongue, no nerves of taste, no
special means of discrimination of any kind ; and yet, so
long as it meets only grains of sand or bits of shell, it
makes no effort in any way to swallow them ; but, the
moment it comes across a bit of material fit for its food, it
begins at once to spread its clammy fingers around the
nutritious morsel. The fact is, every part of the amœba's
body apparently possesses, in a very vague form, the first
beginnings of those senses which in us are specialised and
confined to a single spot. And it is because of the light
which the amœba thus incidentally casts upon the nature
of the specialised senses in higher animals that I have ventured once more to drag out of the private life of his native
pond that already too notorious and obtrusive rhizopod.

With us lordly human beings, at the extreme opposite
end in the scale of being from the microscopic jelly-specks,
the art of feeding and the mechanism which provides for
it have both reached a very high state of advanced perfection. We have slowly evolved a tongue and palate on the
one hand, and French cooks and *pâté de foie gras* on the
other. But while everybody knows practically how things
taste to us, and which things respectively we like and dislike, comparatively few people ever recognise that the sense
of taste is not merely intended as a source of gratification,
but serves a useful purpose in our bodily economy, in informing us what we ought to eat and what to refuse.
Paradoxical as it may sound at first to most people, nice
things are, in the main, things that are good for us, and
nasty things are poisonous or otherwise injurious. That
we often practically find the exact contrary the case (alas!)
is due, not to the provisions of nature, but to the artificial
surroundings in which we live, and to the cunning way in

which we flavour up unwholesome food, so as to deceive
and cajole the natural palate. Yet, after all, it is a pleasant
gospel that what we like is really good for us, and, when
we have made some small allowances for artificial conditions, it is in the main a true one also.

The sense of taste, which in the lowest animals is dif-
fused equally over the whole frame, is in ourselves and
other higher creatures concentrated in a special part of
the body, namely the mouth, where the food about to be
swallowed is chewed and otherwise prepared beforehand for
the work of digestion. Now it is, of course, quite clear
that some sort of supervision must be exercised by the
body over the kind of food that is going to be put into it.
Common experience teaches us that prussic acid and pure
opium are undesirable food-stuffs in large quantities ; that
raw spirits, petroleum, and red lead should be sparingly
partaken of by the judicious feeder ; and that even green
fruit, the bitter end of cucumber, and the berries of deadly
nightshade are unsatisfactory articles of diet when continuously persisted in. If, at the very outset of our
digestive apparatus, we hadn't a sort of automatic premoni-
tory adviser upon the kinds of food we ought or ought not
to indulge in, we should naturally commit considerable
imprudences in the way of eating and drinking—even
more than we do at present. Natural selection has therefore provided us with a fairly efficient guide in this respect
in the sense of taste, which is placed at the very threshold,
as it were, of our digestive mechanism. It is the duty of
taste to warn us against uneatable things, and to recommend to our favourable attention eatable and wholesome
ones ; and, on the whole, in spite of small occasional
remissness, it performs this duty with creditable success.

Taste, however, is not equally distributed over the
whole surface of the tongue alike. There are three

distinct regions or tracts, each of which has to perform its
own special office and function. The tip of the tongue is
concerned mainly with pungent and acrid tastes; the
middle portion is sensitive chiefly to sweets and bitters;
while the back or lower portion confines itself almost
entirely to the flavours of roast meats, butter, oils, and
other rich or fatty substances. There are very good reasons
for this subdivision of faculties in the tongue, the object
being, as it were, to make each piece of food undergo three
separate examinations (like ' smalls,' ' mods,' and ' greats '
at Oxford), which must be successively passed before it is
admitted into full participation in the human economy.
The first examination, as we shall shortly see, gets rid at
once of substances which would be actively and immediately destructive to the very tissues of the mouth and
body; the second discriminates between poisonous and
chemically harmless food-stuffs; and the third merely
decides the minor question whether the particular food is
likely to prove then and there wholesome or indigestible to
the particular person. The sense of taste proceeds, in fact,
upon the principle of gradual selection and elimination; it
refuses first what is positively destructive, next what is
more remotely deleterious, and finally what is only undesirable or over-luscious.

When we want to assure ourselves, by means of taste,
about any unknown object—say a lump of some white
stuff, which may be crystal, or glass, or alum, or borax, or
quartz, or rocksalt—we put the tip of the tongue against it
gingerly. If it begins to burn us, we draw it away more
or less rapidly with an accompaniment in language strictly
dependent upon our personal habits and manners. The
test we thus occasionally apply, even in the civilised adult
state, to unknown bodies is one that is being applied every
day and all day long by children and savages. Unsophis-

ticated humanity is constantly putting everything it sees
up to its mouth in a frank spirit of experimental inquiry as
to its gustatory properties.   In civilised life we find everything ready labelled and assorted for us ; we comparatively
seldom require to roll the contents of a suspicious bottle
(in very small quantities) doubtfully upon the tongue in
order to discover whether it is pale sherry or Chili vinegar,
Dublin stout or mushroom ketchup.   But in the savage
state, from which, geologically and biologically speaking,
we have only just emerged, bottles and labels do not exist.
Primitive man, therefore, in his sweet simplicity, has only
two modes open before him for deciding whether the
things he finds are or are not strictly edible.   The first
thing he does is to sniff at them ; and smell, being, as Mr.
Herbert Spencer has well put it, an anticipatory taste,
generally gives him some idea of what the thing is likely
to prove.   The second thing he does is to pop it into his
mouth, and proceed practically to examine its further
characteristics.

Strictly speaking, with the tip of the tongue one can't
really taste at all.   If you put a small drop of honey or of
oil of bitter almonds on that part of the mouth, you will find
(no doubt to your great surprise) that it produces no effect of
any sort ; you only taste it when it begins slowly to diffuse
itself, and reaches the true tasting region in the middle
distance.   But if you put a little cayenne or mustard on
the same part, you will find that it bites you immediately
--the experiment should be tried sparingly—while if you
put it lower down in the mouth you will swallow it almost
without noticing the pungency of the stimulant.   The
reason is, that the tip of the tongue is supplied only with
nerves which are really nerves of touch, not nerves of
taste proper ; they belong to a totally different main branch,
and they go to a different centre in the brain, together

with the very similar threads which supply the nerves of smell for mustard and pepper. That is why the smell and taste of these pungent substances are so much alike, as everybody must have noticed, a good sniff at a mustard-pot producing almost the same irritating effects as an incautious mouthful. As a rule we don't accurately distinguish, it is true, between these different regions of taste in the mouth in ordinary life; but that is because we usually roll our food about instinctively, without paying much attention to the particular part affected by it. Indeed, when one is trying deliberate experiments in the subject, in order to test the varying sensitiveness of the different parts to different substances, it is necessary to keep the tongue quite dry, in order to isolate the thing you are experimenting with, and prevent its spreading to all parts of the mouth together. In actual practice this result is obtained in a rather ludicrous manner — by blowing upon the tongue, between each experiment, with a pair of bellows. To such undignified expedients does the pursuit of science lead the ardent modern psychologist. Those domestic rivals of Dr. Forbes Winslow, the servants, who behold the enthusiastic investigator alternately drying his tongue in this ridiculous fashion, as if he were a blacksmith's fire, and then squeezing out a single drop of essence of pepper, vinegar, or beef-tea from a glass syringe upon the dry surface, not unnaturally arrive at the conclusion that master has gone stark mad, and that, in their private opinion, it's the microscope and the skeleton as has done it.

Above all things, we don't want to be flayed alive. So the kinds of tastes discriminated by the tip of the tongue are the pungent, like pepper, cayenne and mustard; the astringent, like borax and alum; the alkaline, like soda and potash; the acid, like vinegar and green fruit; and the saline, like salt and ammonia. Almost all the bodies likely to give rise to such tastes (or, more correctly, sensations of touch in the tongue) are obviously unwholesome and destructive in their character, at least when taken in large quantities. Nobody wishes to drink nitric acid by the quart. The first business of this part of the tongue is, therefore, to warn us emphatically against caustic substances and corrosive acids, against vitriol and kerosene, spirits of wine and ether, capsicums and burning leaves or roots, such as those of the common English lords-and-ladies. Things of this sort are immediately destructive to the very tissues of the tongue and palate; if taken incautiously in too large doses, they burn the skin off the roof of the mouth; and when swallowed they play havoc, of course, with our internal arrangements. It is highly advisable, therefore, to have an immediate warning of these extremely dangerous substances, at the very outset of our feeding apparatus.

This kind of taste hardly differs from touch or burning. The sensibility of the tip of the tongue is only a very slight modification of the sensibility possessed by the skin generally, and especially by the inner folds over all delicate parts of the body. We all know that common caustic burns us wherever it touches; and it burns the tongue only in a somewhat more marked manner. Nitric or sulphuric acid attacks the fingers each after its own kind. A mustard plaster makes us tingle almost immediately; and the action of mustard on the tongue hardly differs, except in being more instantaneous and more discriminative. Cantharides work in just the same way. If you cut a red pepper in two and rub it on your neck, it will sting just as it does when put into soup (this experiment, however, is best tried upon one's younger brother; if made personally, it hardly repays the trouble and annoyance). Even vinegar and other acids, rubbed into the skin, are followed by a slight tingling; while the

effect of brandy, applied, say, to the arms, is gently stimulating and pleasurable, somewhat in the same way as when
normally swallowed in conjunction with the habitual
seltzer. In short, most things which give rise to distinct
tastes when applied to the tip of the tongue give rise to
fainter sensations when applied to the skin generally. And
one hardly needs to be reminded that pepper or vinegar
placed (accidentally as a rule) on the inner surface of the
eyelids produces a very distinct and unpleasant smart.

The fact is, the liability to be chemically affected by
pungent or acid bodies is common to every part of the
skin; but it is least felt where the tough outer skin is
thickest, and most felt where that skin is thinnest, and
the nerves are most plentifully distributed near the surface.
A mustard plaster would probably fail to draw at all on
one's heel or the palm of one's hand ; while it is decidedly
painful on one's neck or chest ; and a mere speck of mustard inside the eyelid gives one positive torture for hours
together. Now, the tip of the tongue is just a part of one's
body specially set aside for this very object, provided with
an extremely thin skin, and supplied with an immense
number of nerves, on purpose so as to be easily affected by
all such pungent, alkaline, or spirituous substances. Sir
Wilfrid Lawson would probably conclude that it was
deliberately designed by Providence to warn us against a
wicked indulgence in the brandy and seltzer aforesaid.

At first sight it might seem as though there were
hardly enough of such pungent and fiery things in existence to make it worth while for us to be provided with a
special mechanism for guarding against them. That is
true enough, no doubt, as regards our modern civilised life ;
though, even now, it is perhaps just as well that our children should have an internal monitor (other than conscience) to dissuade them immediately from indiscriminate

indulgence in photographic chemicals, the contents of stray medicine bottles, and the best dried West India chilies. But in an earlier period of progress, and especially in tropical countries (where the Darwinians have now decided the human race made its first *début* upon this or any other stage), things were very different indeed. Pungent and poisonous plants and fruits abounded on every side. We have all of us in our youth been taken in by some too cruelly waggish companion, who insisted upon making us eat the bright, glossy leaves of the common English arum, which without look pretty and juicy enough, but within are full of the concentrated essence of pungency and profanity. Well, there are hundreds of such plants, even in cold climates, to tempt the eyes and poison the veins of unsuspecting cattle or childish humanity. There is buttercup, so horribly acrid that cows carefully avoid it in their closest cropped pastures ; and yet your cow is not usually a too dainty animal. There is aconite, the deadly poison with which Dr. Lamson removed his troublesome relatives. There is baneberry, whose very name sufficiently describes its dangerous nature. There are horse-radish, and stinging rocket, and biting wall-pepper, and still smarter water-pepper, and worm-wood, and nightshade, and spurge, and hemlock, and half a dozen other equally unpleasant weeds. All of these have acquired their pungent and poisonous properties, just as nettles have acquired their sting, and thistles their thorns, in order to prevent animals from browsing upon them and destroying them. And the animals in turn have acquired a very delicate sense of pungency on purpose to warn them beforehand of the existence of such dangerous and undesirable qualities in the plants which they might otherwise be tempted incautiously to swallow.

In tropical woods, where our 'hairy quadrumanous

ancestor ' (Darwinian for the primæval monkey, from whom
we are presumably descended) used playfully to disport
himself, as yet unconscious of his glorious destiny as the
remote progenitor of Shakespeare, Milton, and the late
Mr. Peace—in tropical woods, such acrid or pungent fruits
and plants are particularly common, and correspondingly
annoying. The fact is, our primitive forefather and all
the other monkeys are, or were, confirmed fruit-eaters.
But to guard against their depredations a vast number of
tropical fruits and nuts have acquired disagreeable or fiery
rinds and shells, which suffice to deter the bold aggressor.
It may not be nice to get your tongue burnt with a root or
fruit, but it is at least a great deal better than getting
poisoned ; and, roughly speaking, pungency in external
nature exactly answers to the rough gaudy labels which
some chemists paste on bottles containing poisons. It
means to say, ' This fruit or leaf, if you eat it in any quantities, will kill you.' That is the true explanation of
capsicums, pimento, colocynth, croton oil, the upas tree,
and the vast majority of bitter, acrid, or fiery fruits and
leaves. If we had to pick up our own livelihood, as our
naked ancestors had to do, from roots, seeds, and berries,
we should far more readily appreciate this simple truth.
We should know that a great many more plants than we
now suspect are bitter or pungent, and therefore poisonous.
Even in England we are familiar enough with such defences
as those possessed by the outer rind of the walnut ; but
the tropical cashew-nut has a rind so intensely acrid that
it blisters the lips and fingers instantaneously, in the same
way as cantharides would do. I believe that on the whole,
taking nature throughout, more fruits and nuts are poisonous, or intensely bitter, or very fiery, than are sweet,
luscious, and edible.

' But,' says that fidgety person, the hypothetical objector

(whom one always sets up for the express purpose of promptly knocking him down again), 'if it be the business of the fore part of the tongue to warn us against pungent and acrid substances, how comes it that we purposely use such things as mustard, pepper, curry-powder, and vinegar?' Well, in themselves all these things are, strictly speaking, bad for us; but in small quantities they act as agreeable stimulants; and we take care in preparing most of them to get rid of the most objectionable properties. Moreover, we use them, not as foods, but merely as condiments. One drop of oil of capsicums is enough to kill a man, if taken undiluted; but in actual practice we buy it in such a very diluted form that comparatively little harm arises from using it. Still, very young children dislike all these violent stimulants, even in small quantities; they won't touch mustard, pepper, or vinegar, and they recoil at once from wine or spirits. It is only by slow degrees that we learn these unnatural tastes, as our nerves get blunted and our palates jaded; and we all know that the old Indian who can eat nothing but dry curries, devilled biscuits, anchovy paste, pepper-pot, mulligatawny soup, Worcestershire sauce, preserved ginger, hot pickles, fiery sherry, and neat cognac, is also a person with no digestion, a fragmentary liver, and very little chance of getting himself accepted by any safe and solvent insurance office. Throughout, the warning in itself is a useful one; it is we who foolishly and persistently disregard it. Alcohol, for example, tells us at once that it is bad for us; yet we manage so to dress it up with flavouring matters and dilute it with water that we overlook the fiery character of the spirit itself. But that alcohol is in itself a bad thing (when freely indulged in) has been so abundantly demonstrated in the history of mankind that it hardly needs any further proof.

The middle region of the tongue is the part with which

we experience sensations of taste proper—that is to say, of sweetness and bitterness. In a healthy, natural state all sweet things are pleasant to us, and all bitters (even if combined with sherry) unpleasant. The reason for this is easy enough to understand. It carries us back at once into those primæval tropical forests, where our 'hairy ancestor' used to diet himself upon the fruits of the earth in due season. Now, almost all edible fruits, roots, and tubers contain sugar; and therefore the presence of sugar is, in the wild condition, as good a rough test of whether anything is good to eat as one could easily find. In fact, the argument cuts both ways: edible fruits are sweet because they are intended for man and other animals to eat; and man and other animals have a tongue pleasurably affected by sugar because sugary things in nature are for them in the highest degree edible. Our early progenitors formed their taste upon oranges, mangoes, bananas, and grapes; upon sweet potatoes, sugar-cane, dates, and wild honey. There is scarcely anything fitted for human food in the vegetable world (and our earliest ancestors were most undoubted vegetarians) which does not contain sugar in considerable quantities. In temperate climates (where man is but a recent intruder), we have taken, it is true, to regarding wheaten bread as the staff of life; but in our native tropics enormous populations still live almost exclusively upon plantains, bananas, bread-fruit, yams, sweet potatoes, dates, cocoanuts, melons, cassava, pine-apples, and figs. Our nerves have been adapted to the circumstances of our early life as a race in tropical forests; and we still retain a marked liking for sweets of every sort. Not content with our strawberries, raspberries, gooseberries, currants, apples, pears, cherries, plums and other northern fruits, we ransack the world for dates, figs, raisins, and oranges. Indeed, in spite of our acquired meat-eating propensities, it may be fairly said that fruits and seeds (including wheat, rice, peas beans, and other grains and pulse) still form by far the most important element in the food-stuffs of human populations generally.

But besides the natural sweets, we have also taken to producing artificial ones. Has any housewife ever realised the alarming condition of cookery in the benighted generations before the invention of sugar? It is really almost too appalling to think about. So many things that we now look upon as all but necessaries—cakes, puddings, made dishes, confectionery, preserves, sweet biscuits, jellies, cooked fruits, tarts, and so forth—were then practically quite impossible. Fancy attempting nowadays to live a single day without sugar; no tea, no coffee, no jam, no pudding, no cake, no sweets, no hot toddy before one goes to bed; the bare idea of it is too terrible. And yet that was really the abject condition of all the civilised world up to the middle of the middle ages. Horace's punch was sugarless and lemonless; the gentle Virgil never tasted the congenial cup of afternoon tea; and Socrates went from his cradle to his grave without ever knowing the flavour of peppermint bull's eyes. How the children managed to spend their Saturday *as*, or their weekly *obolus*, is a profound mystery. To be sure, people had honey; but honey is rare, dear, and scanty; it can never have filled one quarter the place that sugar fills in our modern affections. Try for a moment to realise drinking honey with one's whisky-and-water, or doing the year's preserving with a pot of best Narbonne, and you get at once a common measure of the difference between the two as practical sweeteners. Nowadays, we get sugar from cane and beet-root in abundance, while sugar-maples and palm-trees of various sorts afford a considerable supply to remoter countries. But the childhood of the little Greeks and

Romans must have been absolutely unlighted by a single ray of joy from chocolate creams or Everton toffee.

The consequence of this excessive production of sweets in modern times is, of course, that we have begun to distrust the indications afforded us by the sense of taste in this particular as to the wholesomeness of various objects. We can mix sugar with anything we like, whether it had sugar in it to begin with or otherwise ; and by sweetening and flavouring we can give a false palatableness to even the worst and most indigestible rubbish, such as plaster-of-Paris, largely sold under the name of sugared almonds to the ingenuous youth of two hemispheres. But in untouched nature the test rarely or never fails. As long as fruits are unripe and unfit for human food, they are green and sour ; as soon as they ripen they become soft and sweet, and usually acquire some bright colour as a sort of advertisement of their edibility. In the main, bar the accidents of civilisation, whatever is sweet is good to eat—nay more, is meant to be eaten ; it is only our own perverse folly that makes us sometimes think all nice things bad for us, and all wholesome things nasty. In a state of nature, the exact opposite is really the case. One may observe, too, that children, who are literally young savages in more senses than one, stand nearer to the primitive feeling in this respect than grown-up people. They unaffectedly like sweets ; adults, who have grown more accustomed to the artificial meat diet, don't, as a rule, care much for puddings, cakes, and made dishes. (May I venture parenthetically to add, any appearance to the contrary notwithstanding, that I am not a vegetarian, and that I am far from desiring to bring down upon my devoted head the imprecation pronounced against the rash person who would rob a poor man of his beer. It is quite possible to believe that vegetarianism was the starting point of the race, without wishing to consider it also as the goal ; just as it is quite possible to regard clothes as purely artificial products of civilisation, without desiring personally to return to the charming simplicity of the Garden of Eden.)

Bitter things in nature at large, on the contrary, are almost invariably poisonous. Strychnia, for example, is intensely bitter, and it is well known that life cannot be supported on strychnia alone for more than a few hours. Again, colocynth and aloes are far from being wholesome food stuffs, for a continuance ; and the bitter end of cucumber does not conduce to the highest standard of good living. The bitter matter in decaying apples is highly injurious when swallowed, which it isn't likely to be by anybody who ever tastes it. Wormwood and walnut-shells contain other bitter and poisonous principles ; absinthe, which is made from one of them, is a favourite slow poison with the fashionable young men of Paris, who wish to escape prematurely from ' Le monde où l'on s'ennuie.' But prussic acid is the commonest component in all natural bitters, being found in bitter almonds, apple pips, the kernels of mangosteens, and many other seeds and fruits. Indeed, one may say roughly that the object of nature generally is to prevent the actual seeds of edible fruits from being eaten and digested ; and for this purpose, while she stores the pulp with sweet juices, she encloses the seed itself in hard stony coverings, and makes it nasty with bitter essences. Eat an orange-pip, and you will promptly observe how effectual is this arrangement. As a rule, the outer rind of nuts is bitter, and the inner kernel of edible fruits. The tongue thus warns us immediately against bitter things, as being poisonous, and prevents us automatically from swallowing them.

' But how is it,' asks our objector again, ' that so many poisons are tasteless, or even, like sugar of lead, pleasant

P

to the palate ? ' The answer is (you see, we knock him
down again, as usual) because these poisons are themselves
for the most part artificial products ; they do not occur in
a state of nature, at least in man's ordinary surroundings.
Almost every poisonous thing that we are really liable to
meet with in the wild state we are warned against at once
by the sense of taste ; but of course it would be absurd to
suppose that natural selection could have produced a mode
of warning us against poisons which have never before
occurred in human experience. One might just as well
expect that it should have rendered us dynamite-proof, or
have given us a skin like the hide of a rhinoceros to protect us against the future contingency of the invention of
rifles.

Sweets and bitters are really almost the only tastes
proper, almost the only ones discriminated by this central
and truly gustatory region of the tongue and palate. Most
so-called flavourings will be found on strict examination
to be nothing more than mixtures with these of certain
smells, or else of pungent, salty, or alkaline matters, distinguished as such by the tip of the tongue. For instance,
paradoxical as it sounds to say so, cinnamon has really no
taste at all, but only a smell. Nobody will ever believe
this on first hearing, but nothing on earth is easier than to
put it to the test. Take a small piece of cinnamon, hold
your nose tightly, rather high up, between the thumb and
finger, and begin chewing it. You will find that it is
absolutely tasteless ; you are merely chewing a perfectly
insipid bit of bark. Then let go your nose, and you will
find immediately that it ' tastes ' strongly, though in
reality it is only the perfume from it that you now permit
to rise into the smelling-chamber in the nose. So, again,
cloves have only a pungent taste and a peculiar smell, and
the same is the case more or less with almost all distinctive

flavourings. When you come to find of what they are made up, they consist generally of sweets or bitters, intermixed with certain ethereal perfumes, or with pungent or acid tastes, or with both or several such together. In this way, a comparatively small number of original elements, variously combined, suffice to make up the whole enormous mass of recognisably different tastes and flavours.

The third and lowest part of the tongue and throat is the seat of those peculiar tastes to which Professor Bain, the great authority upon this important philosophical subject, has given the names of relishes and disgusts. It is here, chiefly, that we taste animal food, fats, butters, oils, and the richer class of vegetables and made dishes. If we like them, we experience a sensation which may be called a relish, and which induces one to keep rolling the morsel farther down the throat, till it passes at last beyond the region of our voluntary control. If we don't like them, we get the sensation which may be called a disgust, and which is very different from the mere unpleasantness of excessively pungent or bitter things. It is far less of an intellectual and far more of a physical and emotional feeling. We say, and say rightly, of such things that we find it hard to swallow them; a something within us (of a very tangible nature) seems to rise up bodily and protest against them. As a very good example of this experience, take one's first attempt to swallow cod-liver oil. Other things may be unpleasant or unpalatable, but things of this class are in the strictest sense nasty and disgusting.

The fact is, the lower part of the tongue is supplied with nerves in close sympathy with the digestion. If the food which has been passed by the two previous examiners is found here to be simple and digestible, it is permitted to go on unchallenged; if it is found to be too rich, too bilious, or too indigestible, a protest is promptly entered

P 2

against it, and if we are wise we will immediately desist from eating any more of it. It is here that the impartial tribunal of nature pronounces definitely against roast goose, mince pies, *pâté de foie gras*, sally lunn, muffins and crumpets, and creamy puddings. It is here, too, that the slightest taint in meat, milk, or butter is immediately detected ; that rancid pastry from the pastrycook's is ruthlessly exposed ; and that the wiles of the fishmonger are set at naught by the judicious palate. It is the special duty, in fact, of this last examiner to discover, not whether food is positively destructive, not whether it is poisonous or deleterious in nature, but merely whether it is then and there digestible or undesirable.

As our state of health varies greatly from time to time, however, so do the warnings of this last sympathetic adviser change and flicker. Sweet things are always sweet, and bitter things always bitter ; vinegar is always sour, and ginger always hot in the mouth, too, whatever our state of health or feeling. But our taste for roast loin of mutton, high game, salmon cutlets, and Gorgonzola cheese varies immensely from time to time, with the passing condition of our health and digestion. In illness, and especially in sea-sickness, one gets the distaste carried to the extreme : you may eat grapes or suck an orange in the chops of the Channel, but you do not feel warmly attached to the steward who offers you a basin of greasy ox-tail, or consoles you with promises of ham sandwiches in half a minute. Under those two painful conditions it is the very light, fresh, and stimulating things that one can most easily swallow—champagne, soda-water, strawberries, peaches ; not lobster salad, sardines on toast, green Chartreuse, or hot brandy-and-water. On the other hand, in robust health, and when hungry with exercise, you can eat fat pork with relish on a Scotch hillside, or dine off fresh

salmon three days running without inconvenience. Even
a Spanish stew, with plenty of garlic in it, and floating in
olive oil, tastes positively delicious after a day's mountain-
eering in the Pyrenees.

The healthy popular belief, still surviving in spite of
cookery, that our likes and dislikes are the best guide to
what is good for us, finds its justification in this fact, that
whatever is relished will prove on the average wholesome,
and whatever rouses disgust will prove on the whole indigestible. Nothing can be more wrong, for example, than
to make children eat fat when they don't want it. A
healthy child likes fat, and eats as much of it as he can
get. If a child shows signs of disgust at fat, that proves
that it is of a bilious temperament, and it ought never to
be forced into eating it against its will. Most of us are
bilious in after-life just because we were compelled to eat
rich food in childhood, which we felt instinctively was un-
suitable for us. We might still be indulging with impunity
in thick turtle, canvas-back ducks, devilled whitebait,
meringues, and Nesselrode puddings, if we hadn't been so
persistently overdosed in our earlier years with things that
we didn't want and knew were indigestible.

Of course, in our existing modern cookery, very few
simple and uncompounded tastes are still left to us; everything is so mixed up together that only by an effort of deliberate experiment can one discover what are the special
effects of special tastes upon the tongue and palate. Salt
is mixed with almost everything we eat—*sal sapit omnia*
—and pepper or cayenne is nearly equally common. Butter
is put into the peas, which have been previously adulterated
by being boiled with mint; and cucumber is unknown except in conjunction with oil and vinegar. This makes it
comparatively difficult for us to realise the distinctness of
the elements which go to make up most tastes as we

actually experience them. Moreover, a great many eatable
objects have hardly any taste of their own, properly speaking, but only a feeling of softness, or hardness, or glutinous-
ness in the mouth, mainly observed in the act of chewing
them. For example, plain boiled rice is almost wholly
insipid ; but even in its plainest form salt has usually been
boiled with it, and in practice we generally eat it with
sugar, preserves, curry, or some other strongly flavoured
condiment. Again, plain boiled tapioca and sago (in
water) are as nearly tasteless as anything can be ; they
merely yield a feeling of gumminess ; but milk, in which
they are oftenest cooked, gives them a relish (in the sense
here restricted), and sugar, eggs, cinnamon, or nutmeg are
usually added by way of flavouring. Even turbot has
hardly any taste proper, except in the glutinous skin,
which has a faint relish ; the epicure values it rather because of. its softness, its delicacy, and its light flesh.
Gelatine by itself is merely very swallowable ; we must mix
sugar, wine, lemon-juice, and other flavourings in order to
make it into good jelly. Salt, spices, essences, vanilla,
vinegar, pickles, capers, ketchups, sauces, chutneys, lime-
juice, curry, and all the rest, are just our civilised expedients
for adding the pleasure of pungency and acidity to naturally
insipid foods, by stimulating the nerves of touch in the
tongue, just as sugar is our tribute to the pure gustatory
sense, and oil, butter, bacon, lard, and the various fats used
in frying to the sense of relish which forms the last
element in our compound taste. A boiled sole is all very
well when one is just convalescent, but in robust health we
demand the delights of egg and bread-crumb, which are
after all only the vehicle for the appetising grease. Plain
boiled macaroni may pass muster in the unsophisticated
nursery, but in the pampered dining-room it requires the
aid of toasted parmesan. Good modern cookery is the

practical result of centuries of experience in this direction ;
the final flower of ages of evolution, devoted to the equalisa-
tion of flavours in all human food.   Think of the generations of fruitless experiment that must have passed before
mankind discovered that mint sauce (itself a cunning compound of vinegar and sugar) ought to be eaten with leg of
lamb, that roast goose required a corrective in the shape
of apple, and that while a pre-established harmony existed
between salmon and lobster, oysters were ordained beforehand by nature as the proper accompaniment of boiled cod.
Whenever I reflect upon such things, I become at once a
good Positivist, and offer up praise in my own private
chapel to the Spirit of Humanity which has slowly perfected
these profound rules of good living.

DE BANANA

THE title which heads this paper is intended to be Latin, and is modelled on the precedent of the De Amicitia, De Senectute, De Corona, and other time-honoured plagues of our innocent boyhood.   It is meant to give dignity and authority to the subject with which it deals, as well as to rouse curiosity in the ingenuous breast of the candid reader, who may perhaps mistake it, at first sight, for negro-English, or for the name of a distinguished Norman family.   In anticipation of the possible objection that the word 'Banana' is not strictly classical, I would humbly urge the precept and example of my old friend Horace —enemy I once thought him—who expresses his approbation of those happy innovations whereby Latium was gradually enriched with a copious vocabulary.   I maintain that if Banana, bananæ, &c., is not already a Latin noun of the first declension, why then it ought to be, and it shall be in future.   Linnæus indeed thought otherwise. He too assigned the plant and fruit to the first declension, but handed it over to none other than our earliest acquaintance in the Latin language, Musa.   He called the banana *Musa sapientum*.   What connection he could possibly conceive between that woolly fruit and the daughters of the ægis-bearing Zeus, or why he should consider it a proof of wisdom to eat a particularly indigestible and nightmare-begetting food-stuff, passes my humble comprehension.

The muses, so far as I have personally noticed their habits, always greatly prefer the grape to the banana, and wise men shun the one at least as sedulously as they avoid the other.

Let it not for a moment be supposed, however, that I wish to treat the useful and ornamental banana with intentional disrespect. On the contrary, I cherish for it— at a distance—feelings of the highest esteem and admiration. We are so parochial in our views, taking us as a species, that I dare say very few English people really know how immensely useful a plant is the common banana. To most of us it envisages itself merely as a curious tropical fruit, largely imported at Covent Garden, and a capital thing to stick on one of the tall dessert-dishes when you give a dinner-party, because it looks delightfully foreign, and just serves to balance the pine-apple at the opposite end of the hospitable mahogany. Perhaps such innocent readers will be surprised to learn that bananas and plantains supply the principal food-stuff of a far larger fraction of the human race than that which is supported by wheaten bread. They form the veritable staff of life to the inhabitants of both eastern and western tropics. What the potato is to the degenerate descendant of Celtic kings; what the oat is to the kilted Highlandman; what rice is to the Bengalee, and Indian corn to the American negro, that is the muse of sages (I translate literally from the immortal Swede) to African savages and Brazilian slaves. Humboldt calculated that an acre of bananas would supply a greater quantity of solid food to hungry humanity than could possibly be extracted from the same extent of cultivated ground by any other known plant. So you see the question is no small one; to sing the praise of this Linnæan muse is a task well worthy of the Pierian muses.

Do you know the outer look and aspect of the banana plant? If not, then you have never voyaged to those

delusive tropics. Tropical vegetation, as ordinarily understood by poets and painters, consists entirely of the coco-
nut palm and the banana bush. Do you wish to paint a
beautiful picture of a rich ambrosial tropical island, *à la*
Tennyson—a summer isle of Eden lying in dark purple
spheres of sea ?—then you introduce a group of coco-nuts,
whispering in odorous heights of even, in the very foreground of your pretty sketch, just to let your public understand at a glance that these are the delicious poetical tropics.
Do you desire to create an ideal paradise, *à la* Bernardin
de St. Pierre, where idyllic Virginies die of pure modesty
rather than appear before the eyes of their beloved but un-
wedded Pauls in a lace-bedraped *peignoir* ?—then you
strike the keynote by sticking in the middle distance a hut
or cottage, overshadowed by the broad and graceful foliage
of the picturesque banana. ('Hut' is a poor and chilly word
for these glowing descriptions, far inferior to the pretty
and high-sounding original *chaumière*.) That is how we
do the tropics when we want to work upon the emotions of
the reader. But it is all a delicate theatrical illusion ; a
trick of art meant to deceive and impose upon the unwary
who have never been there, and would like to think
it all genuine. In reality, nine times out of ten, you
might cast your eyes casually around you in any tropical
valley, and, if there didn't happen to be a native cottage
with a coco-nut grove and banana patch anywhere in the
neighbourhood, you would see nothing in the way of vegetation which you mightn't see at home any day in Europe.
But what painter would ever venture to paint the tropics
without the palm trees ? He might just as well try to
paint the desert without the camels, or to represent St.
Sebastian without a sheaf of arrows sticking unperceived in
the calm centre of his unruffled bosom, to mark and empha-
sise his Sebastianic personality.

Still, I will frankly admit that the banana itself, with its practically almost identical relation, the plantain, is a real bit of tropical foliage. I confess to a settled prejudice against the tropics generally, but I allow the sunsets, the coco-nuts, and the bananas. The true stem creeps underground, and sends up each year an upright branch, thickly covered with majestic broad green leaves, somewhat like those of the canna cultivated in our gardens as ' Indian shot,' but far larger, nobler, and handsomer. They sometimes measure from six to ten feet in length, and their thick midrib and strongly marked diverging veins give them a very lordly and graceful appearance. But they are apt in practice to suffer much from the fury of the tropical storms. The wind rips the leaves up between the veins as far as the midrib in tangled tatters ; so that after a good hurricane they look more like coco-nut palm leaves than like single broad masses of foliage as they ought properly to do. This, of course, is the effect of a gentle and balmy hurricane—a mere capful of wind that tears and tatters them. After a really bad storm (one of the sort when you tie ropes round your wooden house to prevent its falling bodily to pieces, I mean) the bananas are all actually blown down, and the crop for that season utterly destroyed. The apparent stem, being merely composed of the overlapping and sheathing leaf-stalks, has naturally very little stability ; and the soft succulent trunk accordingly gives way forthwith at the slightest onslaught. This liability to be blown down in high winds forms the weak point of the plantain, viewed as a food-stuff crop. In the South Sea Islands, where there is little shelter, the poor Fijian, in cannibal days, often lost his one means of subsistence from this cause, and was compelled to satisfy the pangs of hunger on the plump persons of his immediate relatives. But since the introduction of Christianity, and of a dwarf stout windproof variety of banana, his condition in this respect, I am glad to say, has been greatly ameliorated.

By descent the banana bush is a developed tropical lily, not at all remotely allied to the common iris, only that its flowers and fruit are clustered together on a hanging spike, instead of growing solitary and separate as in the true irises. The blossoms, which, though pretty, are comparatively inconspicuous for the size of the plant, show the extraordinary persistence of the lily type; for almost all the vast number of species, more or less directly descended from the primitive lily, continue to the very end of the chapter to have six petals, six stamens, and three rows of seeds in their fruits or capsules. But practical man, with his eye always steadily fixed on the one important quality of edibility—the sum and substance to most people of all botanical research—has confined his attention almost entirely to the fruit of the banana. In all essentials (other than the systematically unimportant one just alluded to) the banana fruit in its original state exactly resembles the capsule of the iris—that pretty pod that divides in three when ripe, and shows the delicate orange-coated seeds lying in triple rows within—only, in the banana, the fruit does not open ; in the sweet language of technical botany, it is an indehiscent capsule ; and the seeds, instead of standing separate and distinct, as in the iris, are embedded in a soft and pulpy substance which forms the edible and practical part of the entire arrangement.

This is the proper appearance of the original and natural banana, before it has been taken in hand and cultivated by tropical man. When cut across the middle, it ought to show three rows of seeds, interspersed with pulp, and faintly preserving some dim memory of the dividing wall which once separated them. In practice, however, the banana differs widely from this theoretical ideal, as practice often *will* differ from theory; for it has been so long cultivated and selected by man—being probably one of the very oldest, if not actually quite the oldest, of domesticated plants—that it has all but lost the original habit of producing seeds. This is a common effect of cultivation on fruits, and it is of course deliberately aimed at by horticulturists, as the seeds are generally a nuisance, regarded from the point of view of the eater, and their absence improves the fruit, as long as one can manage to get along somehow without them. In the pretty little Tangierine oranges (so ingeniously corrupted by fruiterers into mandarins) the seeds have almost been cultivated out; in the best pine-apples, and in the small grapes known in the dried state as currants, they have quite disappeared; while in some varieties of pears they survive only in the form of shrivelled, barren, and useless pips. But the banana, more than any other plant we know of, has managed for many centuries to do without seeds altogether. The cultivated sort, especially in America, is quite seedless, and the plants are propagated entirely by suckers.

Still, you can never wholly circumvent nature. Expel her with a pitchfork, *tamen usque recurrit*. Now nature has settled that the right way to propagate plants is by means of seedlings. Strictly speaking, indeed, it is the only way; the other modes of growth from bulbs or cuttings are not really propagation, but mere reduplication by splitting, as when you chop a worm in two, and a couple of worms wriggle off contentedly forthwith in either direction. Just so when you divide a plant by cuttings, suckers, slips, or runners; the two apparent plants thus produced are in the last resort only separate parts of the same individual—one and indivisible, like the French Republic. Seedlings are absolutely distinct indi-

viduals ; they are the product of the pollen of one plant
and the ovules of another, and they start afresh in life with
some chance of being fairly free from the hereditary taints
or personal failings of either parent. But cuttings or
suckers are only the same old plant over and over again in
fresh circumstances, transplanted as it were, but not truly
renovated or rejuvenescent. That is the real reason why
our potatoes are now all going to—well, the same place as
the army has been going ever since the earliest memories
of the oldest officer in the whole service. We have gone
on growing potatoes over and over again from the tubers
alone, and hardly ever from seed, till the whole constitution
of the potato kind has become permanently enfeebled by
old age and dotage. The eyes (as farmers call them) are
only buds or underground branches ; and to plant potatoes
as we usually do is nothing more than to multiply the
apparent scions by fission. Odd as it may sound to say so,
all the potato vines in a whole field are often, from the
strict biological point of view, parts of a single much-
divided individual. It is just as though one were to go on
cutting up a single worm, time after time, as soon as he
grew again, till at last the one original creature had multiplied into a whole colony of apparently distinct individuals. Yet, if the first worm happened to have the gout
or the rheumatism (metaphorically speaking), all the other
worms into which his compound personality had been
divided would doubtless suffer from the same complaints
throughout the whole of their joint lifetimes.

The banana, however, has very long resisted the inevitable tendency to degeneration in plants thus artificially and
unhealthily propagated. Potatoes have only been in cultivation for a few hundred years ; and yet the potato
constitution has become so far enfeebled by the practice of
growing from the tuber that the plants now fall an easy

prey to potato fungus, Colorado beetles, and a thousand other persistent enemies. It is just the same with the vine—propagated too long by layers or cuttings, its health has failed entirely, and it can no longer resist the ravages of the phylloxera or the slow attacks of the vine-disease fungus. But the banana, though of very ancient and positively immemorial antiquity as a cultivated plant, seems somehow gifted with an extraordinary power of holding its own in spite of long-continued unnatural propagation. For thousands of years it has been grown in Asia in the seedless condition, and yet it springs as heartily as ever still from the underground suckers. Nevertheless, there must in the end be some natural limit to this wonderful power of reproduction, or rather of longevity; for, in the strictest sense, the banana bushes that now grow in the negro gardens of Trinidad and Demerara are part and parcel of the very same plants which grew and bore fruit a thousand years ago in the native compounds of the Malay Archipelago.

In fact, I think there can be but little doubt that the banana is the very oldest product of human tillage. Man, we must remember, is essentially by origin a tropical animal, and wild tropical fruits must necessarily have formed his earliest food-stuffs. It was among them of course that his first experiments in primitive agriculture would be tried; the little insignificant seeds and berries of cold northern regions would only very slowly be added to his limited stock in husbandry, as circumstances pushed some few outlying colonies northward and ever northward toward the chillier unoccupied regions. Now, of all tropical fruits, the banana is certainly the one that best repays cultivation. It has been calculated that the same area which will produce thirty-three pounds of wheat or ninety-nine pounds of potatoes will produce 4,400 pounds of plantains or bananas.

The cultivation of the various varieties in India, China, and the Malay Archipelago dates, says De Candolle, 'from an epoch impossible to realise.' Its diffusion, as that great but very oracular authority remarks, may go back to a period 'contemporary with or even anterior to that of the human races.' What this remarkably illogical sentence may mean I am at a loss to comprehend; perhaps M. de Candolle supposes that the banana was originally cultivated by pre-human gorillas; perhaps he merely intends to say that before men began to separate they sent special messengers on in front of them to diffuse the banana in the different countries they were about to visit. Even legend retains some trace of the extreme antiquity of the species as a cultivated fruit, for Adam and Eve are said to have reclined under the shadow of its branches, whence Linnæus gave to the sort known as the plantain the Latin name of *Musa paradisiaca*. If a plant was cultivated in Eden by the grand old gardener and his wife, as Lord Tennyson democratically styled them (before his elevation to the peerage), we may fairly conclude that it possesses a very respectable antiquity indeed.

The wild banana is a native of the Malay region, according to De Candolle, who has produced by far the most learned and unreadable work on the origin of domestic plants ever yet written. (Please don't give me undue credit for having heroically read it through out of pure love of science : I was one of its unfortunate reviewers.) The wild form produces seed, and grows in Cochin China, the Philippines, Ceylon, and Khasia. Like most other large tropical fruits, it no doubt owes its original development to the selective action of monkeys, hornbills, parrots and other big fruit-eaters; and it shares with all fruits of similar origin one curious tropical peculiarity. Most northern berries, like the strawberry, the raspberry, the currant, and the blackberry, developed by the selective action of small northern birds, can be popped at once into the mouth and eaten whole; they have no tough outer rind or defensive covering of any sort. But big tropical fruits, which lay themselves out for the service of large birds or monkeys, have always hard outer coats, because they could only be injured by smaller animals, who would eat the pulp without helping in the dispersion of the useful seeds, the one object really held in view by the mother plant. Often, as in the case of the orange, the rind even contains a bitter, nauseous, or pungent juice, while at times, as in the pine-apple, the prickly pear, the sweet-sop, and the cherimoyer, the entire fruit is covered with sharp projections, stinging hairs, or knobby protuberances, on purpose to warn off the unauthorised depredator. It was this line of defence that gave the banana in the first instance its thick yellow skin; and, looking at the matter from the epicure's point of view, one may say roughly that all tropical fruits have to be skinned before they can be eaten. They are all adapted for being cut up with a knife and fork, or dug out with a spoon, on a civilised dessert-plate. As for that most delicious of Indian fruits, the mango, it has been well said that the only proper way to eat it is over a tub of water, with a couple of towels hanging gracefully across the side.

The varieties of the banana are infinite in number, and, as in most other plants of ancient cultivation, they shade off into one another by infinitesimal gradations. Two principal sorts, however, are commonly recognised—the true banana of commerce, and the common plantain. The banana proper is eaten raw, as a fruit, and is allowed accordingly to ripen thoroughly before being picked for market; the plantain, which is the true food-stuff of all the equatorial region in both hemispheres, is gathered green and

Q

roasted as a vegetable, or, to use the more expressive West Indian negro phrase, as a bread-kind. Millions of human beings in Asia, Africa, America, and the islands of the Pacific Ocean live almost entirely on the mild and succulent but tasteless plantain. Some people like the fruit; to me personally it is more suggestive of a very flavourless over-ripe pear than of anything else in heaven or earth or the waters' that are under the earth—the latter being the most probable place to look for it, as its taste and substance are decidedly watery. Baked dry in the green state ' it resembles roasted chestnuts,' or rather baked parsnip; pulped and boiled with water it makes ' a very agreeable sweet soup,' almost as nice as peasoup with brown sugar in it; and cut into slices, sweetened, and fried, it forms ' an excellent substitute for fruit pudding,' having a flavour much like that of potatoes *à la maitre d'hôtel* served up in treacle.

Altogether a fruit to be sedulously avoided, the plantain, though millions of our spiritually destitute African brethren haven't yet for a moment discovered that it isn't every bit as good as wheaten bread and fresh butter. Missionary enterprise will no doubt before long enlighten them on this subject, and create a good market in time for American flour and Manchester piece-goods.

Though by origin a Malayan plant, there can be little doubt that the banana had already reached the mainland of America and the West India Islands long before the voyage of Columbus. When Pizarro disembarked upon the coast of Peru on his desolating expedition, the mild-eyed, melancholy, doomed Peruvians flocked down to the shore and offered him bananas in a lordly dish. Beds composed of banana leaves have been discovered in the tombs of the Incas, of date anterior, of course, to the Spanish conquest. How did they get there? Well, it is clearly an absurd mistake to suppose that Columbus discovered America; as Artemus Ward pertinently remarked, the noble Red Indian had obviously discovered it long before him. There had been intercourse of old, too, between Asia and the Western Continent; the elephant-headed god of Mexico, the debased traces of Buddhism in the Aztec religion, the singular coincidences between India and Peru, all seem to show that a stream of communication, however faint, once existed between the Asiatic and American worlds. Garcilaso himself, the half-Indian historian of Peru, says that the banana was well known in his native country before the conquest, and that the Indians say 'its origin is Ethiopia.' In some strange way or other, then, long before Columbus set foot upon the low sandbank of Cat's Island, the banana had been transported from Africa or India to the Western hemisphere.

If it were a plant propagated by seed, one would suppose that it was carried across by wind or waves, wafted on the feet of birds, or accidentally introduced in the crannies of drift timber. So the coco-nut made the tour of the world ages before either of the famous Cooks—the Captain or the excursion agent—had rendered the same feat easy and practicable; and so, too, a number of American plants have fixed their home in the tarns of the Hebrides or among the lonely bogs of Western Galway. But the banana must have been carried by man, because it is unknown in the wild state in the Western Continent; and, as it is practically seedless, it can only have been transported entire, in the form of a root or sucker. An exactly similar proof of ancient intercourse between the two worlds is afforded us by the sweet potato, a plant of undoubted American origin, which was nevertheless naturalised in China as early as the first centuries of the Christian era. Now that we all know how the Scandinavians of the eleventh century went to Massachusetts, which they called

Vineland, and how the Mexican empire had some knowledge of Accadian astronomy, people are beginning to discover that Columbus himself was after all an egregious
humbug.

In the old world the cultivation of the banana and the
plantain goes back, no doubt, to a most immemorial antiquity. Our Aryan ancestor himself, Professor Max Müller's
especial *protégé*, had already invented several names for it,
which duly survive in very classical Sanskrit. The Greeks
of Alexander's expedition saw it in India, where ' sages
reposed beneath its shade and ate of its fruit, whence the
botanical name, *Musa sapientum.*' As the sages in question were lazy Brahmans, always celebrated for their
immense capacity for doing nothing, the report, as quoted
by Pliny, is no doubt an accurate one. But the accepted
derivation of the word *Musa* from an Arabic original seems
to me highly uncertain ; for Linnæus, who first bestowed
it on the genus, called several other allied genera by such
cognate names as Urania and Heliconia. If, therefore,
the father of botany knew that his own word was originally
Arabic, we cannot acquit him of the high crime and
misdemeanour of deliberate punning. Should the Royal
Society get wind of this, something serious would doubtless happen ; for it is well known that the possession of a
sense of humour is absolutely fatal to the pretensions of a
man of science.

Besides its main use as an article of food, the banana
serves incidentally to supply a valuable fibre, obtained from
the stem, and employed for weaving into textile fabrics and
making paper. Several kinds of the plantain tribe are
cultivated for this purpose exclusively, the best known
among them being the so-called manilla hemp, a plant
largely grown in the Philippine Islands. Many of the
finest Indian shawls are woven from banana stems, and

much of the rope that we use in our houses comes from the
same singular origin. I know nothing more strikingly
illustrative of the extreme complexity of our modern civilisation than the way in which we thus every day employ
articles of exotic manufacture in our ordinary life without
ever for a moment suspecting or inquiring into their true
nature. What lady knows when she puts on her delicate
wrapper, from Liberty's or from Swan and Edgar's, that
the material from which it is woven is a Malayan plantain
stalk? Who ever thinks that the glycerine for our chapped
hands comes from Travancore coco-nuts, and that the
pure butter supplied us from the farm in the country is
coloured yellow with Jamaican annatto? We break a
tooth, as Mr. Herbert Spencer has pointed out, because
the grape-curers of Zante are not careful enough about
excluding small stones from their stock of currants; and
we suffer from indigestion because the Cape wine-grower
has doctored his light Burgundies with Brazilian logwood
and white rum, to make them taste like Portuguese port.
Take merely this very question of dessert, and how intensely complicated it really is. The West Indian bananas
keep company with sweet St. Michaels from the Azores,
and with Spanish cobnuts from Barcelona. Dried fruits
from Metz, figs from Smyrna, and dates from Tunis lie
side by side on our table with Brazil nuts and guava jelly
and damson cheese and almonds and raisins. We forget
where everything comes from nowadays, in our general
consciousness that they all come from the Queen Victoria
Street Stores, and any real knowledge of common objects
is rendered every day more and more impossible by the
bewildering complexity and variety, every day increasing,
of the common objects themselves, their substitutes,
adulterates, and spurious imitations. Why, you probably
never heard of manilla hemp before, until this very minute,

and yet you have been familiarly using it all your lifetime, while 400,000 hundredweights of that useful article are annually imported into this country alone. It is an interesting study to take any day a list of market quotations, and ask oneself about every material quoted, what it is and what they do with it.

For example, can you honestly pretend that you really understand the use and importance of that valuable object of everyday demand, fustic ? I remember an ill-used telegraph clerk in a tropical colony once complaining to me that English cable operators were so disgracefully ignorant about this important staple as invariably to substitute for its name the word ' justice ' in all telegrams which originally referred to it. Have you any clear and definite notions as to the prime origin and final destination of a thing called jute, in whose sole manufacture the whole great and flourishing town of Dundee lives and moves and has its being ? What is turmeric ? Whence do we obtain vanilla ? How many commercial products are yielded by the orchids ? How many totally distinct plants in different countries afford the totally distinct starches lumped together in grocers' lists under the absurd name of arrowroot ? When you ask for sago do you really see that you get it ? and how many entirely different objects described as sago are known to commerce ? Define the uses of partridge canes and cohune oil. What objects are generally manufactured from tucum ? Would it surprise you to learn that English door-handles are commonly made out of coquilla nuts ? that your wife's buttons are turned from the indurated fruit of the Tagua palm ? and that the knobs of umbrellas grew originally in the remote depths of Guatemalan forests ? Are you aware that a plant calle d manioc supplies the starchy food of about one-half the population of tropical America ? These are the sort of inquiries with

which a new edition of ' Mangnall's Questions ' would have
to be filled; and as to answering them—why, even the
pupil-teachers in a London Board School (who represent,
I suppose, the highest attainable level of human knowledge) would often find themselves completely nonplussed.
The fact is, tropical trade has opened out so rapidly and so
wonderfully that nobody knows much about the chief
articles of tropical growth; we go on using them in an un-
inquiring spirit of childlike faith, much as the Jamaica
negroes go on using articles of European manufacture
about whose origin they are so ridiculously ignorant that
one young woman once asked me whether it was really true
that cotton handkerchiefs were dug up out of the ground
over in England. Some dim confusion between coal or
iron and Manchester piece-goods seemed to have taken firm
possession of her infantile imagination.

That is why I have thought that a treatise De Banana
might not, perhaps, be wholly without its usefulness to the
modern English reading world. After all, a food-stuff
which supports hundreds of millions among our beloved
tropical fellow-creatures ought to be very dear to the heart
of a nation which governs (and annually kills) more black
people, taken in the mass, than all the other European
powers put together. We have introduced the blessings of
British rule—the good and well-paid missionary, the Rem-
ington rifle, the red-cotton pocket-handkerchief, and the
use of ' the liquor called rum '—into so many remote
corners of the tropical world that it is high time we should
begin in return to learn somewhat about fetiches and fustic,
Jamaica and jaggery, bananas and Buddhism. We know
too little still about our colonies and dependencies. ' Cape
Breton an island!' cried King George's Minister, the Duke
of Newcastle, in the well-known story, ' Cape Breton an
island! Why, so it is! God bless my soul! I must go and

tell the King that Cape Breton's an island.   That was a hundred years ago ; but only the other day the Board of Trade placarded all our towns and villages with a flaming notice to the effect that the Colorado beetle had made its appearance at ' a town in Canada called Ontario,' and might soon be expected to arrive at Liverpool by Cunard steamer. The right honourables and other high mightinesses who put forth the notice in question were evidently unaware that Ontario is a province as big as England, including in its borders Toronto, Ottawa, Kingston, London, Hamilton, and other large and flourishing towns.   Apparently, in spite of competitive examinations, the schoolmaster is still abroad in the Government offices.

GO TO THE ANT

In the market-place at Santa Fé, in Mexico, peasant women from the neighbouring villages bring in for sale trayfuls of living ants, each about as big and round as a large white currant, and each entirely filled with honey or grape sugar, much appreciated by the ingenuous Mexican youth as an excellent substitute for Everton toffee. The method of eating them would hardly command the approbation of the Society for the Prevention of Cruelty to Animals. It is simple and primitive, but decidedly not humane. Ingenuous youth holds the ant by its head and shoulders, sucks out the honey with which the back part is absurdly distended, and throws away the empty body as a thing with which it has now no further sympathy. Maturer age buys the ants by the quart, presses out the honey through a muslin strainer, and manufactures it into a very sweet intoxicating drink, something like shandygaff, as I am credibly informed by bold persons who have ventured to experiment upon it, taken internally.

The curious insect which thus serves as an animated sweetmeat for the Mexican children is the honey-ant of the Garden of the Gods ; and it affords a beautiful example of Mandeville's charming paradox that personal vices are public benefits—*vitia privata humana commoda*. The honey-ant is a greedy individual who has nevertheless nobly devoted himself for the good of the community by

converting himself into a living honey-jar, from which all
the other ants in his own nest may help themselves freely
from time to time, as occasion demands. The tribe to
which he belongs lives underground, in a dome-roofed
vault, and only one particular caste among the workers,
known as rotunds from their expansive girth, is told off
for this special duty of storing honey within their own
bodies. Clinging to the top of their nest, with their round,
transparent abdomens hanging down loosely, mere globules
of skin enclosing the pale amber-coloured honey, these
Daniel Lamberts of the insect race look for all the world
like clusters of the little American Delaware grapes, with
an ant's legs and head stuck awkwardly on to the end
instead of a stalk. They have, in fact, realised in everyday life the awful fate of Mr. Gilbert's discontented sugar-
broker, who laid on flesh and 'adipose deposit' until he
became converted at last into a perfect rolling ball of
globular humanity.

The manners of the honey-ant race are very simple.
Most of the members of each community are active and
roving in their dispositions, and show no tendency to undue
distension of the nether extremities. They go out at
night and collect nectar or honey-dew from the gall-insects
on oak-trees ; for the gall-insect, like love in the old Latin
saw, is fruitful both in sweets and bitters, *melle et felle*.
This nectar they then carry home, and give it to the rotunds
or honey-bearers, who swallow it and store it in their round
abdomen until they can hold no more, having stretched
their skins literally to the very point of bursting. They
pass their time, like the Fat Boy in 'Pickwick,' chiefly in
sleeping, but they cling upside down meanwhile to the
roof of their residence. When the workers in turn
require a meal, they go up to the nearest honey-bearer and
stroke her gently with their antennæ. The honey-bearer

thereupon throws up her head and regurgitates a large drop of the amber liquid. (' Regurgitates ' is a good word which I borrow from Dr. McCook, of Philadelphia, the great authority upon honey-ants; and it saves an immense deal of trouble in looking about for a respectable periphrasis.) The workers feed upon the drops thus exuded, two or three at once often standing around the living honey-jar, and lapping nectar together from the lips of their devoted comrade. This may seem at first sight rather an unpleasant practice on the part of the ants; but after all, how does it really differ from our own habit of eating honey which has been treated in very much the same unsophisticated manner by the domestic bee?

Worse things than these, however, Dr. McCook records to the discredit of the Colorado honey-ant. When he was opening some nests in the Garden of the Gods, he happened accidentally to knock down some of the rotunds, which straightway burst asunder in the middle, and scattered their store of honey on the floor of the nest. At once the other ants, tempted away from their instinctive task of carrying off the cocoons and young grubs, clustered around their unfortunate companion, like street boys around a broken molasses barrel, and, instead of forming themselves forthwith into a volunteer ambulance company, proceeded immediately to lap up the honey from their dying brother. On the other hand it must be said, to the credit of the race, that (unlike the members of Arctic expeditions) they never desecrate the remains of the dead. When a honey-bearer dies at his post, a victim to his zeal for the common good, the workers carefully remove his cold corpse from the roof where it still clings, clip off the head and shoulders from the distended abdomen, and convey their deceased brother piecemeal, in two detachments, to the formican cemetery, undisturbed. If they chose, they might only bury the front half of their late relation, while they retained his remaining moiety as an available honey-bag: but from this cannibal proceeding ant-etiquette recoils in decent horror; and the amber globes are ' pulled up galleries, rolled along rooms, and bowled into the graveyard, along with the juiceless heads, legs, and other members.' Such fraternal conduct would be very creditable to the worker honey-ants, were it not for a horrid doubt insinuated by Dr. McCook that perhaps the insects don't know they could get at the honey by breaking up the body of their lamented relative. If so, their apparent disregard of utilitarian considerations may really be due not to their sentimentality but to their hopeless stupidity.

The reason why the ants have taken thus to storing honey in the living bodies of their own fellows is easy enough to understand. They want to lay up for the future like prudent insects that they are; but they can't make wax, as the bees do, and they have not yet evolved the purely human art of pottery. Consequently—happy thought —why not tell off some of our number to act as jars on behalf of the others? Some of the community work by going out and gathering honey; they also serve who only stand and wait—who receive it from the workers, and keep it stored up in their own capacious indiarubber maws till further notice. So obvious is this plan for converting ants into animated honey-jars, that several different kinds of ants in different parts of the world, belonging to the most widely distinct families, have independently hit upon the very self-same device. Besides the Mexican species, there is a totally different Australian honey-ant, and another equally separate in Borneo and Singapore. This last kind does not store the honey in the hind part of the body technically known as the abdomen, but in the middle division which naturalists call the thorax, where it forms a transparent bladder-like swelling, and makes the creature look as though it were suffering with an acute attack of dropsy. In any case, the life of a honey-bearer must be singularly uneventful, not to say dull and monotonous ; but no doubt any small inconvenience in this respect must be more than compensated for by the glorious consciousness that one is sacrificing one's own personal comfort for the common good of universal anthood. Perhaps, however, the ants have not yet reached the Positivist stage, and may be totally ignorant of the enthusiasm of formicity.

Equally curious are the habits and manners of the harvesting ants, the species which Solomon seems to have had specially in view when he advised his hearers to go to the ant—a piece of advice which I have also adopted as the title of the present article, though I by no means intend thereby to insinuate that the readers of this volume ought properly to be classed as sluggards. These industrious little creatures abound in India : they are so small that it takes eight or ten of them to carry a single grain of wheat or barley ; and yet they will patiently drag along their big burden for five hundred or a thousand yards to the door of their formicary. To prevent the grain from germinating, they bite off the embryo root—a piece of animal intelligence outdone by another species of ant, which actually allows the process of budding to begin, so as to produce sugar, as in malting. After the last thunderstorms of the monsoon the little proprietors bring up all the grain from their granaries to dry in the tropical sunshine. The quantity of grain stored up by the harvesting ants is often so large that the hair-splitting Jewish casuists of the Mishna have seriously discussed the question whether it belongs to the landowner or may lawfully be appropriated by the gleaners. ' They do not appear,' says Sir John Lubbock, ' to have considered the rights of the ants.' Indeed our duty towards insects is a question which seems hitherto to have escaped the notice of all moral philosophers. Even Mr. Herbert Spencer, the prophet of individualism, has never taken exception to our gross disregard of the proprietary rights of bees in their honey, or of silkworms in their cocoons. There are signs, however, that the obtuse human conscience is awakening in this respect ; for when Dr. Loew suggested to bee-keepers the desirability of testing the commercial value of honey-ants, as rivals to the bee, Dr. McCook replied that ' the sentiment against the use of honey thus taken from living insects, which is worthy of all respect, would not be easily overcome.'

There are no harvesting ants in Northern Europe, though they extend as far as Syria, Italy, and the Riviera, in which latter station I have often observed them busily working. What most careless observers take for grain in the nests of English ants are of course really the cocoons of the pupæ. For many years, therefore, entomologists were under the impression that Solomon had fallen into this popular error, and that when he described the ant as ' gathering her food in the harvest ' and ' preparing her meat in the summer,' he was speaking rather as a poet than as a strict naturalist. Later observations, however, have vindicated the general accuracy of the much-married king by showing that true harvesting ants do actually occur in Syria, and that they lay by stores for the winter in the very way stated by that early entomologist, whose knowledge of ' creeping things ' is specially enumerated in the long list of his universal accomplishments.

Dr. Lincecum of Texan fame has even improved upon Solomon by his discovery of those still more interesting and curious creatures, the agricultural ants of Texas. America is essentially a farming country, and the agricultural ants are born farmers. They make regular clearings around their nests, and on these clearings they allow

nothing to grow except a particular kind of grain, known
as ant-rice. Dr. Lincecum maintains that the tiny farmers
actually sow and cultivate the ant-rice. Dr. McCook, on
the other hand, is of opinion that the rice sows itself, and
that the insects' part is limited to preventing any other
plants or weeds from encroaching on the appropriated area.
In any case, be they squatters or planters, it is certain that
the rice, when ripe, is duly harvested, and that it is, to say
the least, encouraged by the ants, to the exclusion of all
other competitors. 'After the maturing and harvesting of
the seed,' says Dr. Lincecum, 'the dry stubble is cut away
and removed from the pavement, which is thus left fallow
until the ensuing autumn, when the same species of grass,
and in the same circle, appears again, and receives the
same agricultural care as did the previous crop.' Sir
John Lubbock, indeed, goes so far as to say that the three
stages of human progress—the hunter, the herdsman, and
the agriculturist—are all to be found among various species
of existing ants.

The Saüba ants of tropical America carry their agricultural operations a step further. Dwelling in underground
nests, they sally forth upon the trees, and cut out of the
leaves large round pieces, about as big as a shilling. These
pieces they drop upon the ground, where another detachment is in waiting to convey them to the galleries of the
nest. There they store enormous quantities of these
round pieces, which they allow to decay in the dark, so
as to form a sort of miniature mushroom bed. On the
mouldering vegetable heap they have thus piled up, they
induce a fungus to grow, and with this fungus they feed
their young grubs during their helpless infancy. Mr. Belt,
the 'Naturalist in Nicaragua,' found that native trees
suffered far less from their depredations than imported
ones. The ants hardly touched the local forests, but they

stripped young plantations of orange, coffee, and mango trees stark naked. He ingeniously accounts for this curious fact by supposing that an internecine struggle has long been going on in the countries inhabited by the Saübas between the ants and the forest trees. Those trees that best resisted the ants, owing either to some unpleasant taste or to hardness of foliage, have in the long run survived destruction; but those which were suited for the purpose of the ants have been reduced to nonentity, while the ants in turn were getting slowly adapted to attack other trees. In this way almost all the native trees have at last acquired some special means of protection against the ravages of the leaf-cutters; so that they immediately fall upon all imported and unprotected kinds as their natural prey. This ingenious and wholly satisfactory explanation must of course go far to console the Brazilian planters for the frequent loss of their orange and coffee crops.

Mr. Alfred Russel Wallace, the co-discoverer of the Darwinian theory (whose honours he waived with rare generosity in favour of the older and more distinguished naturalist), tells a curious story about the predatory habits of these same Saübas. On one occasion, when he was wandering about in search of specimens on the Rio Negro, he bought a peck of rice, which was tied up, Indian fashion, in the local bandanna of the happy plantation slave. At night he left his rice incautiously on the bench of the hut where he was sleeping; and next morning the Saübas had riddled the handkerchief like a sieve, and carried away a gallon of the grain for their own felonious purposes. The underground galleries which they dig can often be traced for hundreds of yards; and Mr. Hamlet Clarke even asserts that in one case they have tunnelled under the bed of a river where it is a quarter of a mile wide. This beats

Brunel on his own ground into the proverbial cocked hat, both for depth and distance.

Within doors, in the tropics, ants are apt to put themselves obtrusively forward in a manner little gratifying to any except the enthusiastically entomological mind. The winged females, after their marriage flight, have a disagreeable habit of flying in at the open doors and windows at lunch time, settling upon the table like the Harpies in the Æneid, and then quietly shuffling off their wings one at a time, by holding them down against the table-cloth with one leg, and running away vigorously with the five others. As soon as they have thus disembarrassed themselves of their superfluous members, they proceed to run about over the lunch as if the house belonged to them, and to make a series of experiments upon the edible qualities of the different dishes. One doesn't so much mind their philosophical inquiries into the nature of the bread or even the meat; but when they come to drowning themselves by dozens, in the pursuit of knowledge, in the soup and sherry, one feels bound to protest energetically against the spirit of martyrdom by which they are too profoundly animated. That is one of the slight drawbacks of the realms of perpetual summer; in the poets you see only one side of the picture—the palms, the orchids, the humming-birds, the great trailing lianas : in practical life you see the reverse side—the thermometer at 98°, the tepid drinking-water, the prickly heat, the perpetual languor, the endless shoals of aggressive insects. A lady of my acquaintance, indeed, made a valuable entomological collection in her own dining-room, by the simple process of consigning to pill-boxes all the moths and flies and beetles that settled upon the mangoes and star-apples in the course of dessert.

Another objectionable habit of the tropical ants,

R

viewed practically, is their total disregard of vested interests
in the case of house property.   Like Mr. George and his
communistic friends, they disbelieve entirely in the principle
of private rights in real estate.   They will eat their way
through the beams of your house till there is only a slender
core of solid wood left to support the entire burden.   I
have taken down a rafter in my own house in Jamaica,
originally 18 inches thick each way, with a sound circular
centre of no more than 6 inches in diameter, upon which all
the weight necessarily fell.   With the material extracted from
the wooden beams they proceed to add insult to injury by building long covered galleries right across the ceiling of your drawing-room.   As may be easily imagined, these galleries do not
tend to improve the appearance of the ceiling ; and it
becomes necessary to form a Liberty and Property Defence
League for the protection of one's personal interests against
the insect enemy.   I have no objection to ants building
galleries on their own freehold, or even to their nationalising
the land in their native forests ; but I do object strongly
to their unwarrantable intrusion upon the domain of private life.   Expostulation and active warfare, however, are
equally useless.   The carpenter-ant has no moral sense,
and is not amenable either to kindness or blows.   On one
occasion, when a body of these intrusive creatures had constructed an absurdly conspicuous brown gallery straight
across the ceiling of my drawing-room, I determined to
declare open war against them, and, getting my black servant to bring in the steps and a mop, I proceeded to
demolish the entire gallery just after breakfast.   It was
about 20 feet long, as well as I can remember, and perhaps
an inch in diameter.   At one o'clock I returned to lunch.
My black servant pointed, with a broad grin on his intelligent features, to the wooden ceiling.   I looked up ; in
those three hours the carpenter-ants had reconstructed the

entire gallery, and were doubtless mocking me at their
ease, with their uplifted antennæ, under that safe shelter.
I retired at once from the unequal contest. It was clearly
impossible to go on knocking down a fresh gallery every
three hours of the day or night throughout a whole lifetime.

Ants, says Mr. Wallace, without one touch of satire,
' force themselves upon the attention of everyone who visits
the tropics.' They do, indeed, and that most pungently ;
if by no other method, at least by the simple and effectual
one of stinging. The majority of ants in every nest are of
course neuters, or workers, that is to say, strictly speaking,
undeveloped females, incapable of laying eggs. But they
still retain the ovipositor, which is converted into a sting,
and supplied with a poisonous liquid to eject afterwards
into the wound. So admirably adapted to its purpose is
this beautiful provision of nature, that some tropical ants
can sting with such violence as to make your leg swell and
confine you for some days to your room ; while cases have
even been known in which the person attacked has fainted
with pain, or had a serious attack of fever in consequence.
It is not every kind of ant, however, that can sting ; a
great many can only bite with their little hard horny jaws,
and then eject a drop of formic poison afterwards into the
hole caused by the bite. The distinction is a delicate
physiological one, not much appreciated by the victims of
either mode of attack. The perfect females can also sting,
but not, of course, the males, who are poor, wretched, useless creatures, only good as husbands for the community,
and dying off as soon as they have performed their part in
the world—another beautiful provision, which saves the
workers the trouble of killing them off, as bees do with
drones after the marriage flight of the queen bee.

The blind driver-ants of West Africa are among the

very few species that render any service to man, and that, of course, only incidentally. Unlike most other members of their class, the driver-ants have no settled place of residence ; they are vagabonds and wanderers upon the face of the earth, formican tramps, blind beggars, who lead a gipsy existence, and keep perpetually upon the move, smelling their way cautiously from one camping-place to another. They march by night, or on cloudy days, like wise tropical strategists, and never expose themselves to the heat of the day in broad sunshine, as though they were no better than the mere numbered British Tommy Atkins at Coomassie or in the Soudan. They move in vast armies across country, driving everything before them as they go ; for they belong to the stinging division, and are very voracious in their personal habits. Not only do they eat up the insects in their line of march, but they fall even upon larger creatures and upon big snakes, which they attack first in the eyes, the most vulnerable portion. When they reach a negro village the inhabitants turn out *en masse*, and run away, exactly as if the visitors were English explorers or brave Marines, bent upon retaliating for the theft of a knife by nobly burning down King Tom's town or King Jumbo's capital. Then the negroes wait in the jungle till the little black army has passed on, after clearing out the huts by the way of everything eatable. When they return they find their calabashes and saucepans licked clean, but they also find every rat, mouse, lizard, cockroach, gecko, and beetle completely cleared out from the whole village. Most of them have cut and run at the first approach of the drivers ; of the remainder, a few blanched and neatly-picked skeletons alone remain to tell the tale.

As I wish to be considered a veracious historian, I will not retail the further strange stories that still find their

way into books of natural history about the manners and
habits of these blind marauders. They cross rivers, the
West African gossips declare, by a number of devoted individuals flinging themselves first into the water as a
living bridge, like so many six-legged Marcus Curtiuses,
while over their drowning bodies the heedless remainder
march in safety to the other side. If the story is not true,
it is at least well invented; for the ant-commonwealth
everywhere carries to the extremest pitch the old Roman
doctrine of the absolute subjection of the individual to the
State. So exactly is this the case that in some species
there are a few large, overgrown, lazy ants in each
nest, which do no work themselves, but accompany the
workers on their expeditions; and the sole use of these
idle mouths seems to be to attract the attention of birds
and other enemies, and so distract it from the useful
workers, the mainstay of the entire community. It is
almost as though an army, marching against a tribe of
cannibals, were to place itself in the centre of a hollow
square formed of all the fattest people in the country,
whose fine condition and fitness for killing might immediately engross the attention of the hungry enemy. Ants,
in fact, have, for the most part, already reached the
goal set before us as a delightful one by most current
schools of socialist philosophers, in which the individual
is absolutely sacrificed in every way to the needs of the
community.

The most absurdly human, however, among all the
tricks and habits of ants are their well known cattle-
farming and slave-holding instincts. Everybody has heard,
of course, how they keep the common rose-blight as milch
cows, and suck from them the sweet honey-dew. But
everybody, probably, does not yet know the large number
of insects which they herd in one form or another as

domesticated animals. Man has, at most, some twenty or thirty such, including cows, sheep, horses, donkeys, camels, llamas, alpacas, reindeer, dogs, cats, canaries, pigs, fowl, ducks, geese, turkeys, and silkworms. But ants have hundreds and hundreds, some of them kept obviously for purposes of food ; others apparently as pets ; and yet others again, as has been plausibly suggested, by reason of superstition or as objects of worship. There is a curious blind beetle which inhabits ants' nests, and is so absolutely dependent upon its hosts for support that it has even lost the power of feeding itself. It never quits the nest, but the ants bring it in food and supply it by putting the nourishment actually into its mouth. But the beetle, in return, seems to secrete a sweet liquid (or it may even be a stimulant like beer, or a narcotic like tobacco) in a tuft of hairs near the bottom of the hard wing-cases, and the ants often lick this tuft with every appearance of satisfaction and enjoyment. In this case, and in many others, there can be no doubt that the insects are kept for the sake of food or some other advantage yielded by them.

But there are other instances of insects which haunt ants' nests, which it is far harder to account for on any hypothesis save that of superstitious veneration. There is a little weevil that runs about by hundreds in the galleries of English ants, in and out among the free citizens, making itself quite at home in their streets and public places, but as little noticed by the ants themselves as dogs are in our own cities. Then, again, there is a white woodlouse, something like the common little armadillo, but blind from having lived so long underground, which walks up and down the lanes and alleys of antdom, without ever holding any communication of any sort with its hosts and neighbours. In neither case has Sir John Lubbock ever seen an ant take the slightest notice of the presence of these strange fellow-lodgers. 'One might almost imagine,' he says, 'that they had the cap of invisibility.' Yet it is quite clear that the ants deliberately sanction the residence of the weevils and woodlice in their nests, for any unauthorised intruder would immediately be set upon and massacred outright.

Sir John Lubbock suggests that they may perhaps be tolerated as scavengers : or, again, it is possible that they may prey upon the eggs or larvæ of some of the parasites to whose attacks the ants are subject. In the first case, their use would be similar to that of the wild dogs in Constantinople or the common black John-crow vultures in tropical America : in the second case, they would be about equivalent to our own cats or to the hedgehog often put in farmhouse kitchens to keep down cockroaches.

The crowning glory of owning slaves, which many philosophic Americans (before the war) showed to be the highest and noblest function of the most advanced humanity, has been attained by more than one variety of anthood. Our great English horse-ant is a moderate slaveholder ; but the big red ant of Southern Europe carries the domestic institution many steps further. It makes regular slave-raids upon the nests of the small brown ants, and carries off the young in their pupa condition. By-and-by the brown ants hatch out in the strange nest, and never having known any other life except that of slavery, accommodate themselves to it readily enough. The red ant, however, is still only an occasional slaveowner ; if necessary, he can get along by himself, without the aid of his little brown servants. Indeed, there are free states and slave states of red ants side by side with one another, as of old in Maryland and Pennsylvania : in the first, the red ants do their work themselves, like mere vulgar Ohio farmers ; in the second, they get their work done for them by their industrious little brown servants, like the aristocratic first families of Virginia before the earthquake of emancipation.

But there are other degraded ants, whose life-history may be humbly presented to the consideration of the Anti-Slavery Society, as speaking more eloquently than any other known fact for the demoralising effect of slaveowning upon the slaveholders themselves. The Swiss rufescent ant is a species so long habituated to rely entirely upon the services of slaves that it is no longer able to manage its own affairs when deprived by man of its hereditary bonds-men. It has lost entirely the art of constructing a nest ; it can no longer tend its own young, whom it leaves entirely to the care of negro nurses ; and its bodily structure even has changed, for the jaws have lost their teeth, and have been converted into mere nippers, useful only as weapons of war. The rufescent ant, in fact, is a purely military caste, which has devoted itself entirely to the pursuit of arms, leaving every other form of activity to its slaves and dependents. Officers of the old school will be glad to learn that this military insect is dressed, if not in scarlet, at any rate in very decent red, and that it refuses to be bothered in any way with questions of transport or commissariat. If the community changes its nest, the masters are carried on the backs of their slaves to the new position, and the black ants have to undertake the entire duty of foraging and bringing in stores of supply for their gentlemanly pro-prietors. Only when war is to be made upon neighbouring nests does the thin red line form itself into long file for active service. Nothing could be more perfectly aristocratic than the views of life entertained and acted upon by these distinguished slaveholders.

On the other hand, the picture has its reverse side, exhibiting clearly the weak points of the slaveholding system. The rufescent ant has lost even the very power of feeding itself. So completely dependent is each upon his little black valet for daily bread, that he cannot so much as help himself to the food that is set before him. Hüber put a few slaveholders into a box with some of their own larvæ and pupæ, and a supply of honey, in order to see what they would do with them. Appalled at the novelty of the situation, the slaveholders seemed to come to the conclusion that something must be done; so they began carrying the larvæ about aimlessly in their mouths, and rushing up and down in search of the servants. After a while, however, they gave it up and came to the conclusion that life under such circumstances was clearly intolerable. They never touched the honey, but resigned themselves to their fate like officers and gentlemen. In less than two days, half of them had died of hunger, rather than taste a dinner which was not supplied to them by a properly constituted footman. Admiring their heroism or pitying their incapacity, Hüber at last gave them just one slave between them all. The plucky little negro, nothing daunted by the gravity of the situation, set to work at once, dug a small nest, gathered together the larvæ, helped several pupæ out of the cocoon, and saved the lives of the surviving slaveowners. Other naturalists have tried similar experiments, and always with the same result. The slaveowners will starve in the midst of plenty rather than feed themselves without attendance. Either they cannot or will not put the food into their own mouths with their own mandibles.

There are yet other ants, such as the workerless *Anergates*, in which the degradation of slaveholding has gone yet further. These wretched creatures are the formican representatives of those Oriental despots who are no longer even warlike, but are sunk in sloth and luxury, and pass their lives in eating bang or smoking opium. Once upon a time, Sir John Lubbock thinks, the ancestors of *Anergates* were marauding slaveowners, who attacked and made serfs of other ants. But gradually they lost not only their arts but even their military prowess, and were reduced to making war by stealth instead of openly carrying off their slaves in fair battle. It seems probable that they now creep into a nest of the far more powerful slave ants, poison or assassinate the queen, and establish themselves by sheer usurpation in the queenless nest. 'Gradually,' says Sir John Lubbock, ' even their bodily force dwindled away under the enervating influence to which they had subjected themselves, until they sank to their present degraded condition—weak in body and mind, few in numbers, and apparently nearly extinct, the miserable representatives of far superior ancestors maintaining a precarious existence as contemptible parasites of their former slaves.' One may observe in passing that these wretched do-nothings cannot have been the ants which Solomon commended to the favourable consideration of the sluggard ; though it is curious that the text was never pressed into the service of defence for the peculiar institution by the advocates of slavery in the South, who were always most anxious to prove the righteousness of their cause by most sure and certain warranty of Holy Scripture.

BIG ANIMALS

' THE Atlantosaurus,' said I, pointing affectionately with a wave of my left hand to all that was immortal of that extinct reptile, ' is estimated to have had a total length of one hundred feet, and was probably the very biggest lizard that ever lived, even in Western America, where his earthly remains were first disinhumed by an enthusiastic explorer.'

' Yes, yes,' my friend answered abstractedly. ' Of course, of course; things were all so very big in those days, you know, my dear fellow.'

' Excuse me,' I replied with polite incredulity ; ' I really don't know to what particular period of time the phrase " in those days " may be supposed precisely to refer.'

My friend shuffled inside his coat a little uneasily. (I will admit that I was taking a mean advantage of him. The professorial lecture in private life, especially when followed by a strict examination, is quite undeniably a most intolerable nuisance. ' Well,' he said, in a crusty voice, after a moment's hesitation, ' I mean, you know, in geological times . . . well, there, my dear fellow, things used all to be so *very* big in those days, usedn't they ? '

I took compassion upon him and let him off easily. ' You've had enough of the museum,' I said with magnanimous self-denial. ' The Atlantosaurus has broken the camel's back. Let's go and have a quiet cigarette in the park outside.'

But if you suppose, reader, that I am going to carry my forbearance so far as to let you, too, off the remainder of that geological disquisition, you are certainly very much mistaken. A discourse which would be quite unpardonable in social intercourse may be freely admitted in the privacy of print ; because, you see, while you can't easily tell a man that his conversation bores you (though some people just avoid doing so by an infinitesimal fraction), you can shut up a book whenever you like, without the very faintest or remotest risk of hurting the author's delicate susceptibilities.

The subject of my discourse naturally divides itself, like the conventional sermon, into two heads—the precise date of ' geological times,' and the exact bigness of the animals that lived in them. And I may as well begin by announcing my general conclusion at the very outset ; first, that ' those days ' never existed at all ; and, secondly, that the animals which now inhabit this particular planet are, on the whole, about as big, taken in the lump, as any previous contemporary fauna that ever lived at any one time together upon its changeful surface. I know that to announce this sad conclusion is to break down one more universal and cherished belief ; everybody considers that ' geological animals ' were ever so much bigger than their modern representatives ; but the interests of truth should always be paramount, and, if the trade of an iconoclast is a somewhat cruel one, it is at least a necessary function in a world so ludicrously overstocked with popular delusions as this erring planet.

What, then, is the ordinary idea of ' geological time ' in the minds of people like my good friend who refused to discuss with me the exact antiquity of the Atlantosaurian ? They think of it all as immediate and contemporaneous, a vast panorama of innumerable ages being all crammed for them on to a single mental sheet, in which the dodo and the moa hob-an'-nob amicably with the pterodactyl and the ammonite ; in which the tertiary megatherium goes cheek by jowl with the secondary deinosaurs and the primary trilobites ; in which the huge herbivores of the Paris Basin are supposed to have browsed beneath the gigantic club-mosses of the Carboniferous period, and to have been successfully hunted by the great marine lizards and flying dragons of the Jurassic Epoch. Such a picture is really just as absurd, or, to speak more correctly, a thousand times absurder, than if one were to speak of those grand old times when Homer and Virgil smoked their pipes together in the Mermaid Tavern, while Shakespeare and Molière, crowned with summer roses, sipped their Falernian at their ease beneath the whispering palmwoods of the Nevsky Prospect, and discussed the details of the play they were to produce to-morrow in the crowded Colosseum, on the occasion of Napoleon's reception at Memphis by his victorious brother emperors, Ramses and Sardanapalus. This is not, as the inexperienced reader may at first sight imagine, a literal transcript from one of the glowing descriptions that crowd the beautiful pages of Ouida ; it is a faint attempt to parallel in the brief moment of historical time the glaring anachronisms perpetually committed as regards the vast lapse of geological chronology even by well-informed and intelligent people.

We must remember, then, that in dealing with geological time we are dealing with a positively awe-inspiring and unimaginable series of æons, each of which occupied its own enormous and incalculable epoch, and each of which saw the dawn, the rise, the culmination, and the downfall of innumerable types of plant and animal. On the cosmic clock, by whose pendulum alone we can faintly measure the dim ages behind us, the brief lapse of historical time,

from the earliest of Egyptian dynasties to the events nar-
rated in this evening's *Pall Mall*, is less than a second, less
than a unit, less than the smallest item by which we can
possibly guide our blind calculations.   To a geologist the
temples of Karnak and the New Law Courts would be
absolutely contemporaneous; he has no means by which
he could discriminate in date between a scarabæus of
Thothmes, a denarius of Antonine, and a bronze farthing of
her Most Gracious Majesty Queen Victoria.   Competent
authorities have shown good grounds for believing that the
Glacial Epoch ended about 80,000 years ago; and everything that has happened since the Glacial Epoch is, from
the geological point of view, described as ' recent.'   A shell
embedded in a clay cliff sixty or seventy thousand years
ago, while short and swarthy Mongoloids still dwelt undisturbed in Britain, ages before the irruption of the
' Ancient Britons ' of our inadequate school-books, is, in
the eyes of geologists generally, still regarded as purely
modern.

But behind that indivisible moment of recent time,
that eighty thousand years which coincides in part with the
fraction of a single swing of the cosmical pendulum, there
lie hours, and days, and weeks, and months, and years,
and centuries, and ages of an infinite, an illimitable, an inconceivable past, whose vast divisions unfold themselves
slowly, one beyond the other, to our aching vision in the
half-deciphered pages of the geological record.   Before the
Glacial Epoch there comes the Pliocene, immeasurably
longer than the whole expanse of recent time ; and before
that again the still longer Miocene, and then the Eocene,
immeasurably longer than all the others put together.
These three make up in their sum the Tertiary period,
which entire period can hardly have occupied more time
in its passage than a single division of the Secondary,

such as the Cretaceous, or the Oolite, or the Triassic ; and the Secondary period, once more, though itself of positively appalling duration, seems but a patch (to use the expressive modernism) upon the unthinkable and unrealisable vastness of the endless successive Primary æons. So that in the end we can only say, like Michael Scott's mystic head, ' Time was, Time is, Time will be.' The time we know affords us no measure at all for even the nearest and briefest epochs of the time we know not ; and the time we know not seems to demand still vaster and more inexpressible figures as we pry back curiously, with wondering eyes, into its dimmest and earliest recesses.

These efforts to realise the unrealisable make one's head swim ; let us hark back once more from cosmical time to the puny bigness of our earthly animals, living or extinct.

If we look at the whole of our existing fauna, marine and terrestrial, we shall soon see that we could bring together at the present moment a very goodly collection of extant monsters, most parlous monsters, too, each about as fairly big in its own kind as almost anything that has ever preceded it. Every age has its own *specialité* in the way of bigness ; in one epoch it is the lizards that take suddenly to developing overgrown creatures, the monarchs of creation in their little day ; in another, it is the fishes that blossom out unexpectedly into Titanic proportions ; in a third, it is the sloths or the proboscideans that wax fat and kick with gigantic members ; in a fourth, it may be the birds or the men that are destined to evolve with future ages into veritable rocs or purely realistic Gargantuas or Brobdingnagians. The present period is most undoubtedly the period of the cetaceans ; and the future geologist who goes hunting for dry bones among the ooze of the Atlantic, now known to us only by the scanty dredgings of our ' Alerts ' and ' Challengers,' but then upheaved into snow-clad Alps or vine-covered Apennines, will doubtless stand aghast at the huge skeletons of our whales and our razorbacks, and will mutter to himself in awe-struck astonishment, in the exact words of my friend at South Kensington, ' Things used all to be so very big in those days, usedn't they ? '

Now, the fact as to the comparative size of our own cetaceans and of ' geological ' animals is just this. The Atlantosaurus of the Western American Jurassic beds, a great erect lizard, is the very largest creature ever known to have inhabited this sublunary sphere. His entire length is supposed to have reached about a hundred feet (for no complete skeleton has ever been discovered), while in stature he appears to have stood some thirty feet high, or over. In any case, he was undoubtedly a very big animal indeed, for his thigh-bone alone measures eight feet, or two feet taller than that glory of contemporary civilisation, a British Grenadier. This, of course, implies a very decent total of height and size; but our own sperm whale frequently attains a good length of seventy feet, while the rorquals often run up to eighty, ninety, and even a hundred feet. We are thus fairly entitled to say that we have at least one species of animal now living which, occasionally at any rate, equals in size the very biggest and most colossal form known inferentially to geological science. Indeed when we consider the extraordinary compactness and rotundity of the modern cetaceans, as compared with the tall limbs and straggling skeleton of the huge Jurassic deinosaurs, I am inclined to believe that the tonnage of a decent modern rorqual must positively exceed that of the gigantic Atlantosaurus, the great lizard of the west, *in propria persona*. I doubt, in short, whether even the solid thigh-bone of the deinosaur could ever have supported the prodigious weight of a full-grown family razor-back whale. The mental picture of these unwieldy monsters hopping casually about, like

Alice's Gryphon in Tenniel's famous sketch, or like that still more parlous brute, the chortling Jabberwock, must be left to the vivid imagination of the courteous reader, who may fill in the details for himself as well as he is able.

If we turn from the particular comparison of selected specimens (always an unfair method of judging) to the general aspect of our contemporary fauna, I venture confidently to claim for our own existing human period as fine a collection of big animals as any other ever exhibited on this planet by any one single rival epoch. Of course, if you are going to lump all the extinct monsters and horrors into one imaginary unified fauna, regardless of anachronisms, I have nothing more to say to you; I will candidly admit that there were more great men in all previous generations put together, from Homer to Dickens, from Agamemnon to Wellington, than there are now existing in this last quarter of our really very respectable nineteenth century. But if you compare honestly age with age, one at a time, I fearlessly maintain that, so far from there being any falling off in the average bigness of things generally in these latter days, there are more big things now living than there ever were in any one single epoch, even of much longer duration than the 'recent' period.

I suppose we may fairly say, from the evidence before us, that there have been two Augustan Ages of big animals in the history of our earth—the Jurassic period, which was the zenith of the reptilian type, and the Pliocene, which was the zenith of the colossal terrestrial tertiary mammals. I say on purpose, 'from the evidence before us,' because, as I shall go on to explain hereafter, I do not myself believe that any one age has much surpassed another in the general size of its fauna, since the Permian Epoch at least; and where we do not get geological evidence of the

s

existence of big animals in any particular deposit, we may take it for granted, I think, that that deposit was laid down under conditions unfavourable to the preservation of the remains of large species. For example, the sediment now being accumulated at the bottom of the Caspian cannot ·possibly contain the bones of any creature much larger than the Caspian seal, because there are no big species there swimming; and yet that fact does not negative the existence in other places of whales, elephants, giraffes, buffaloes, and hippopotami. Nevertheless, we can only go upon the facts before us; and if we compare our existing fauna with the fauna of Jurassic and Pliocene times, we shall at any rate be putting it to the test of the severest competition that lies within our power under the actual circumstances.

In the Jurassic age there were undoubtedly a great many very big reptiles. ' A monstrous eft was of old the lord and master of earth : For him did his high sun flame and his river billowing ran : And he felt himself in his pride to be nature's crowning race.' There was the ichthyosaurus, a fishlike marine lizard, familiar to us all from a thousand reconstructions, with his long thin body, his strong flippers, his stumpy neck, and his huge pair of staring goggle eyes. The ichthyosaurus was certainly a most unpleasant creature to meet alone in a narrow strait on a dark night ; but if it comes to actual measurement, the very biggest ichthyosaurian skeleton ever unearthed does not exceed twenty-five feet from snout to tail. Now, this is an extremely decent size for a reptile, as reptiles go ; for the crocodile and alligator, the two biggest existing lizards, seldom attain an extreme length of sixteen feet. But there are other reptiles now living that easily beat the ichthyosaurus, such, for example, as the larger pythons or rock-snakes, which not infrequently reach to thirty feet, and measure round the waist as much as a London alderman of the noblest proportions. Of course, other Jurassic saurians easily beat this simple record. Our British Megalosaurus only extended twenty-five feet in length, and carried weight not exceeding three tons; but his rival Ceteosaurus stood ten feet high, and measured fifty feet from the tip of his snout to the end of his tail; while the dimensions of Titanosaurus may be briefly described as sixty feet by thirty, and those of Atlantosaurus as one hundred by thirty-two. Viewed as reptiles, we have certainly nothing at all to come up to these; but our cetaceans, as a group, show an assemblage of species which could very favourably compete with the whole lot of Jurassic saurians at any cattle show. Indeed, if it came to tonnage, I believe a good blubbery right-whale could easily give points to any deinosaur that ever moved upon oolitic continents.

The great mammals of the Pliocene age, again, such as the deinotherium and the mastodon, were also, in their way, very big things in livestock; but they scarcely exceeded the modern elephant, and by no means came near the modern whales. A few colossal ruminants of the same period could have held their own well against our existing giraffes, elks, and buffaloes; but, taking the group as a group, I don't think there is any reason to believe that it beat in general aspect the living fauna of this present age.

For few people ever really remember how very many big animals we still possess. We have the Indian and the African elephant, the hippopotamus, the various rhinoceroses, the walrus, the giraffe, the elk, the bison, the musk ox, the dromedary, and the camel. Big marine animals are generally in all ages bigger than their biggest terrestrial rivals, and most people lump all our big existing cetaceans under the common and ridiculous title of whales, which makes this vast and varied assortment of gigantic species seem all reducible to a common form. As a matter of fact, however, there are several dozen colossal marine animals now sporting and spouting in all oceans, as distinct from one another as the camel is from the ox, or the elephant from the hippopotamus. Our New Zealand Berardius easily beats the ichthyosaurus; our sperm whale is more than a match for any Jurassic European deinosaur; our rorqual, one hundred feet long, just equals the dimensions of the gigantic American Atlantosaurus himself. Besides these exceptional monsters, our bottleheads reach to forty feet, our California whales to forty-four, our hump-backs to fifty, and our razor-backs to sixty or seventy. True fish generally fall far short of these enormous dimensions, but some of the larger sharks attain almost equal size with the biggest cetaceans. The common blue shark, with his twenty-five feet of solid rapacity, would have proved a tough antagonist, I venture to believe, for the best bred enaliosaurian that ever munched a lias ammonite. I would back our modern carcharodon, who grows to forty feet, against any plesiosaurus that ever swam the Jurassic sea. As for rhinodon, a gigantic shark of the Indian Ocean, he has been actually measured to a length of fifty feet, and is stated often to attain seventy. I will stake my reputation upon it that he would have cleared the secondary seas of their great saurians in less than a century. When we come to add to these enormous marine and terrestrial creatures such other examples as the great snakes, the gigantic cuttle-fish, the grampuses, and manatees, and sea-lions, and sunfish, I am quite prepared fearlessly to challenge any other age that ever existed to enter the lists against our own for colossal forms of animal life.

Again, it is a point worth noting that a great many of the very big animals which people have in their minds when they talk vaguely about everything having been so very much bigger 'in those days' have become extinct within a very late period, and are often, from the geological point of view, quite recent.

For example, there is our friend the mammoth. I suppose no animal is more frequently present to the mind of the non-geological speaker, when he talks indefinitely about the great extinct monsters, than the familiar figure of that huge-tusked, hairy northern elephant. Yet the mammoth, chronologically speaking, is but a thing of yesterday. He was hunted here in England by men whose descendants are probably still living—at least so Professor Boyd Dawkins solemnly assures us ; while in Siberia his frozen body, flesh and all, is found so very fresh that the wolves devour it, without raising any unnecessary question as to its fitness for lupine food. The Glacial Epoch is the yesterday of geological time, and it was the Glacial Epoch that finally killed off the last mammoth. Then, again, there is his neighbour, the mastodon. That big tertiary proboscidean did not live quite long enough, it is true, to be hunted by the cavemen of the Pleistocene age, but he survived at any rate as long as the Pliocene—our day before yesterday—and he often fell very likely before the fire-split flint weapons of the Abbé Bourgeois' Miocene men. The period that separates him from our own day is as nothing compared with the vast and immeasurable interval that separates him from the huge marine saurians of the Jurassic world. To compare the relative lapses of time with human chronology, the mastodon stands to our own fauna as Beau Brummel stands to the modern masher, while the saurians stand to it as the Egyptian and Assyrian warriors stand to Lord Wolseley and the followers of the Mahdi.

Once more, take the gigantic moa of New Zealand, that

enormous bird who was to the ostrich as the giraffe is to
the antelope ; a monstrous emu, as far surpassing the
ostriches of to-day as the ostriches surpass all the other
fowls of the air. Yet the moa, though now extinct, is in
the strictest sense quite modern, a contemporary very
likely of Queen Elizabeth or Queen Anne, exterminated by
the Maoris only a very little time before the first white
settlements in the great southern archipelago. It is even
doubtful whether the moa did not live down to the days of
the earliest colonists, for remains of Maori encampments
are still discovered, with the ashes of the fireplace even now
unscattered, and the close-gnawed bones of the gigantic
bird lying in the very spot where the natives left them after
their destructive feasts. So, too, with the big sharks.
Our modern carcharodon, who runs (as I have before noted)
to forty feet in length, is a very respectable monster indeed,
as times go ; and his huge snapping teeth, which measure
nearly two inches long by one and a half broad, would
disdain to make two bites of the able-bodied British seaman. But the naturalists of the 'Challenger' expedition
dredged up in numbers from the ooze of the Pacific similar
teeth, five inches long by four wide, so that the sharks to
which they originally belonged must, by parity of reasoning,
have measured nearly a hundred feet in length. This, no
doubt, beats our biggest existing shark, the rhinodon, by
some thirty feet. Still, the ooze of the Pacific is a quite
recent or almost modern deposit, which is even now being
accumulated on the sea bottom, and there would be really
nothing astonishing in the discovery that some representatives of these colossal carcharodons are to this day swimming about at their lordly leisure among the coral reefs of
the South Sea Islands. That very cautious naturalist, Dr.
Günther, of the British Museum, contents himself indeed
by merely saying : ' As we have no record of living indi-

viduals of that bulk having been observed, the gigantic
species to which these teeth belonged must probably have
become extinct within a comparatively recent period.'

If these things are so, the question naturally suggests
itself : Why should certain types of animals have attained
their greatest size at certain different epochs, and been replaced at others by equally big animals of wholly unlike
sorts ? The answer, I believe, is simply this : Because
there is not room and food in the world at any one time
for more than a certain relatively small number of gigantic
species. Each great group of animals has had successively
its rise, its zenith, its decadence, and its dotage ; each at
the period of its highest development has produced a considerable number of colossal forms ; each has been sup-
planted in due time by higher groups of totally different
structure, which have killed off their predecessors, not
indeed by actual stress of battle, but by irresistible compe-
tion for food and prey. The great saurians were thus
succeeded by the great mammals, just as the great mammals
are themselves in turn being ousted, from the land at least,
by the human species.

Let us look briefly at the succession of big animals in
the world, so far as we can follow it from the mutilated and
fragmentary record of the geological remains.

The very earliest existing fossils would lead us to believe what is otherwise quite probable, that life on our
planet began with very small forms—that it passed at first
through a baby stage. The animals of the Cambrian
period are almost all small mollusks, star-fishes, sponges,
and other simple, primitive types of life. There were as
yet no vertebrates of any sort, not even fishes, far less
amphibians, reptiles, birds, or mammals. The veritable
giants of the Cambrian world were the crustaceans, and
especially the trilobites, which, nevertheless, hardly ex-

ceeded in size a good big modern lobster. The biggest
trilobite is some two feet long ; and though we cannot by
any means say that this was really the largest form of animal
life then existing, owing to the extremely broken nature of
the geological record, we have at least no evidence that
anything bigger as yet moved upon the face of the waters.
The trilobites, which were a sort of triple-tailed crabs (to
speak very popularly), began in the Cambrian Epoch,
attained their culminating point in the Silurian, waned in
the Devonian, and died out utterly in the Carboniferous
seas.

It is in the second great epoch, the Silurian, that the
cuttle-fish tribe, still fairly represented by the nautilus,
the argonaut, the squid, and the octopus, first began to
make their appearance upon this or any other stage.   The
cuttle-fishes are among the most developed of invertebrate
animals ; they are rapid swimmers ; they have large and
powerful eyes ; and they can easily enfold their prey (*teste*
Victor Hugo) in their long and slimy sucker-clad arms.
With these natural advantages to back them up, it is not
surprising that the cuttle family rapidly made their mark
in the world.   They were by far the most advanced thinkers
and actors of their own age, and they rose almost at once
to be the dominant creatures of the primæval ocean in
which they swam.   There were as yet no saurians or
whales to dispute the dominion with these rapacious
cephalopods, and so the cuttle family had things for the
time all their own way.   Before the end of the Silurian
Epoch, according to that accurate census-taker, M. Barrande,
they had blossomed·forth into no less than 1,622 distinct
species.   For a single family to develop so enormous a
variety of separate forms, all presumably derived from a
single common ancestor, argues, of course, an immense
success in life ; and it also argues a vast lapse of time

during which the different species were gradually demarcated from one another.

Some of the ammonites, which belonged to this cuttlefish group, soon attained a very considerable size ; but a shell known as the orthoceras (I wish my subject didn't compel me to use such *very* long words, but I am not personally answerable, thank heaven, for the vagaries of modern scientific nomenclature) grew to a bigger size than that of any other fossil mollusk, sometimes measuring as much as six feet in total length. At what date the gigantic cuttles of the present day first began to make their appearance it would be hard to say, for their shell-less bodies are so soft that they could leave hardly anything behind in a fossil state ; but the largest known cuttle, measured by Mr. Gabriel, of Newfoundland, was eighty feet in length, including the long arms.

These cuttles are the only invertebrates at all in the running so far as colossal size is concerned, and it will be observed that here the largest modern specimen immeasurably beats the largest fossil form of the same type. I do not say that there were not fossil forms quite as big as the gigantic calamaries of our own time—on the contrary, I believe there were ; but if we go by the record alone we must confess that, in the matter of invertebrates at least, the balance of size is all in favour of our own period.

The vertebrates first make their appearance, in the shape of fishes, towards the close of the Silurian period, the second of the great geological epochs. The earliest fish appear to have been small, elongated, eel-like creatures, closely resembling the lampreys in structure ; but they rapidly developed in size and variety, and soon became the ruling race in the waters of the ocean, where they maintained their supremacy till the rise of the great secondary saurians. Even then, in spite of the severe competition thus introduced, and still later, in spite of the struggle ... life against the huge modern cetaceans (the true monarchs of the recent seas), the sharks continued to hold their own as producers of gigantic forms ; and at the present day their largest types probably rank second only to the whales in the whole range of animated nature. There seems no reason to doubt that modern fish, as a whole, quite equal in size the piscine fauna of any previous geological age.

It is somewhat different with the next great vertebrate group, the amphibians, represented in our own world only by the frogs, the toads, the newts, and the axolotls. Here we must certainly with shame confess that the amphibians of old greatly surpassed their degenerate descendants in our modern waters. The Japanese salamander, by far the biggest among our existing newts, never exceeds a yard in length from snout to tail; whereas some of the labyrin-thodonts (forgive me once more) of the Carboniferous Epoch must have reached at least seven or eight feet from stem to stern. But the reason of this falling off is not far to seek. When the adventurous newts and frogs of that remote period first dropped their gills and hopped about inquir-ingly on the dry land, under the shadow of the ancient tree-ferns and club-mosses, they were the only terrestrial vertebrates then existing, and they had the field (or, rather, the forest) all to themselves. For a while, therefore, like all dominant races for the time being, they blossomed forth at their ease into relatively gigantic forms. Frogs as big as donkeys, and efts as long as crocodiles, luxuriated to their hearts' content in the marshy lowlands, and lorded it freely over the small creatures which they found in undis-turbed possession of the Carboniferous isles. But as ages passed away, and new improvements were slowly invented and patented by survival of the fittest in the offices of nature, their own more advanced and developed descendants, the reptiles and mammals, got the upper hand with them, and soon lived them down in the struggle for life, so that this essentially intermediate form is now almost entirely restricted to its one adapted seat, the pools and ditches that dry up in summer.

The reptiles, again, are a class in which the biggest modern forms are simply nowhere beside the gigantic extinct species. First appearing on the earth at the very close of the vast primary periods—in the Permian age— they attained in secondary times the most colossal proportions, and have certainly never since been exceeded in size by any later forms of life in whatever direction. But one must remember that during the heyday of the great saurians, there were as yet no birds and no mammals. The place now filled in the ocean by the whales and grampuses, as well as the place now filled in the great continents by the elephants, the rhinoceroses, the hippopotami, and the other big quadrupeds, was then filled exclusively by huge reptiles, of the sort rendered familiar to us all by the restored effigies on the little island in the Crystal Palace grounds. Every dog has his day, and the reptiles had *their* day in the secondary period. The forms into which they developed were certainly every whit as large as any ever seen on the surface of this planet, but not, as I have already shown, appreciably larger than those of the biggest cetaceans known to science in our own time.

During the very period, however, when enaliosaurians and pterodactyls were playing such pranks before high heaven as might have made contemporary angels weep, if they took any notice of saurian morality, a small race of unobserved little prowlers was growing up in the dense shades of the neighbouring forests which was destined at last to oust the huge reptiles from their empire over earth, and to become in the fulness of time the exclusively dominant type of the whole planet. In the trias we get the first remains of mammalian life in the shape of tiny rat-like animals, marsupial in type, and closely related to the banded ant-eaters of New South Wales at the present day. Throughout the long lapse of the secondary ages, across the lias, the oolite, the wealden, and the chalk, we find the mammalian race slowly developing into opossums and kangaroos, such as still inhabit the isolated and anti-quated continent of Australia. Gathering strength all the time for the coming contest, increasing constantly in size of brain and keenness of intelligence, the true mammals were able at last, towards the close of the secondary ages, to enter the lists boldly against the gigantic saurians. With the dawn of the tertiary period, the reign of the rep-tiles begins to wane, and the reign of the mammals to set in at last in real earnest. In place of the ichthyosaurs we get the huge cetaceans; in place of the deinosaurs we get the mammoth and the mastodon; in place of the domi-nant reptile groups we get the first precursors of man himself.

The history of the great birds has been somewhat more singular. Unlike the other main vertebrate classes, the birds (as if on purpose to contradict the proverb) seem never yet to have had their day. Unfortunately for them, or at least for their chance of producing colossal species, their evolution went on side by side, apparently, with that of the still more intelligent and more powerful mammals; so that, wherever the mammalian type had once firmly established itself, the birds were compelled to limit their aspirations to a very modest and humble standard. Ter-restrial mammals, however, cannot cross the sea; so in isolated regions, such as New Zealand and Madagascar, the birds had things all their own way. In New Zealand, there are no indigenous quadrupeds at all; and there the huge moa attained to dimensions almost equalling those of the giraffe. In Madagascar, the mammalian life was small and of low grade, so the gigantic æpyornis became the very biggest of all known birds. At the same time, these big species acquired their immense size at the cost of the distinctive birdlike habit of flight. A flying moa is almost an impossible conception ; even the ostriches compete practically with the zebras and antelopes rather than with the eagles, the condors, or the albatrosses. In like manner, when a pigeon found its way to Mauritius, it developed into the practically wingless dodo ; while in the northern penguins, on their icy perches, the fore limbs have been gradually modified into swimming organs, exactly analogous to the flippers of the seal.

Are the great animals now passing away and leaving no representatives of their greatness to future ages ? On land at least that is very probable. Man, diminutive man, who, if he walked on all fours, would be no bigger than a silly sheep, and who only partially disguises his native smallness by his acquired habit of walking erect on what ought to be his hind legs—man has upset the whole balanced economy of nature, and is everywhere expelling and exterminating before him the great herbivores, his predecessors. He needs for his corn and his bananas the fruitful plains which were once laid down in prairie or scrubwood. Hence it seems not unlikely that the elephant, the hippopotamus, the rhinoceros, and the buffalo must go. But we are still a long way off from that final consummation, even on dry land ; while as for the water, it appears highly probable that there are as good fish still in the sea as ever came out of it. Whether man himself, now become the sole dominant animal of our poor old planet, will ever develop into Titanic proportions, seems far more problematical. The race is now no longer to the swift, nor the battle to the

strong. Brain counts for more than muscle, and mind has
gained the final victory over mere matter. Goliath of Gath
has shrunk into insignificance before the Gatling gun ; as
in the fairy tales of old, it is cunning little Jack with his
clever devices who wins the day against the heavy, clumsy,
muddle-headed giants. Nowadays it is our ' Minotaurs '
and ' Warriors ' that are the real leviathans and behemoths
of the great deep ; our Krupps and Armstrongs are the
fire-breathing krakens of the latter-day seas. Instead of
developing individually into huge proportions, the human
race tends rather to aggregate into vast empires, which
compete with one another by means of huge armaments,
and invent mitrailleuses and torpedos of incredible ferocity
for their mutual destruction. The dragons of the prime
that tare each other in their slime have yielded place to
eighty-ton guns and armour-plated turret-ships. Those are
the genuine lineal representatives on our modern seas of
the secondary saurians. Let us hope that some coming
geologist of the dim future, finding the fossil remains of
the sunken ' Captain,' or the plated scales of the ' Comte
de Grasse,' firmly embedded in the upheaved ooze of the
existing Atlantic, may shake his head in solemn deprecation
at the horrid sight, and thank heaven that such hideous
carnivorous creatures no longer exist in his own day.

FOSSIL FOOD

THERE is something at first sight rather ridiculous in the idea of eating a fossil. To be sure, when the frozen mammoths of Siberia were first discovered, though they had been dead for at least 80,000 years (according to Dr. Croll's minimum reckoning for the end of the great ice age), and might therefore naturally have begun to get a little musty, they had nevertheless been kept so fresh, like a sort of prehistoric Australian mutton, in their vast natural refrigerators, that the wolves and bears greedily devoured the precious relics for which the naturalists of Europe would have been ready gladly to pay the highest market price of best beefsteak. Those carnivorous vandals gnawed off the skin and flesh with the utmost appreciation, and left nothing but the tusks and bones to adorn the galleries of the new Natural History Museum at South Kensington. But then wolves and bears, especially in Siberia, are not exactly fastidious about the nature of their meat diet. Furthermore, some of the bones of extinct animals found beneath the stalagmitic floor of caves, in England and elsewhere, presumably of about the same age as the Siberian mammoths, still contain enough animal matter to produce a good strong stock for antediluvian broth, which has been scientifically described by a high authority as pre-Adamite jelly. The congress of naturalists at Tübingen a few years since had a smoking tureen of this cave-bone soup placed upon the dinner-table at their hotel one evening, and pronounced it with geological enthusiasm ' scarcely inferior to prime ox-tail.' But men of science, too, are accustomed to trying unsavoury experiments, which would go sadly against the grain with less philosophic and more squeamish palates. They think nothing of tasting a caterpillar that birds will not touch, in order to discover whether it owes its immunity from attack to some nauseous, bitter, or pungent flavouring ; and they even advise you calmly to discriminate between two closely similar species of snails by trying which of them when chewed has a delicate *soupçon* of oniony aroma. So that naturalists in this matter, as the children say, don't count : their universal thirst for knowledge will prompt them to drink anything, down even to *consommé* of quaternary cave-bear.

There is one form of fossil food, however, which appears constantly upon all our tables at breakfast, lunch, and dinner, every day, and which is so perfectly familiar to every one of us that we almost forget entirely its immensely remote geological origin. The salt in our salt-cellars is a fossil product, laid down ages ago in some primæval Dead Sea or Caspian, and derived in all probability (through the medium of the grocer) from the triassic rocks of Cheshire or Worcestershire. Since that thick bed of rock-salt was first precipitated upon the dry floor of some old evaporated inland sea, the greater part of the geological history known to the world at large has slowly unrolled itself through incalculable ages. The dragons of the prime have begun and finished their long (and Lord Tennyson says slimy) race. The fish-like saurians and flying pterodactyls of the secondary period have come into existence and gone out of it gracefully again. The whole family of birds has been developed and diversified into its modern variety of eagles and titmice. The beasts of the field have passed through sundry stages of mammoth and mastodon, of sabre-toothed lion and huge rhinoceros. Man himself has progressed gradually from the humble condition of a ' hairy arboreal quadruped '—these bad words are Mr. Darwin's own—to the glorious elevation of an erect, two-handed creature, with a county suffrage question and an intelligent interest in the latest proceedings of the central divorce court. And after all those manifold changes, compared to which the entire period of English history, from the landing of Julius Cæsar to the appearance of this present volume (to take two important landmarks), is as one hour to a human lifetime, we quietly dig up the salt to-day from that dry lake bottom and proceed to eat it with the eggs laid by the hens this morning for this morning's breakfast, just as though the one food-stuff were not a whit more ancient or more dignified in nature than the other. Why, mammoth steak is really quite modern and common-place by the side of the salt in the salt-cellar that we treat so cavalierly every day of our ephemeral existence.

The way salt got originally deposited in these great rock beds is very well illustrated for us by the way it is still being deposited in the evaporating waters of many inland seas. Every schoolboy knows of course (though some persons who are no longer schoolboys may just possibly have forgotten) that the Caspian is in reality only a little bit of the Mediterranean, which has been cut off from the main sea by the gradual elevation of the country between them. For many ages the intermediate soil has been quite literally rising in the world; but to this day a continuous chain of salt lakes and marshes runs between the Caspian and the Black Sea, and does its best to keep alive the memory of the time when they were both united in a single basin. All along this intervening tract, once sea but now dry land, banks of shells belonging to kinds still living in the Caspian and the Black Sea alike testify to the old line of water communication. One fine morning (date unknown) the intermediate belt began to rise up between chem; the water was all pushed off into the Caspian, but the shells remained to tell the tale even unto this day.

Now, when a bit of the sea gets cut off in this way from the main ocean, evaporation of its waters generally takes place rather faster than the return supply of rain by rivers and lesser tributaries. In other words, the inland sea or salt lake begins slowly to dry up. This is now just happening in the Caspian, which is in fact a big pool in course of being slowly evaporated. By-and-by a point is reached when the water can no longer hold in solution the amount of salts of various sorts that it originally contained. In the technical language of chemists and physicists it begins to get supersaturated. Then the salts are thrown down as a sediment at the bottom of the sea or lake, exactly as crust formed on the bottom of a kettle. Gypsum is the first material to be so thrown down, because it is less soluble than common salt, and therefore sooner got rid of. It forms a thick bottom layer in the bed of all evaporating inland seas; and as plaster of Paris it not only gives rise finally to artistic monstrosities hawked about the streets for the degradation of national taste, but also plays an important part in the manufacture of bonbons, the destruction of the human digestion, and the ultimate ruin of the dominant white European race. Only about a third of the water in a salt lake need be evaporated before the gypsum begins to be deposited in a solid layer over its whole bed; it is not till 93 per cent. of the water has gone, and only 7 per cent. is left, that common salt begins to be thrown down. When that point of intensity is reached, the salt, too, falls as a sediment to the bottom, and there overlies the gypsum deposit. Hence all the world over, wherever we come upon a bed of rock salt, it almost invariably lies upon a floor of solid gypsum.

The Caspian, being still a very respectable modern sea, constantly supplied with fresh water from the surrounding. rivers, has not yet begun by any means to deposit salt on its bottom from its whole mass; but the shallow pools and long bays around its edge have crusts of beautiful rose-coloured salt-crystals forming upon their sides; and as these lesser basins gradually dry up, the sand, blown before the wind, slowly drifts over them, so as to form miniature rock-salt beds on a very small scale. Nevertheless, the young and vigorous Caspian only represents the first stage in the process of evaporation of an inland sea. It is still fresh enough to form the abode of fish and mollusks; and the irrepressible young lady of the present generation is perhaps even aware that it contains numbers of seals, being in fact the seat of one of the most important and valuable seal-fisheries in the whole world. It may be regarded as a typical example of a yet youthful and lively inland sea.

The Dead Sea, on the other hand, is an old and de-crepit salt lake in a very advanced state of evaporation. It lies several feet below the level of the Mediterranean, just as the Caspian lies several feet below the level of the Black Sea; and as in both cases the surface must once have been con-tinuous, it is clear that the water of either sheet must have dried up to a very considerable extent. But, while the Caspian has shrunk only to 85 feet below the Black Sea, the Dead Sea has shrunk to the enormous depth of 1,292 feet below the Mediterranean. Every now and then, some enterprising De Lesseps or other proposes to dig a canal from the Mediterranean to the Dead Sea, and so re-esta-blish the old high level. The effect of this very revolutionary proceeding would be to flood the entire Jordan Valley, connect the Sea of Galilee with the Dead Sea, and play the dickens generally with Scripture geography, to the infinite delight of Sunday school classes. Now, when the Dead Sea first began its independent career as a separate sheet of water on its own account, it no doubt occupied the whole bed of this imaginary engineers' lake—spreading, if not from Dan to Beersheba, at any rate from Dan to Edom, or, in other words, along the whole Jordan Valley from the Sea of Galilee and even the Waters of Merom to the southern desert. (I will not insult the reader's intelligence and orthodoxy by suggesting that perhaps he may not be precisely certain as to the exact position of the Waters of Merom ; but I will merely recommend him just to refresh his memory by turning to his atlas, as this is an opportunity which may not again occur.)   The modern Dead Sea is the last shrunken relic of such a considerable ancient lake. Its waters are now so very concentrated and so very nasty that no fish or other self-respecting animal can consent to live in them ; and so buoyant that a man can't drown himself, even if he tries, because the sea is saturated with salts of various sorts till it has become a kind of soup or porridge, in which a swimmer floats, will he nill he.   Persons in the neighbourhood who wish to commit suicide are therefore obliged to go elsewhere : much as in Tasmania, the healthiest climate in the world, people who want to die are obliged to run across for a week to Sydney or Melbourne.

The waters of the Dead Sea are thus in the condition of having already deposited almost all their gypsum, as well as the greater part of the salt they originally contained.   They are, in fact, much like sea water which has been boiled down till it has reached the state of a thick salty liquid ; and though most of the salt is now already deposited in a deep layer on the bottom, enough still remains in solution to make the Dead Sea infinitely salter than the general ocean.   At the same time, there are a good many other things in solution in sea water besides, gypsum and common salt; such as chloride of magnesia sulphate of potassium, and other interesting substances with pretty chemical names, well calculated to endear them at first sight to the sentimental affections of the general public. These other by-contents of the water are often still longer in getting deposited than common salt; and, owing to their intermixture in a very concentrated form with the mother liquid of the Dead Sea, the water of that evaporating lake is not only salt but also slimy and fetid to the last degree, its taste being accurately described as half brine, half rancid oil. Indeed, the salt has been so far precipitated already that there is now five times as much chloride of magnesium left in the water as there is common salt. By the way, it is a lucky thing for us that these various soluble minerals are of such constitution as to be thrown down separately at different stages of concentration in the evaporating liquid; for, if it were otherwise, they would all get deposited together, and we should find on all old salt lake beds only a mixed layer of gypsum, salt, and other chlorides and sulphates, absolutely useless for any practical human purpose. In that case, we should be entirely dependent upon marine salt pans and artificial processes for our entire salt supply. As it is, we find the materials deposited one above another in regular layers; first, the gypsum at the bottom; then the rock-salt; and last of all, on top, the more soluble mineral constituents.

The Great Salt Lake of Utah, sacred to the memory of Brigham Young, gives us an example of a modern saline sheet of very different origin, since it is in fact not a branch of the sea at all, but a mere shrunken remnant of a very large fresh-water lake system, like that of the still-existing St. Lawrence chain. Once upon a time, American geologists say, a huge sheet of water, for which they have even invented a definite name, Lake Bonneville, occupied a far larger valley among the outliers of the Rocky Mountains, measuring 300 miles in one direction by 180 miles in the other. Beside this primitive Superior lay a second great sheet—an early Huron—(Lake Lahontan, the geologists call it) almost as big, and equally of fresh water. By-and-by—the precise dates are necessarily indefinite—some change in the rainfall, unregistered by any contemporary ' New York Herald,' made the waters of these big lakes shrink and evaporate. Lake Lahontan shrank away like Alice in Wonderland, till there was absolutely nothing left of it ; Lake Bonneville shrank till it attained the diminished size of the existing Great Salt Lake. Terrace after terrace, running in long parallel lines on the sides of the Wahsatch Mountains around, mark the various levels at which it rested for awhile on its gradual downward course. It is still falling indeed ; and the plain around is being gradually uncovered, forming the white salt-encrusted shore with which all visitors to the Mormon city are so familiar.

But why should the water have become briny ? Why should the evaporation of an old Superior produce at last a Great Salt Lake ? Well, there is a small quantity of salt in solution even in the freshest of lakes and ponds, brought down to them by the streams or rivers ; and, as the water of the hypothetical Lake Bonneville slowly evaporated, the salt and other mineral constituents remained behind. Thus the solution grew constantly more and more concentrated, till at the present day it is extremely saline. Professor Geikie (to whose works the present paper is much indebted) found that he floated on the water in spite of himself ; and the under sides of the steps at the bathing-places are all encrusted with short stalactites of salt, produced from the drip of the bathers as they leave the water.

The mineral constituents, however, differ considerably in their proportions from those found in true salt lakes of marine origin ; and the point at which the salt is thrown down is still far from having been reached. Great Salt Lake must simmer in the sun for many centuries yet before the point arrives at which (as cooks say) it begins to settle.

That is the way in which deposits of salt are being now produced on the world's surface, in preparation for that man of the future who, as we learn from a duly constituted authority, is to be hairless, toothless, web-footed, and far too respectable ever to be funny. Man of the present derives his existing salt-supply chiefly from beds of rock-salt similarly laid down against his expected appearance some hundred thousand æons or so ago. (An æon is a very convenient geological unit indeed to reckon by ; as nobody has any idea how long it is, they can't carp at you for a matter of an æon or two one way or the other.) Rock-salt is found in most parts of the world, in beds of very various ages. The great Salt Range of the Punjaub is probably the earliest in date of all salt deposits ; it was laid down at the bottom of some very ancient Asiatic Mediterranean, whose last shrunken remnant covered the upper basin of the Indus and its tributaries during the Silurian age. Europe had then hardly begun to be ; and England was probably still covered from end to end by the primæval ocean. From this very primitive salt deposit the greater part of India and Central Asia is still supplied ; and the Indian Government makes a pretty penny out of the dues in the shape of the justly detested salt-tax—a tax especially odious because it wrings the fraction of a farthing even from those unhappy agricultural labourers who have never tasted ghee with their rice.

The thickness of the beds in each salt deposit of course

depends entirely upon the area of the original sea or salt-lake, and the length of time during which the evaporation went on. Sometimes we may get a mere film of salt; sometimes a solid bed six hundred feet thick. Perfectly pure rock-salt is colourless and transparent; but one doesn't often find it pure. Alas for a degenerate world! even in its original site, Nature herself has taken the trouble to adulterate it beforehand. (If she hadn't done so, one may be perfectly sure that commercial enterprise would have proved equal to the occasion in the long run.) But the adulteration hasn't spoilt the beauty of the salt; on the contrary, it serves, like rouge, to give a fine fresh colour where none existed. When iron is the chief colouring matter, rock-salt assumes a beautiful clear red tint; in other cases it is emerald green or pale blue. As a rule, salt is prepared from it for table by a regular process; but it has become a fad of late with a few people to put crystals of native rock-salt on their tables; and they decidedly look very pretty, and have a certain distinctive flavour of their own that is not unpleasant.

Our English salt supply is chiefly derived from the Cheshire and Worcestershire salt-regions, which are of triassic age. Many of the places at which the salt is mined have names ending in *wich*, such as Northwich, Middlewich, Nantwich, Droitwich, Netherwich, and Shirleywich. This termination *wich* is itself curiously significant, as Canon Isaac Taylor has shown, of the necessary connection between salt and the sea. The earliest known way of producing salt was of course in shallow pans on the sea-shore, at the bottom of a shoal bay, called in Norse and Early English a wick or wich; and the material so produced is still known in trade as bay-salt. By-and-by, when people came to discover the inland brine-pits and salt mines, they transferred to them the familiar name, a wich; and the places where the salt was manufactured came to be known as wych-houses. Droitwich, for example, was originally such a wich, where the droits or dues on salt were paid at the time when William the Conqueror's commissioners drew up their great survey for Domesday Book. But the good, easy-going mediæval people who gave these quaint names to the inland wiches had probably no idea that they were really and truly dried-up bays, and that the salt they mined from their pits was genuine ancient bay-salt, the deposit of an old inland sea, evaporated by slow degrees a countless number of ages since, exactly as the Dead Sea and the Great Salt Lake are getting evaporated in our own time.

Such, nevertheless, is actually the case. A good-sized Caspian used to spread across the centre of England and north of Ireland in triassic times, bounded here and there, as well as Dr. Hull can make out, by the Welsh Mountains, the Cheviots, and the Donegal Hills, and with the Peak of Derbyshire and the Isle of Man standing out as separate islands from its blue expanse. (We will beg the question that the English seas were then blue. They are certainly marked so in a very fine cerulean tint on Dr. Hull's map of Triassic Britain.) Slowly, like most other inland seas, this early British Caspian began to lose weight and to shrivel away to ever smaller dimensions. In Devonshire, where it appears to have first dried up, we get no salt, but only red marl, with here and there a cubical cast, filling a hole once occupied by rock-salt, though the percolation of the rain has long since melted out that very soluble sub-stance, and replaced it by a mere mould in the character-istic square shape of salt crystals. But Worcestershire and Cheshire were the seat of the inland sea when it had con-tracted to the dimensions of a mere salt lake, and begun to throw down its dissolved saline materials. One of the Cheshire beds is sometimes a hundred feet thick of almost

pure and crystalline rock-salt. The absence of fossils shows
that animals must have had as bad a time of it there as in
the Dead Sea of our modern Palestine. The Droitwich
brine-pits have been known for many centuries, since they
were worked (and taxed) even before the Norman Conquest,
as were many other similar wells elsewhere. But the
actual mining of rock-salt as such in England dates back
only as far as the reign of King Charles II. of blessed
memory, or more definitely to the very year in which the
'Pilgrim's Progress' was conceived and written by John
Bunyan. During that particular summer, an enterprising
person at Nantwich had sunk a shaft for coal, which he
failed to find; but on his way down he came unexpectedly
across the bed of rock-salt, then for the first time discovered
as a native mineral. Since that fortunate accident the beds
have been so energetically worked and the springs so
energetically pumped that some of the towns built on top
of them have got undermined, and now threaten from year
to year, in the most literal sense, to cave in. In fact, one
or two subsidences of considerable extent have already taken
place, due in part no doubt to the dissolving action of rain
water, but in part also to the mode of working. The mines
are approached by a shaft; and, when you get down to the
level of the old sea bottom, you find yourself in a sort of
artificial gallery, whose roof, with all the world on top of
it, is supported every here and there by massive pillars
about fifteen feet thick. Considering that the salt lies
often a hundred and fifty yards deep, and that these pillars
have to bear the weight of all that depth of solid rock, it
is not surprising that subsidences should sometimes occur
in abandoned shafts, where the water is allowed to collect,
and slowly dissolve away the supporting columns.

Salt is a necessary article of food for animals, but in a
far less degree than is commonly supposed. Each of us

eats on an average about ten times as much salt as we actually require. In this respect popular notions are as inexact as in the very similar case of the supply of phosphorus. Because phosphorus is needful for brain action, people jump forthwith to the absurd conclusion that fish and other foods rich in phosphates ought to be specially good for students preparing for examination, great thinkers, and literary men. Mark Twain indeed once advised a poetical aspirant, who sent him a few verses for his critical opinion, that fish was very feeding for the brains ; he would recommend a couple of young whales to begin upon. As a matter of fact, there is more phosphorus in our daily bread than would have sufficed Shakespeare to write ' Hamlet,' or Newton to discover the law of gravitation. It isn't phosphorus that most of us need, but brains to burn it in. A man might as well light a fire in a carriage, because coal makes an engine go, as hope to mend the pace of his dull pate by eating fish for the sake of the phosphates.

The question still remains, How did the salt originally get there ? After all, when we say that it was produced, as rock-salt, by evaporation of the water in inland seas, we leave unanswered the main problem, How did the brine in solution get into the sea at all in the first place ? Well, one might almost as well ask, How did anything come to be upon the earth at any time, in any way ? How did the sea itself get there ? How did this planet swim into existence at all ? In the Indian mythology the world is supported upon the back of an elephant, who is supported upon the back of a tortoise ; but what the tortoise in the last resort is supported upon the Indian philosophers prudently say not. If we once begin thus pushing back our inquiries into the genesis of the cosmos, we shall find our search retreating step after step *ad infinitum*. The negro preacher, describing the creation of Adam, and drawing slightly

upon his imagination, observed that when our prime forefather first came to consciousness he found himself ' sot up
agin a fence.'　　One of his hearers ventured sceptically to
ejaculate, ' Den whar dat fence come from, ministah ? ' The
outraged divine scratched his grey wool reflectively for a
moment, and replied, after a pause, with stern solemnity,
' Tree more ob dem questions will undermine de whole
system ob teology.'

However, we are not permitted humbly to imitate the
prudent reticence of the Indian philosophers.　In these
days of evolution hypotheses, and nebular theories, and
kinetic energy, and all the rest of it, the question why the
sea is salt rises up irrepressible and imperatively demands
to get itself answered.　There was a sapient inquirer,
recently deceased, who had a short way out of this difficulty.　He held that the sea was only salt because of all
the salt rivers that run into it.　Considering that the
salt rivers are themselves salted by passing through salt
regions, or being fed by saline springs, all of which derive
their saltness from deposits laid down long ago by evaporation from earlier seas or lake basins, this explanation
savours somewhat of circularity.　It amounts in effect
to saying that the sea is salt because of the large amount
of saline matter which it holds in solution.　Cheese is also
a caseous preparation of milk ; the duties of an archdeacon
are to perform archidiaconal functions ; and opium puts one
to sleep because it possesses a soporific virtue.

Apart from such purely verbal explanations of the saltness of the sea, however, one can only give some such
account of the way it came to be ' the briny ' as the
following :—

This world was once a haze of fluid light, as the poets
and the men of science agree in informing us.　As soon as it
began to cool down a little, the heavier materials naturally

sank towards the centre, while the lighter, now represented
by the ocean and the atmosphere, floated in a gaseous condition on the outside. But the great envelope of vapour
thus produced did not consist merely of the constituents of
air and water ; many other gases and vapours mingled with
them, as they still do to a far less extent in our existing
atmosphere. By-and-by, as the cooling and condensing process continued, the water settled down from the condition of
steam into one of a liquid at a dull red heat. As it condensed,
it carried down with it a great many other substances, held in
solution, whose component elements had previously existed
in the primitive gaseous atmosphere. Thus the early ocean
which covered the whole earth was in all probability not
only very salt, but also quite thick with other mineral matters close up to the point of saturation. It was full of lime,
and raw flint, and sulphates, and many other miscellaneous
bodies. Moreover, it was not only just as salt as at the present day, but even a great deal salter. For from that time
to this evaporation has constantly been going on in certain
shallow isolated areas, laying down great beds of gypsum
and then of salt, which still remain in the solid condition,
while the water has, of course, been correspondingly purified. The same thing has likewise happened in a slightly
different way with the lime and flint, which have been
separated from the water chiefly by living animals, and
afterwards deposited on the bottom of the ocean in immense
layers as limestone, chalk, sandstone, and clay.

Thus it turns out that in the end all our sources of
salt-supply are alike ultimately derived from the briny
ocean. Whether we dig it out as solid rock-salt from the
open quarries of the Punjaub, or pump it up from brine-
wells sunk into the triassic rocks of Cheshire, or evaporate
it direct in the salt-pans of England and the shallow *salines*
of the Mediterranean shore, it is still at bottom essentially

sea-salt. However distant the connection may seem, our salt is always in the last resort obtained from the material held in solution in some ancient or modern sea. Even the saline springs of Canada and the Northern States of America, where the wapiti love to congregate, and the noble hunter lurks in the thicket to murder them unperceived, derive their saltness, as an able Canadian geologist has shown, from the thinly scattered salts still retained among the sediments of that very archaic sea whose precipitates form the earliest known life-bearing rocks. To the Homeric Greek, as to Mr. Dick Swiveller, the ocean was always the briny : to modern science, on the other hand (which neither of those worthies would probably have appreciated at its own valuation), the briny is always the oceanic. The fossil food which we find to-day on all our dinner-tables dates back its origin primarily to the first seas that ever covered the surface of our planet, and secondarily to the great rock deposits of the dried-up triassic inland sea. And yet even our men of science habitually describe that ancient mineral as common salt.

OGBURY BARROWS

WE went to Ogbury Barrows on an archæological expedition. And as the very name of archæology, owing to a serious misconception incidental to human nature, is enough to deter most people from taking any further interest in our proceedings when once we got there, I may as well begin by explaining, for the benefit of those who have never been to one, the method and manner of an archæological outing.

The first thing you have to do is to catch your secretary. The genuine secretary is born, not made; and therefore you have got to catch him, not to appoint him. Appointing a secretary is pure vanity and vexation of spirit; you must find the right man made ready to your hand; and when you have found him you will soon see that he slips into the onerous duties of the secretariat as if to the manner born, by pure instinct. The perfect secretary is an urbane old gentleman of mature years and portly bearing, a dignified representative of British archæology, with plenty of money and plenty of leisure, possessing a heaven-born genius for organisation, and utterly unhampered by any foolish views of his own about archæological research or any other kindred subject. The secretary who archæologises is lost. His business is not to discourse of early English windows or of palæolithic hatchets, of buried villas or of Plantagenet pedigrees, of Roman tile-

work or of dolichocephalic skulls, but to provide abundant
brakes, drags, and carriages, to take care that the owners
of castles and baronial residences throw them open (with
lunch provided) to the ardent student of British antiquities,
to see that all the old ladies have somebody to talk to, and
all the young ones somebody to flirt with, and generally to
superintend the morals, happiness, and personal comfort of
some fifty assorted scientific enthusiasts. The secretary
who diverges from these his proper and elevated functions
into trivial and puerile disquisitions upon the antiquity of
man (when he ought rather to be admiring the juvenility
of woman), or the precise date of the Anglo-Saxon conquest (when he should by rights be concentrating the whole
force of his massive intellect upon the arduous task of
arranging for dinner), proves himself at once unworthy of
his high position, and should forthwith be deposed from
the secretariat by public acclamation.

Having once entrapped your perfect secretary, you set
him busily to work beforehand to make all the arrangements for your expected excursion, the archæologists
generally cordially recognising the important principle
that he pays all the expenses he incurs out of his own
pocket, and drives splendid bargains on their account with
hotel-keepers, coachmen, railway companies, and others to
feed, lodge, supply, and convey them at fabulously low
prices throughout the whole expedition. You also understand that the secretary will call upon everybody in the
neighbourhood you propose to visit, induce the rectors to
throw open their churches, square the housekeepers of
absentee dukes, and beard the owners of Elizabethan
mansions in their own dens. These little preliminaries
being amicably settled, you get together your archæologists
and set out upon your intended tour.

An archæologist, it should be further premised, has no

necessary personal connection with archæology in any way. He (or she) is a human being, of assorted origin, age, and sex, known as an archæologist then and there on no other ground than the possession of a ticket (price half-a-guinea) for that particular archæological meeting. Who would not be a man (or woman) of science on such easy and unexacting terms? Most archæologists within my own private experience, indeed, are ladies of various ages, many of them elderly, but many more young and pretty, whose views about the styles of English architecture or the exact distinction between Durotriges and Damnonians are of the vaguest and most shadowy possible description. You all drive in brakes together to the various points of interest in the surrounding country. When you arrive at a point of interest, somebody or other with a bad cold in his head reads a dull paper on its origin and nature, in which there is fortunately no subsequent examination. If you are burning to learn all about it, you put your hand up to your ear, and assume an attitude of profound attention. If you are not burning with the desire for information, you stroll off casually about the grounds and gardens with the prettiest and pleasantest among the archæological sisters, whose acquaintance you have made on the way thither. Sometimes it rains, and then you obtain an admirable chance of offering your neighbour the protection afforded by your brand-new silk umbrella. By-and-by the dull paper gets finished, and somebody who lives in an adjoining house volunteers to provide you with luncheon. Then you adjourn to the parish church, where an old gentleman of feeble eyesight reads a long and tedious account of all the persons whose monuments are or are not to be found upon the walls of that poky little building. Nobody listens to him; but everybody carries away a vague impression that some one or other, temp. Henry the Second,

U

married Adeliza, daughter and heiress of Sir Ralph de Thingumbob, and had issue thirteen stalwart sons and twenty-seven beautiful daughters, each founders of a noble family with a correspondingly varied pedigree. Finally, you take tea and ices upon somebody's lawn, by special invitation, and drive home, not without much laughter, in the cool of the evening to an excellent table d'hôte dinner at the marvellously cheap hotel, presided over by the ever-smiling and urbane secretary. That is what we mean now-adays by being a member of an archæological association.

It was on just such a pleasant excursion that we all went to Ogbury Barrows. I was overflowing, myself, with bottled-up information on the subject of those two pre-historic tumuli; for Ogbury Barrows have been the hobby of my lifetime; but I didn't read a paper upon their origin and meaning, first, because the secretary very happily forgot to ask me, and secondly, because I was much better employed in psychological research into the habits and manners of an extremely pretty pink-and-white archæo-logist who stood beside me. Instead, therefore, of boring her and my other companions with all my accumulated store of information about Ogbury Barrows, I locked it up securely in my own bosom, with the fell design of finally venting it all at once in one vast flood upon the present article.

Ogbury Barrows, I would have said (had it not been for the praiseworthy negligence of our esteemed secretary), stand upon the very verge of a great chalk-down, over-looking a broad and fertile belt of valley, whose slopes are terraced in the quaintest fashion with long parallel lines of obviously human and industrial origin. The terracing must have been done a very long time ago indeed, for it is a device for collecting enough soil on a chalky hillside to grow corn in. Now, nobody ever tried to grow corn on

open chalk-downs in any civilised period of history until
the present century, because the downs are so much more
naturally adapted for sheep-walks that the attempt to turn
them into waving cornfields would never occur to anybody
on earth except a barbarian or an advanced agriculturist.
But when Ogbury Downs were originally terraced, I don't
doubt that the primitive system of universal tribal warfare
still existed everywhere in Britain.   This system is aptly
summed up in the familiar modern Black Country
formula, ' Yon's a stranger. 'Eave 'arf a brick at him.'
Each tribe was then perpetually at war with every other
tribe on either side of it : a simple plan which rendered
foreign tariffs quite unnecessary, and most effectually protected home industries. The consequence was, each district had to produce for its own tribe all the necessaries
of life, however ill-adapted by nature for their due production : because traffic and barter did not yet exist, and
the only form ever assumed by import trade was that of
raiding on your neighbours' territories, and bringing back
with you whatever you could lay hands on.   So the people
of the chalky Ogbury valley had perforce to grow corn for
themselves, whether nature would or nature wouldn't ;
and, in order to grow it under such very unfavourable circumstances of soil and climate, they terraced off the entire
hillside, by catching the silt as it washed slowly down, and
keeping it in place by artificial barriers.

On the top of the down, overlooking this curious vale
of prehistoric terraces, rise the twin heights of Ogbury
Barrows, familiar landmarks to all the country side around
for many miles.   One of them is a tall, circular mound or
tumulus surrounded by a deep and well-marked trench :
the other, which stands a little on one side, is long and
narrow, shaped exactly like a modern grave, but of comparatively gigantic and colossal proportions.   Even the

little children of Ogbury village have noticed its close resemblance of shape and outline to the grassy hillocks in their own churchyard, and whisper to one another when they play upon its summit that a great giant in golden armour lies buried in a stone vault underneath. But if only they knew the real truth, they would say instead that that big, ungainly, overgrown grave covers the remains of a short, squat, dwarfish chieftain, akin in shape and feature to the Lapps and Finns, and about as much unlike a giant as human nature could easily manage. It may be regarded as a general truth of history that the greatest men don't by any means always get the biggest monument.

The archæologists in becoming prints who went with us to the top of Ogbury Barrows sagaciously surmised (with demonstrative parasol) that 'these mounds must have been made a very long time ago, indeed.' So in fact they were : but though they stand now so close together, and look so much like sisters and contemporaries, one is ages older than the other, and was already green and grass-grown with immemorial antiquity when the fresh earth of its neighbour tumulus was first thrown up by its side, above the buried urn of some long-forgotten Celtic warrior. Let us begin by considering the oldest first, and then pass on to its younger sister.

. Ogbury Long Barrow is a very ancient monument indeed. Not, to be sure, one quarter so ancient as the days of the extremely old master who carved the mammoth on the fragments of his own tusk in the caves of the Dordogne, and concerning whom I have indited a discourse in an earlier portion of this volume : compared with that very antique personage, our long barrow on Ogbury hill-top may in fact be looked upon as almost modern. Still, when one isn't talking in geological language, ten or twenty thousand years may be fairly considered a very long time as time

goes : and I have little doubt that from ten to twenty
thousand years have passed since the short, squat chieftain
aforesaid was first committed to his final resting-place in
Ogbury Long Barrow. Two years since, we local archæologists—*not* in becoming prints this time—opened the
barrow to see what was inside it. We found, as we expected, the ' stone vault ' of the popular tradition, proving
conclusively that some faint memory of the original inter-
ment had clung for all those long years around the grassy
pile of that ancient tumulus. Its centre, in fact, was
occupied by a sepulchral chamber built of big Sarsen
stones from the surrounding hillsides ; and in the midst of
the house of death thus rudely constructed lay the mouldering skeleton of its original possessor—an old prehistoric
Mongoloid chieftain. When I stood for the first moment
within that primæval palace of the dead, never before
entered by living man for a hundred centuries, I felt, I
must own, something like a burglar, something like a body-
snatcher, something like a resurrection man, but most of
all like a happy archæologist.

The big stone hut in which we found ourselves was, in
fact, a buried cromlech, covered all over (until we opened
it) by the earth of the barrow. Almost every cromlech,
wherever found, was once, I believe, the central chamber
of just such a long barrow : but in some instances wind
and rain have beaten down and washed away the surrounding earth (and then we call it a ' Druidical monument '), while in others the mound still encloses its
original deposit (and then we call it merely a prehistoric
tumulus). As a matter of fact, even the Druids themselves
are quite modern and common-place personages compared
with the short, squat chieftains of the long barrows. For
all the indications we found in the long barrow at Ogbury
(as in many others we had opened elsewhere) led us at

once to the strange conclusion that our new acquaintance, the skeleton, had once been a living cannibal king of the newer stone-age in Britain.

The only weapons or implements we could discover in the barrow were two neatly chipped flint arrowheads, and a very delicate ground greenstone hatchet, or tomahawk. These were the weapons of the dead chief, laid beside him in the stone chamber where we found his skeleton, for his future use in his underground existence. A piece or two of rude hand-made pottery, no doubt containing food and drink for the ghost, had also been placed close to his side : but they had mouldered away with time and damp, till it was quite impossible to recover more than a few broken and shapeless fragments. There was no trace of metal in any way : whereas if the tribesmen of our friend the skeleton had known at all the art of smelting, we may be sure some bronze axe or spearhead would have taken the place of the flint arrows and the greenstone tomahawk : for savages always bury a man's best property together with his corpse, while civilised men take care to preserve it with pious care in their own possession, and to fight over it strenuously in the court of probate.

The chief's own skeleton lay, or rather squatted, in the most undignified attitude, in the central chamber. His people when they put him there evidently considered that he was to sit at his ease, as he had been accustomed to do in his lifetime, in the ordinary savage squatting position, with his knees tucked up till they reached his chin, and his body resting entirely on the heels and haunches. The skeleton was entire : but just outside and above the stone vault we came upon a number of other bones, which told another and very different story. Some of them were the bones of the old prehistoric short-horned ox : others belonged to wild boars, red deer, and sundry similar animals, for the most part skulls and feet only, the relics of the savage funeral feast. It was clear that as soon as the builders of the barrow had erected the stone chamber of their dead chieftain, and placed within it his honoured remains, they had held a great banquet on the spot, and, after killing oxen and chasing red deer, had eaten all the eatable portions, and thrown the skulls, horns, and hoofs on top of the tomb, as offerings to the spirit of their departed master. But among these relics of the funeral baked meats there were some that specially attracted our attention—a number of broken human skulls, mingled indiscriminately with the horns of deer and the bones of oxen. It was impossible to look at them for a single moment, and not to recognise that we had here the veritable remains of a cannibal feast, a hundred centuries ago, on Ogbury hill-top.

Each skull was split or fractured, not clean cut, as with a sword or bullet, but hacked and hewn with some blunt implement, presumably either a club or a stone tomahawk. The skull of the great chief inside was entire and his skeleton unmutilated : but we could see at a glance that the remains we found huddled together on the top were those of slaves or prisoners of war, sacrificed beside the dead chieftain's tomb, and eaten with the other products of the chase by his surviving tribesmen. In an inner chamber behind the chieftain's own hut we came upon yet a stranger relic of primitive barbarism. Two complete human skeletons squatted there in the same curious attitude as their lord's, as if in attendance upon him in a neighbouring ante-chamber. They were the skeletons of women—so our professional bone-scanner immediately told us—and each of their skulls had been carefully cleft right down the middle by a single blow from a sharp stone hatchet. But they were not the victims intended for the *pièce de résistance* at the funeral banquet.   They were clearly the two wives of the deceased chieftain, killed on his tomb by his son and successor, in order to accompany their lord and master in his new life underground as they had hitherto done in his rude wooden palace on the surface of the middle earth.

We covered up the reopened sepulchre of the old cannibal savage king (after abstracting for our local museum the arrowheads and tomahawk, as well as the skull of the very ancient Briton himself), and when our archæological society, ably led by the esteemed secretary, stood two years later on the desecrated tomb, the grass had grown again as green as ever, and not a sign remained of the sacrilegious act in which one of the party then assembled there had been a prime actor.   Looking down from the summit of the long barrow on that bright summer morning, over the gay group of picnicking archæologists, it was a curious contrast to reinstate in fancy the scene at that first installation of the Ogbury monument.   In my mind's eye I saw once more the howling band of naked, yellow-faced and yellow-limbed savages surge up the terraced slopes of Ogbury Down ; I saw them bear aloft, with beating of breasts and loud gesticulations, the bent corpse of their dead chieftain ; I saw the terrified and fainting wives haled along by thongs of raw oxhide, and the weeping prisoners driven passively like sheep to the slaughter ; I saw the fearful orgy of massacre and rapine around the open tumulus, the wild priest shattering with his gleaming tomahawk the skulls of his victims, the fire of gorse and low brushwood prepared to roast them, the heads and feet flung carelessly on top of the yet uncovered stone chamber, the awful dance of blood-stained cannibals around the mangled remains of men and oxen, and finally the long task of heaping up above the stone hut of the dead king the earthen mound that was never again to be opened to the light of day till, ten thousand years later, we modern Britons invaded with our prying, sacrilegious mattock the sacred privacy of that cannibal ghost. All this passed like a vision before my mind's eye; but I didn't mention anything of it at that particular moment to my fellow-archæologists, because I saw they were all much more interested in the pigeon-pie and the funny story about an exalted personage and a distinguished actress with which the model secretary was just then duly entertaining them.

Five thousand years or so slowly wore away, from the date of the erection of the long barrow, and a new race had come to occupy the soil of England, and had driven away or reduced to slavery the short, squat, yellow-skinned cannibals of the earlier epoch. They were a pastoral and agricultural people, these new comers, acquainted with the use and abuse of bronze, and far more civilised in every way than their darker predecessors. No trace remains behind to tell us now by what fierce onslaught the Celtic invaders—for the bronze-age folk were presumably Celts—swept through the little Ogbury valley, and brained the men of the older race, while they made slaves of the younger women and serviceable children. Nothing now stands to tell us anything of the long years of Celtic domination, except the round barrow on the bare down, just as green and as grass-grown nowadays as its far earlier and more primitive neighbour.

We opened the Ogbury round barrow at the same time as the other, and found in it, as we expected, no bones or skeleton of any sort, broken or otherwise, but simply a large cinerary urn. The urn was formed of coarse hand-made earthenware, very brittle by long burial in the earth, but not by any means so old or porous as the fragments we had discovered in the long barrow. A pretty pattern ran round its edge—a pattern in the simplest and most primitive style of ornamentation ; for it consisted merely of the print of the potter's thumb-nail, firmly pressed into the moist clay before baking. Beside the urn lay a second specimen of early pottery, one of those curious perforated jars which antiquaries call by the very question-begging name of incense-cups ; and within it we discovered the most precious part of all our ' find,' a beautiful wedge-shaped bronze hatchet, and three thin gold beads. Having no consideration for the feelings of the ashes, we promptly appropriated both hatchet and beads, and took the urn and cup as a peace-offering to the lord of the manor for our desecration of a tomb (with his full consent) on the land of his fathers.

Why did these bronze-age people burn instead of burying their dead ? Why did they anticipate the latest fashionable mode of disposal of corpses, and go in for cremation with such thorough conviction ? They couldn't have been influenced by those rather unpleasant sanitary considerations which so profoundly agitated the mind of ' Graveyard Walker.' Sanitation was still in a very rudimentary state in the year five thousand B.C.; and the ingenious Celt, who is still given to ' waking ' his neighbours, when they die of small-pox, with a sublime indifference to the chances of infection, must have had some other and more powerful reason for adopting the comparatively unnatural system of cremation in preference to that of simple burial. The change, I believe, was due to a further development of religious ideas on the part of the Celtic tribesmen above that of the primitive stone-age cannibals.

When men began to bury their dead, they did so in the firm belief in another life, which life was regarded as the exact counterpart of this present one. The unsophisticated savage, holding that in that equal sky his faithful dog would bear him company, naturally enough had the dog in question killed and buried with him, in order that it might follow him to the happy hunting-grounds. Clearly, you can't hunt without your arrows and your tomahawk; so the flint weapons and the trusty bow accompanied their owner in his new dwelling-place. The wooden haft, the deer-sinew bow-string, the perishable articles of food and drink have long since decayed within the damp tumulus: but the harder stone and earthenware articles have survived till now, to tell the story of that crude and simple early faith. Very crude and illogical indeed it was, however, for it is quite clear that the actual body of the dead man was thought of as persisting to live a sort of underground life within the barrow. A stone hut was constructed for its use; real weapons and implements were left by its side; and slaves and wives were ruthlessly massacred, as still in Ashantee, in order that their bodies might accompany the corpse of the buried master in his subterranean dwelling. In all this we have clear evidence of a very inconsistent, savage, materialistic belief, not indeed in the immortality of the soul, but in the continued underground life of the dead body.

With the progress of time, however, men's ideas upon these subjects began to grow more definite and more consistent. Instead of the corpse, we get the ghost; instead of the material underground world, we get the idealised and sublimated conception of a shadowy Hades, a world of shades, a realm of incorporeal, disembodied spirits. With the growth of the idea in this ghostly nether world, there arises naturally the habit of burning the dead in order fully to free the liberated spirit from the earthly chains that clog and bind it. It is, indeed, a very noticeable fact that wherever this belief in a world of shades is implicitly accepted, there cremation follows as a matter of course;

while wherever (among savage or barbaric races) burial is practised, there a more materialistic creed of bodily survival necessarily accompanies it. To carry out this theory to its full extent, not only must the body itself be burnt, but also all its belongings with it. Ghosts are clothed in ghostly clothing; and the question has often been asked of modern spiritualists by materialistic scoffers, ' Where do the ghosts get their coats and dresses ? ' The true believer in cremation and the shadowy world has no difficulty at all in answering that crucial inquiry; he would say at once, ' They are the ghosts of the clothes that were burnt with the body.' In the gossiping story of Periander, as veraciously retailed for us by that dear old grandmotherly scandalmonger, Herodotus, the shade of Melissa refuses to communicate with her late husband, by medium or otherwise, on the ground that she found herself naked and shivering with cold, because the garments buried with her had not been burnt, and therefore were of no use to her in the world of shades. So Periander, to put a stop to this sad state of spiritual destitution, requisitioned all the best dresses of the Corinthian ladies, burnt them bodily in a great trench, and received an immediate answer from the gratified shade, who was thenceforth enabled to walk about in the principal promenades of Hades among the best-dressed ghosts of that populous quarter.

The belief which thus survived among the civilised Greeks of the age of the Despots is shared still by Fijis and Karens, and was derived by all in common from early ancestors of like faith with the founders of Ogbury round barrow. The weapons were broken and the clothes burnt, to liberate their ghosts into the world of spirits, just as now, in Fiji, knives and axes have their spiritual counterparts, which can only be released when the material shape is destroyed or purified by the action of fire. Everything, in such a state, is supposed to possess a soul of its own; and the fire is the chosen mode for setting the soul free from all clogging earthly impurities. So till yesterday, in the rite of suttee, the Hindoo widow immolated herself upon her husband's pyre, in order that her spirit might follow him unhampered to the world of ghosts whither he was bound. Thus the twin barrows on Ogbury hillside bridge over for us two vast epochs of human culture, both now so remote as to merge together mentally to the casual eyes of modern observers, but yet in reality marking in their very shape and disposition an immense, long, and slow advance of human reason. For just as the long barrow answers in form to the buried human corpse and the chambered hut that surrounds and encloses it, so does the round barrow answer in form to the urn containing the calcined ashes of the cremated barbarian. And is it not a suggestive fact that when we turn to the little graveyard by the church below we find the Christian belief in the resurrection of the body, as opposed to the pagan belief in the immortality of the soul, once more bringing us back to the small oblong mound which is after all but the dwarfed and humbler modern representative of the long barrow? So deep is the connection between that familiar shape and the practice of inhumation that the dwarf long barrow seems everywhere to have come into use again throughout all Europe, after whole centuries of continued cremation, as the natural concomitant and necessary mark of Christian burial.

This is what I would have said, if I had been asked, at Ogbury Barrows. But I wasn't asked; so I devoted myself instead to psychological research, and said nothing.

FISH OUT OF WATER

STROLLING one day in what is euphemistically termed, in equatorial latitudes, ' the cool of the evening,' along a tangled tropical American field-path, through a low region of lagoons and watercourses, my attention happened to be momentarily attracted from the monotonous pursuit of the nimble mosquito by a small animal scuttling along irregularly before me, as if in a great hurry to get out of my way before I could turn him into an excellent specimen. At first sight I took the little hopper, in the grey dusk, for one of the common, small green lizards, and wasn't much disposed to pay it any distinguished share either of personal or scientific attention. But as I walked on a little further through the dense underbrush, more and more of these shuffling and scurrying little creatures kept crossing the path, hastily, all in one direction, and all, as it were, in a formed body or marching phalanx. Looking closer, to my great surprise, I found they were actually fish out of water, going on a walking tour, for change of air, to a new residence—genuine fish, a couple of inches long each, not eel-shaped or serpentine in outline, but closely resembling a red mullet in miniature, though much more beautifully and delicately coloured, and with fins and tails of the most orthodox spiny and prickly description. They were travelling across country in a bee-line, thousands of them together,

not at all like the helpless fish out of water of popular
imagination, but as unconcernedly and naturally as if they
had been accustomed to the overland route for their whole
lifetimes, and were walking now on the king's highway
without let or hindrance.

I took one up in my hand and examined it more carefully; though the catching it wasn't by any means so easy
as it sounds on paper, for these perambulatory fish are
thoroughly inured to the dangers and difficulties of dry
land, and can get out of your way when you try to capture
them with a rapidity and dexterity which are truly surprising. The little creatures are very pretty, well-formed
catfish, with bright, intelligent eyes, and a body armed all
over, like the armadillo's, with a continuous coat of hard
and horny mail. This coat is not formed of scales, as in
most fish, but of toughened skin, as in crocodiles and
alligators, arranged in two overlapping rows of imbricated
shields, exactly like the round tiles so common on the
roofs of Italian cottages. The fish walks, or rather
shambles along ungracefully, by the shuffling movement
of a pair of stiff spines placed close behind his head, aided
by the steering action of his tail, and a constant snake-like
wriggling motion of his entire body. Leg spines of somewhat the same sort are found in the common English
gurnard, and in this age of Aquariums and Fisheries
Exhibitions, most adult persons above the age of twenty-
one years must have observed the gurnards themselves
crawling along suspiciously by their aid at the bottom of a
tank at the Crystal Palace or the polyonymous South
Kensington building. But while the European gurnard
only uses his substitutes for legs on the bed of the ocean,
my itinerant tropical acquaintance (his name, I regret to
say, is Callichthys) uses them boldly for terrestrial loco-
motion across the dry lowlands of his native country.

And while the gurnard has no less than six of these pro-legs, the American land fish has only a single pair with which to accomplish his arduous journeys. If this be considered as a point of inferiority in the armour-plated American species, we must remember that while beetles and grasshoppers have as many as six legs apiece, man, the head and crown of things, is content to scramble through life ungracefully with no more than two.

There are a great many tropical American pond-fish which share these adventurous gipsy habits of the pretty little Callichthys. Though they belong to two distinct groups, otherwise unconnected, the circumstances of the country they inhabit have induced in both families this queer fashion of waddling out courageously on dry land, and going on voyages of exploration in search of fresh ponds and shallows new, somewhere in the neighbourhood of their late residence. One kind in particular, the Brazilian Doras, takes land journeys of such surprising length, that he often spends several nights on the way, and the Indians who meet the wandering bands during their migrations fill several baskets full of the prey thus dropped upon them, as it were, from the kindly clouds.

Both Doras and Callichthys, too, are well provided with means of defence against the enemies they may chance to meet during their terrestrial excursions ; for in both kinds there are the same bony shields along the sides, securing the little travellers, as far as possible, from attack on the part of hungry piscivorous animals. Doras further utilises its powers of living out of water by going ashore to fetch dry leaves, with which it builds itself a regular nest, like a bird's, at the beginning of the rainy season. In this nest the affectionate parents carefully cover up their eggs, the hope of the race, and watch over them with the utmost attention. Many other fish build nests in the water, of materials naturally found at the bottom ; but Doras, I believe, is the only one that builds them on the beach, of materials sought for on the dry land.

Such amphibious habits on the part of certain tropical fish are easy enough to explain by the fashionable clue of ' adaptation to environment.' Ponds are always very likely to dry up, and so the animals that frequent ponds are usually capable of bearing a very long deprivation of water. Indeed, our evolutionists generally hold that land animals have in every case sprung from pond animals which have gradually adapted themselves to do without water altogether. Life, according to this theory, began in the ocean, spread up the estuaries into the greater rivers, thence extended to the brooks and lakes, and finally migrated to the ponds, puddles, swamps and marshes, whence it took at last, by tentative degrees, to the solid shore, the plains, and the mountains. Certainly the tenacity of life shown by pond animals is very remarkable. Our own English carp bury themselves deeply in the mud in winter, and there remain in a dormant condition many months entirely without food. During this long hibernating period, they can be preserved alive for a considerable time out of water, especially if their gills are, from time to time, slightly moistened. They may then be sent to any address by parcels post, packed in wet moss, without serious damage to their constitution ; though, according to Dr. Günther, these dissipated products of civilisation prefer to have a piece of bread steeped in brandy put intc their mouths to sustain them beforehand. In Holland, where the carp are not so sophisticated, they are often kept the whole winter through, hung up in a net to keep them from freezing. At first they require to be slightly wetted from time to time, just to acclimatise them gradually to so dry an existence ; but after a while they adapt

x

themselves cheerfully to their altered circumstances, and feed on an occasional frugal meal of bread and milk with Christian resignation.

Of all land-frequenting fish, however, by far the most famous is the so-called climbing perch of India, which not only walks bodily out of the water, but even climbs trees by means of special spines, near the head and tail, so arranged as to stick into the bark and enable it to wriggle its way up awkwardly, something after the same fashion as the 'looping' of caterpillars. The tree-climber is a small scaly fish, seldom more than seven inches long; but it has developed a special breathing apparatus to enable it to keep up the stock of oxygen on its terrestrial excursions, which may be regarded as to some extent the exact converse of the means employed by divers to supply themselves with air under water. Just above the gills, which form of course its natural hereditary breathing apparatus, the climbing perch has invented a new and wholly original water chamber, containing within it a frilled bony organ, which enables it to extract oxygen from the stored-up water during the course of its aerial peregrinations. While on shore it picks up small insects, worms, and grubs; but it also has vegetarian tastes of its own, and does not despise fruits and berries. The Indian jugglers tame the climbing perches and carry them about with them as part of their stock in trade; their ability to live for a long time out of water makes them useful confederates in many small tricks which seem very wonderful to people accustomed to believe that fish die almost at once when taken out of their native element.

The Indian snakehead is a closely allied species, common in the shallow ponds and fresh-water tanks of India, where holy Brahmans bathe and drink and die and are buried, and most of which dry up entirely during the dry season. The snakehead, therefore, has similarly accommodated himself to this annual peculiarity in his local habitation by acquiring a special chamber for retaining water to moisten his gills throughout his long deprivation of that prime necessary. He lives composedly in semifluid mud, or lies torpid in the hard baked clay at the bottom of the dry tank from which all the water has utterly evaporated in the drought of summer. As long as the mud remains soft enough to allow the fish to rise slowly through it, they come to the surface every now and then to take in a good hearty gulp of air, exactly as gold fish do in England when confined with thoughtless or ignorant cruelty in a glass globe too small to provide sufficient oxygen for their respiration. But when the mud hardens entirely they hibernate or rather æstivate, in a dormant condition, until the bursting of the monsoon fills the ponds once more with the welcome water. Even in the perfectly dry state, however, they probably manage to get a little air every now and again through the numerous chinks and fissures in the sun-baked mud. Our Aryan brother then goes a-fishing playfully with a spade and bucket, and digs the snakehead in this mean fashion out of his comfortable lair, with an ultimate view to the manufacture of pillau. In Burmah, indeed, while the mud is still soft, the ingenious Burmese catch the helpless creatures by a still meaner and more unsportsmanlike device. They spread a large cloth over the slimy ooze where the snakeheads lie buried, and so cut off entirely for the moment their supply of oxygen. The poor fish, half-asphyxiated by this unkind treatment, come up gasping to the surface under the cloth in search of fresh air, and are then easily caught with the hand and tossed into baskets by the degenerate Buddhists.

Old Anglo-Indians even say that some of these mud

haunting Oriental fish will survive for many years in a state of suspended animation, and that when ponds or jhíls which are known to have been dry for several successive seasons are suddenly filled by heavy rains, they are found to be swarming at once with full-grown snakeheads released in a moment from what I may venture to call their living tomb in the hardened bottom. Whether such statements are absolutely true or not the present deponent would be loth to decide dogmatically; but, if we were implicitly to swallow everything that the old Anglo-Indian in his simplicity assures us he has seen—well, the clergy would have no further cause any longer to deplore the growing scepticism and unbelief of these latter unfaithful ages.

This habit of lying in the mud and there becoming torpid may be looked upon as a natural alternative to the habit of migrating across country, when your pond dries up, in search of larger and more permanent sheets of water. Some fish solve the problem how to get through the dry season in one of these two alternative fashions and some in the other. In flat countries where small ponds and tanks alone exist, the burying plan is almost universal; in plains traversed by large rivers or containing considerable scattered lakes, the migratory system finds greater favour with the piscine population.

One tropical species which adopts the tactics of hiding itself in the hard clay, the African mud-fish, is specially interesting to us human beings on two accounts—first, because, unlike almost all other kinds of fish, it possesses lungs as well as gills; and, secondly, because it forms an intermediate link between the true fish and the frogs or amphibians, and therefore stands in all probability in the direct line of human descent, being the living representative of one among our own remote and early ancestors.

Scientific interest and filial piety ought alike to secure our attention for the African mud-fish. It lives its amphibious life among the rice-fields on the Nile, the Zambesi, and the Gambia, and is so greatly given to a terrestrial existence that its swim-bladder has become porous and cellular, so as to be modified into a pair of true and serviceable lungs. In fact, the lungs themselves in all the higher animals are merely the swim-bladders of fish, slightly altered so as to perform a new but closely allied office. The mud-fish is common enough in all the larger English aquariums, owing to a convenient habit in which it indulges, and which permits it to be readily conveyed to all parts of the globe on the same principle as the vans for furniture. When the dry season comes on and the rice-fields are reduced to banks of baking mud, the mud-fish retire to the bottom of their pools, where they form for themselves a sort of cocoon of hardened clay, lined with mucus, and with a hole at each end to admit the air ; and in this snug retreat they remain torpid till the return of wet weather. As the fish usually reach a length of three or four feet, the cocoons are of course by no means easy to transport entire. Nevertheless the natives manage to dig them up whole, fish and all ; and if the capsules are not broken, the unconscious inmates can be sent across by steamer to Europe with perfect safety. Their astonishment when they finally wake up after their long slumber, and find themselves inspecting the British public, as introduced to them by Mr. Farini, through a sheet of plate-glass, must be profound and interesting.

In England itself, on the other hand, we have at least one kind of fish which exemplifies the opposite or migratory solution of the dry pond problem, and that is our familiar friend the common eel. The ways of eels are indeed mysterious, for nobody has ever yet succeeded in discovering where, when, or how they manage to spawn ; nobody has ever yet seen an eel's egg, or caught a female eel in the spawning condition, or even observed a really adult male or female specimen of perfect development. All the eels ever found in fresh water are immature and undeveloped creatures. But eels do certainly spawn somewhere or other in the deep sea, and every year, in the course of the summer, flocks of young ones, known as elvers, ascend the rivers in enormous quantities, like a vast army under numberless leaders. At each tributary or affluent, be it river, brook, stream, or ditch, a proportionate detachment of the main body is given off to explore the various branches, while the central force wriggles its way up the chief channel, regardless of obstacles, with undiminished vigour. When the young elvers come to a weir, a wall, a floodgate, or a lasher, they simply squirm their way up the perpendicular barrier with indescribable wrigglings, as if they were wholly unacquainted, physically as well as mentally, with Newton's magnificent discovery of gravitation. Nothing stops them ; they go wherever water is to be found ; and though millions perish hopelessly in the attempt, millions more survive in the end to attain their goal in the upper reaches. They even seem to scent ponds or lakes mysteriously, at a distance, and will strike boldly straight across country, to sheets of water wholly cut off from communication with the river which forms their chief highway.

The full-grown eels are also given to journeying across country in a more sober, sedate, and dignified manner, as becomes fish which have fully arrived at years, or rather months, of discretion. When the ponds in which they live dry up in summer, they make in a bee-line for the nearest sheet of fresh water, whose direction and distance they appear to know intuitively, through some strange instinctive geographical faculty. On their way across country, they do not despise the succulent rat, whom they swallow whole when caught with great gusto. To keep their gills wet during these excursions, eels have the power of distending the skin on each side of the neck, just below the head, so as to form a big pouch or swelling. This pouch they fill with water, to carry a good supply along with them, until they reach the ponds for which they are making. It is the pouch alone that enables eels to live so long out of water under all circumstances, and so incidentally exposes them to the disagreeable experience of getting skinned alive, which it is to be feared still forms the fate of most of those that fall into the clutches of the human species.

A far more singular walking fish than any of these is the odd creature that rejoices (unfortunately) in the very classical surname of Periophthalmus, which is, being interpreted, Stare-about. (If he had a recognised English name of his own, I would gladly give it ; but as he hasn't, and as it is clearly necessary to call him something, I fear we must stick to the somewhat alarming scientific nomenclature.) Periophthalmus, then, is an odd fish of the tropical Pacific shores, with a pair of very distinct forelegs (theoretically described as modified pectoral fins), and with two goggle eyes, which he can protrude at pleasure right outside the sockets, so as to look in whatever direction he chooses, without even taking the trouble to turn his head to left or right, backward or forward. At ebb tide this singular peripatetic goby literally walks straight out of the water, and promenades the bare beach erect on two legs, in search of small crabs and other stray marine animals left behind by the receding waters. If you try to catch him, he hops away briskly much like a frog, and stares back at you grimly over his left shoulder, with his squinting optics. So completely adapted is he for this amphibious long-shore existence, that his big eyes, unlike those of most other fish, are formed for seeing in the air as well as in the water. Nothing can be more ludicrous than to watch him suddenly thrusting these very movable orbs right out of their sockets like a pair of telescopes, and twisting them round in all directions so as to see in front, behind, on top, and below, in one delightful circular sweep.

There is also a certain curious tropical American carp which, though it hardly deserves to be considered in the strictest sense as a fish out of water, yet manages to fall nearly half-way under that peculiar category, for it always swims with its head partly above the surface and partly below. But the funniest thing in this queer arrangement is the fact that one half of each eye is out in the air and the other half is beneath in the water. Accordingly, the eye is divided horizontally by a dark strip into two distinct and unlike portions, the upper one of which has a pupil adapted to vision in the air alone, while the lower is adapted to seeing in the water only. The fish, in fact, always swims with its eye half out of the water, and it can see as well on dry land as in its native ocean. Its name is Anableps, but in all probability it does not wish the fact to be generally known.

The flying fish are fish out of water in a somewhat different and more transitory sense. Their aerial excursions are brief and rapid; they can only fly a very little way, and have soon to take once more for safety to their own more natural and permanent element. More than forty kinds of the family are known, in appearance very much like English herrings, but with the front fins expanded and modified into veritable wings. It is fashionable nowadays among naturalists to assert that the flying fish don't fly; that they merely jump horizontally out of the water with a powerful impulse, and fall again as soon as the force of the first impetus is entirely spent. When men endeavour to persuade you to such folly, believe them not. For my own part, I have *seen* the flying fish fly— deliberately fly, and flutter, and rise again, and change the direction of their flight in mid-air, exactly after the fashion of a big dragonfly. If the other people who have watched them haven't succeeded in seeing them fly, that is their own fault, or at least their own misfortune ; perhaps their eyes weren't quick enough to catch the rapid, though to me perfectly recognisable, hovering and fluttering of the gauze-like wings ; but I have seen them myself, and I maintain that on such a question one piece of positive evidence is a great deal better than a hundred negative. The testimony of all the witnesses who didn't see the murder committed is as nothing compared with the single testimony of the one man who really did see it. And in this case I have met with many other quick observers who fully agreed with me, against the weight of scientific opinion, that they have seen the flying fish really fly with their own eyes, and no mistake about it. The German professors, indeed, all think otherwise ; but then the German professors all wear green spectacles, which are the outward and visible sign of ' blinded eyesight poring over miserable books.' The unsophisti-cated vision of the noble British seaman is unanimously with me on the matter of the reality of the fishes' flight.

Another group of very interesting fish out of water are the flying gurnards, common enough in the Mediterranean and the tropical Atlantic. They are much heavier and bigger creatures than the true flying fish of the herring type, being often a foot and a half long, and their wings are much larger in proportion, though not, I think, really so powerful as those of their pretty little silvery rivals. All the flying fish fly only of necessity, not from choice. They leave the water when pursued by their enemies, or when frightened by the rapid approach of a big steamer. So swiftly do they fly, however, that they can far outstrip a ship going at the rate of ten knots an hour ; and I have often watched one keep ahead of a great Pacific liner under full steam for many minutes together in quick successive flights of three or four hundred feet each. Oddly enough, they can fly further against the wind than before it—a fact acknowledged even by the spectacled Germans themselves, and very hard indeed to reconcile with the orthodox belief that they are not flying at all, but only jumping. I don't know whether the flying gurnards are good eating or not ; but the silvery flying fish are caught for market (sad desecration of the poetry of nature !) in the Windward Islands, and when nicely fried in egg and bread-crumb are really quite as good for practical purposes as smelts or whiting or any other prosaic European substitute.

On the whole, it will be clear, I think, to the impartial reader from this rapid survey that the helplessness and awkwardness of a fish out of water has been much exaggerated by the thoughtless generalisation of unscientific humanity. Granting, for argument's sake, that most fish prefer the water, as a matter of abstract predilection, to the dry land, it must be admitted *per contra* that many fish cut a much better figure on terra firma than most of their critics themselves would cut in mid-ocean. There are fish that wriggle across country intrepidly with the dexterity and agility of the most accomplished snakes ; there are fish that walk about on open sand-banks, semi-erect on two legs, as easily as lizards ; there are fish that hop and skip on tail and fins in a manner that the celebrated jumping frog himself might have observed with envy ; and there are fish that fly through the air of heaven with a grace and swiftness that would put to shame innumerable species among their feathered competitors. Nay, there are even fish, like some kinds of eels and the African mud-fish, that scarcely live in the water at all, but merely frequent wet and marshy places, where they lie snugly in the soft ooze and damp earth that line the bottom. If I have only succeeded, therefore, in relieving the mind of one sensitive and retiring fish from the absurd obloquy cast upon its appearance when it ventures away for awhile from its proper element, then, in the pathetic and prophetic words borrowed from a thousand uncut prefaces, this work will not, I trust, have been written in vain.

THE FIRST POTTER

COLLECTIVE humanity owes a great debt of gratitude to the
first potter. Before his days the art of boiling, though in
one sense very simple and primitive indeed, was in another
sense very complex, cumbersome, and lengthy. The unsophisticated savage, having duly speared and killed his
antelope, proceeded to light a roaring fire, with flint or
drill, by the side of some convenient lake or river in his
tropical jungle. Then he dug a big hole in the soft mud
close to the water's edge, and let the water (rather muddy)
percolate into it, or sometimes even he plastered over its
bottom with puddled clay. After that, he heated some
smooth round stones red hot in the fire close by, and
drawing them out gingerly between two pieces of stick,
dropped them one by one, spluttering and fizzing, into his
improvised basin or kettle. This, of course, made the
water in the hole boil; and the unsophisticated savage
thereupon thrust into it his joint of antelope, repeating the
process over and over again until the sodden meat was
completely seethed to taste on the outside. If one application was not sufficient, he gnawed off the cooked meat from
the surface with his stout teeth, innocent as yet of the
dentist's art, and plunged the underdone core back again,
till it exactly suited his not over-delicate or dainty fancy.

To be sure, the primitive savage, unversed as he was in
pastes and glazes, in moulds and ornaments, did not pass

his life entirely devoid of cups and platters. Coconut shell and calabash rind, horn of ox and skull of enemy, bamboo-joint and capacious rhomb-shell, all alike, no doubt, supplied him with congenial implements for drink or storage. Like Eve in the Miltonic Paradise, there lacked him not fit vessels pure ; picking some luscious tropical fruit, the savoury pulp he chewed, and in the rind still as he thirsted scooped the brimming stream. This was satisfactory as far as it went, of course, but it was not pottery. He couldn't boil his joint for dinner in coconut or skull; he had to do it with stone pot-boilers, in a rude kettle of puddled clay.

But at last one day, that inspired barbarian, the first potter, hit by accident upon his grand discovery. He had carried some water in a big calabash—the hard shell of a tropical fruit whose pulpy centre can be easily scooped out —and a happy thought suddenly struck him : why not put the calabash to boil upon the fire with a little clay smeared outside it ? The savage is conservative, but he loves to save trouble. He tried the experiment, and it succeeded admirably. The water boiled, and the calabash was not burnt or broken. Our nameless philosopher took the primitive vessel off the fire with a forked branch and looked at it critically with the delighted eyes of a first inventor. A wonderful change had suddenly come over it. He had blundered accidentally upon the art of pottery. For what is this that has happened to the clay ? It went in soft, brown, and muddy ; it has come out hard, red, and stone-like. The first potter ruminated and wondered. He didn't fully realise, no doubt, what he had actually done; but he knew he had invented a means by which you could put a calabash upon a fire and keep it there without burning or bursting. That, after all, was at least something.

All this, you say (which, in effect, is Dr. Tylor's view),

is purely hypothetical.   In one sense, yes ; but not in
another.   We know that most savage races still use natural
vessels, made of coconuts, gourds, or calabashes, for everyday purposes of carrying water ; and we also know that all
the simplest and earliest pottery is moulded on the shape of
just such natural jars and bottles.   The fact and the theory
based on it are no novelties.   Early in the sixteenth century,
indeed, the Sieur Gonneville, skipper of Honfleur, sailing
round the Cape of Good Hope, made his way right across
the Southern Ocean to some vague point of South America
where he found the people still just in the intermediate
stage between the use of natural vessels and the invention
of pottery.   For these amiable savages (name and habitat
unknown) had wooden pots ' plastered with a kind of clay
a good finger thick, which prevents the fire from burning
them.'   Here we catch industrial evolution in the very act,
and the potter's art in its first infancy, fossilised and
crystallised, as it were, in an embryo condition, and fixed
for us immovably by the unprogressive conservatism of a
savage tribe.   It was this curious early observation of evolving keramic art that made Goguet—an anthropologist born
out of due season—first hit upon that luminous theory of
the origin of pottery now all but universally accepted.

Plenty of evidence to the same effect is now forthcom-
ing for the modern inquirer.   Among the ancient monuments of the Mississippi valley, Squier and Davis found
the kilns in which the primitive pottery had been baked ;
and among their relics were partially burnt pots retaining
in part the rinds of the gourds or calabashes on which they
had been actually modelled.   Along the Gulf of Mexico
gourds were also used to give shape to the pot ; and all
over the world, even to this day, the gourd form is a very
common one for pottery of all sorts, thus pointing back,
dimly and curiously, to the original mode in which fictile

ware generally came to be invented. In Fiji and in many parts of Africa vessels modelled upon natural forms are still universal. Of course all such pots as these are purely hand-made; the invention of the potter's wheel, now so indissolubly associated in all our minds with the production of earthenware, belongs to an infinitely later and almost modern period.

And that consideration naturally suggests the fundamental question, When did the first potter live? The world (as Sir Henry Taylor has oracularly told us) knows nothing of its greatest men; and the very name of the father of all potters has been utterly forgotten in the lapse of ages. Indeed, paradoxical as it may sound to say so, one may reasonably doubt whether there was ever actually any one single man on whom one could definitely lay one's finger, and say with confidence, Here we have the first potter. Pottery, no doubt, like most other things, grew by imperceptible degrees from wholly vague and rudimentary beginnings. Just as there were steam-engines before Watt, and locomotives before Stephenson, so there were pots before the first potter. Many men must have discovered separately, by half-unconscious trials, that a coat of mud rudely plastered over the bottom of a calabash prevented it from catching fire and spilling its contents; other men slowly learned to plaster the mud higher and ever higher up the sides; and yet others gradually introduced and patented new improvements for wholly encasing the entire cup in an inch thickness of carefully kneaded clay. Bit by bit the invention grew, like all great inventions, without any inventor. Thus the question of the date of the first potter practically resolves itself into the simpler question of the date of the earliest known pottery.

Did palæolithic man, that antique naked crouching savage who hunted the mammoth, the reindeer, and the cave-bear among the frozen fields of interglacial Gaul and Britain—did palæolithic man himself, in his rude rock-shelters, possess a knowledge of the art of pottery ? That is a question which has been much debated amongst archæologists, and which cannot even now be considered as finally settled before the tribunal of science. He must have drunk out of something or other, but whether he drank out of earthenware cups is still uncertain. It is pretty clear that the earliest drinking vessels used in Europe were neither bowls of earthenware nor shells of fruits, for the cold climate of interglacial times did not permit the growth in northern latitudes of such large natural vessels as gourds, calabashes, bamboos, or coco-nuts. In all probability the horns of the aurochs and the wild cattle, and the capacious skull of the fellow-man whose bones he had just picked at his ease for his cannibal supper, formed the aboriginal goblets and basins of the old black European savage. A curious verbal relic of the use of horns as drinking-cups survives indeed down to almost modern times in the Greek word *keramic*, still commonly applied to the art of pottery, and derived, of course, from *keras*, a horn ; while as to skulls, not only were they frequently used as drinking-cups by our Scandinavian ancestors. but there still exists a very singular intermediate American vessel in which the clay has actually been moulded on a human skull as model, just as other vessels have been moulded on calabashes or other suitable vegetable shapes.

Still, the balance of evidence certainly seems to show that a little very rude and almost shapeless hand-made pottery has really been discovered amongst the buried caves where palæolithic men made for ages their chief dwelling-places. Fragments of earthenware occurred in the Hohefels cave near Ulm, in company with the bones of reindeer, cave-bears, and mammoths, whose joints had doubtless been duly boiled, a hundred thousand years ago, by the intelligent producer of those identical sun-dried fleshpots ; and M. Joly, of Toulouse, has in his possession portions of an irregularly circular, flat-bottomed vessel, from the cave of Nabrigas, on which the finger-marks of the hand that moulded the clay are still clearly distinguishable on the baked earthenware. That is the great merit of pottery, viewed as an historical document; it retains its shape and peculiarities unaltered through countless centuries, for the future edification of unborn antiquaries. *Litera scripta manet*, and so does baked pottery. The hand itself that formed that rude bowl has long since mouldered away, flesh and bone alike, into the soil around it ; but the print of its fingers, indelibly fixed by fire into the hardened clay, remains for us still to tell the story of that early triumph of nascent keramics.

The relics of palæolithic pottery are, however, so very fragmentary, and the circumstances under which they have been discovered so extremely doubtful, that many cautious and sceptical antiquarians will even now have nothing to say to the suspected impostors. Among the remains of the newer Stone Age, on the other hand, comparatively abundant keramic specimens have been unearthed, without doubt or cavil, from the long barrows— the burial-places of the early Mongoloid race, now represented by the Finns and Lapps, which occupied the whole of Western Europe before the advent of the Aryan vanguard. One of the best bits is a curious wide-mouthed, semi-globular bowl from Norton Bavant, in Wiltshire, whose singular shape suggests almost immediately the idea that it must at least have been based, if not actually modelled, upon a human skull. Its rim is rough and quite irregular, and there is no trace of ornamentation of any sort ; a fact quite in accordance with all the other facts we

Y

know about the men of the newer Stone Age, who were
far less artistic and æsthetic in every way than their ruder
predecessors of the interglacial epoch.

Ornamentation, when it does begin to appear, arises at
first in a strictly practical and unintentional manner.
Later examples elsewhere show us by analogy how it first
came into existence.   The Indians of the Ohio seem to
have modelled their pottery in bags or nettings made of
coarse thread or twisted bark.   Those of the Mississippi
moulded them in baskets of willow or splints.   When the
moist clay thus shaped and marked by the indentations of
the mould was baked in the kiln, it of course retained the
pretty dappling it received from the interlaced and woven
thrums, which were burnt off in the process of firing.
Thus a rude sort of natural diaper ornament was set up,
to which the eye soon became accustomed, and which it
learned to regard as necessary for beauty.   Hence, wherever
newer and more improved methods of modelling came into
use, there would arise an instinctive tendency on the part
of the early potter to imitate the familiar marking by artificial means.   Dr. Klemm long ago pointed out that the
oldest German fictile vases have an ornamentation in which
plaiting is imitated by incised lines.   ' What was no longer
wanted as a necessity,' he says, ' was kept up as an ornament alone.'

Another very simple form of ornamentation, reappearing
everywhere all the world over on primitive bowls and vases,
is the rope pattern, a line or string-course over the whole
surface or near the mouth of the vessel.   Many of the
indented patterns on early British pottery have been produced, as Sir Daniel Wilson has pointed out, by the close
impress of twisted cord on the wet clay.   Sometimes these
cords seem to have been originally left on the clay in the
process of baking, and used as a mould; at other times

they may have been employed afterwards as handles, as is still done in the case of some South African pots : and, when the rope handle wore off, the pattern made by its indentation on the plastic material before sun-baking would still remain as pure ornament. Probably the very common idea of string-course ornamentation just below the mouth or top of vases and bowls has its origin in this early and almost universal practice.

When other conscious and intentional ornamentation began to supersede these rude natural and undesigned patterns, they were at first mere rough attempts on the part of the early potter to imitate, with the simple means at his disposal, the characteristic marks of the ropes or wickerwork by which the older vessels were necessarily surrounded. He had gradually learned, as Mr. Tylor well puts it, that clay alone or with some mixture of sand is capable of being used without any extraneous support for the manufacture of drinking and cooking vessels. He therefore began to model rudely thin globular bowls with his own hands, dispensing with the aid of thongs or basketwork. But he still naturally continued to imitate the original shapes—the gourd, the calabash, the plaited net, the round basket ; and his eye required the familiar decoration which naturally resulted from the use of some one or other among these primitive methods. So he tried his hand at deliberate ornament in his own simple un-tutored fashion.

It was quite literally his hand, indeed, that he tried at first ; for the earliest decoration upon palæolithic pottery is made by pressing the fingers into the clay so as to pro-duce a couple of deep parallel furrows, which is the sole attempt at ornament on M. Joly's Nabrigas specimen ; while the urns and drinking-cups taken from our English long barrows are adorned with really pretty and effective

Y 2

patterns, produced by pressing the tip of the finger and the nail into the plastic material. It is wonderful what capital and varied results you can get with no more recondite graver than the human finger-nail, sometimes turned front downward, sometimes back downward, and sometimes used to egg up the moist clay into small jagged and relieved designs. Most of these patterns are more or less plaitlike in arrangement, evidently suggested to the mind of the potter by the primitive marks of the old basketwork. But, as time went on, the early artist learned to press into his service new implements, pieces of wood, bone scrapers, and the flint knife itself, with which he incised more regular patterns, straight or zigzag lines, rows of dots, squares and triangles, concentric circles, and even the mystic cross and swastika, the sacred symbols of yet unborn and undreamt-of religions. As yet, there was no direct imitation of plant or animal forms ; once only, on a single specimen from a Swiss lake dwelling, are the stem and veins of a leaf dimly figured on the handiwork of the European prehistoric potter. Ornament in its pure form, as pattern merely, had begun to exist ; imitative work as such was yet unknown, or almost unknown, to the eastern hemisphere.

In America, it was quite otherwise. The forgotten people who built the mounds of Ohio and the great tumuli of the Mississippi valley decorated their pottery not only with animal figures, such as snakes, fish, frogs, and turtles, but also with human heads and faces, many of them evidently modelled from the life, and some of them quite unmistakably genuine portraits. On one such vase, found in Arkansas, and figured by the Marquis de Nadaillac in his excellent work on Prehistoric America, the ornamentation consists (in true Red Indian taste) of skeleton hands, interspersed with crossbones; and the delicacy and anatomical correctness of the detail inevitably suggest the idea that the unknown artist must have worked with the actual hand of his slaughtered enemy lying for a model on the table before him. Much of the early American pottery is also coloured as well as figured, and that with considerable real taste ; the pigments were applied, however, after the baking, and so possess little stability or permanence of character. But pots and vases of these advanced styles have got so far ahead of the first potter that we have really little or no business with them in this paper.

Prehistoric European pottery has never a spout, but it often indulges in some simple form of ear or handle. The very ancient British bowl from Bavant Long Barrow —produced by that old squat Finnlike race which preceded the ' Ancient Britons ' of our old-fashioned school-books— has two ear-shaped handles projecting just below the rim, exactly as in the modern form of vessel known as a crock, and still familiarly used for household purposes. This long survival of a common domestic shape from the most remote prehistoric antiquity to our own time is very significant and very interesting. Many of the old British pots have also a hole or two holes pierced through them, near the top, evidently for the purpose of putting in a string or rope by way of a handle. With the round barrows, which belong to the Bronze Age, and contain the remains of a later and more civilised Celtic population, we get far more advanced forms of pottery. Burial here is preceded by cremation, and the ashes are enclosed in urns, many of which are very beautiful in form and exquisitely decorated. Cremation, as Professor Rolleston used feelingly to plead, is bad for the comparative anatomist and ethnographer, but it is passing well for the collector of pottery. Where burning exists as a common practice, there urns are frequent, and pottery an art in great request. Drinking-cups and perforated incense burners accompany the dead in the round barrows; but the use of the potter's wheel is still unknown, and all the urns and vases belonging to this age are still hand-moulded.

It is a curious reflection, however, that in spite of all the later improvements in the fictile art—in spite of wheels and moulds, pastes and glazes, stamps and pigments, and all the rest of it—the most primitive methods of the first potter are still in use in many countries, side by side with the most finished products of modern European skill and industry. I have in my own possession some West Indian calabashes, cut and decorated under my own eye by a Jamaican negro for his personal use, and bought from him by me for the smallest coin there current—calabashes carved round the edge through the rind with a rude string-course, exactly like the common rope pattern of prehistoric pottery. I have seen the same Jamaican negroes kneading their hand-made porous earthenware beside a tropical stream, moulding it on fruits or shaping it inside with a free sweep of the curved hand, and drying it for use in the hot sun, or baking it in a hastily-formed kiln of plastered mud into large coarse jars of prehistoric types, locally known by the quaint West African name of 'yabbas.' Many of these yabbas, if buried in the ground and exposed to damp and frost, till they almost lost the effects of the baking, would be quite indistinguishable, even by the skilled archæologist, from the actual handicraft of the palæolithic potter. The West Indian negroes brought these simple arts with them from their African home, where they have been handed down in unbroken continuity from the very earliest age of fictile industry. New and better methods have slowly grown up everywhere around them, but these simplest, earliest, and easiest plans have survived none the less for the most ordinary domestic uses, and will survive for ages yet, as long as there remain any out-of-the-way places, remote from the main streams of civilised commerce. Thus, while hundreds of thousands of years, in all probability, separate us now from the ancient days of the first potter, it is yet possible for us to see the first potter's own methods and principles exemplified under our very eyes by people who derive them in unbroken succession from the direct teaching of that long-forgotten prehistoric savage.

THE RECIPE FOR GENIUS

LET us start fair by frankly admitting that the genius, like the poet, is born and not made. If you wish to apply the recipe for producing him, it is unfortunately necessary to set out by selecting beforehand his grandfathers and grandmothers, to the third and fourth generation of those that precede him. Nevertheless, there *is* a recipe for the production of genius, and every actual concrete genius who ever yet adorned or disgraced this oblate spheroid of ours has been produced, I believe, in strict accordance with its unwritten rules and unknown regulations. In other words, geniuses don't crop up irregularly anywhere, ' quite promiscuous like ' ; they have their fixed laws and their adequate causes : they are the result and effect of certain fairly demonstrable concatenations of circumstance : they are, in short, a natural product, not a *lusus naturæ*. You get them only under sundry relatively definite and settled conditions ; and though it isn't (unfortunately) quite true that the conditions will always infallibly bring forth the genius, it is quite true that the genius can never be brought forth at all without the conditions. Do men gather grapes of thorns, or figs of thistles ? No more can you get a poet from a family of stockbrokers who have intermarried with the daughters of an eminent alderman, or make a philosopher out of a country grocer's eldest son whose amiable mother had no soul above the half-pounds of tea and sugar.

In the first place, by way of clearing the decks for action, I am going to start even by getting rid once for all (so far as we are here concerned) of that famous but misleading old distinction between genius and talent. It is really a distinction without a difference. I suppose there is probably no subject under heaven on which so much high-flown stuff and nonsense has been talked and written as upon this well-known and much-debated hair-splitting discrimination. It is just like that other great distinction between fancy and imagination, about which poets and essayists discoursed so fluently at the beginning of the present century, until at last one fine day the world at large woke up suddenly to the unpleasant consciousness that it had been wasting its time over a non-existent difference, and that fancy and imagination were after all absolutely identical. Now, I won't dogmatically assert that talent and genius are exactly one and the same thing ; but I do assert that genius is simply talent raised to a slightly higher power ; it differs from it not in kind but merely in degree : it is talent at its best. There is no drawing a hard-and-fast line of demarcation between the two. You might just as well try to classify all mankind into tall men and short men, and then endeavour to prove that a real distinction existed in nature between your two artificial classes. As a matter of fact, men differ in height and in ability by infinitesimal gradations : some men are very short, others rather short, others medium-sized, others tall, and yet others again of portentous stature like Mr. Chang and Jacob Omnium. So, too, some men are idiots, some are next door to a fool, some are stupid, some are worthy people, some are intelligent, some are clever, and some geniuses. But genius is only the culminating point of ordinary cleverness, and if you were to try and draw up a list of all the real geniuses in the last hundred years, no two people could ever be found to agree among themselves as to which should be included and which excluded from the artificial catalogue. I have heard Kingsley and Charles Lamb described as geniuses, and I have heard them both absolutely denied every sort of literary merit. Carlyle thought Darwin a poor creature, and Comte regarded Hegel himself as an empty wind-bag.

The fact is, most of the grandiose talk about the vast gulf which separates genius·from mere talent has been published and set abroad by those fortunate persons who fell, or fancied themselves to fall, under the former highly satisfactory and agreeable category. Genius, in short, real or self-suspected, has always been at great pains to glorify itself at the expense of poor, common-place, inferior talent. There is a certain type of great man in particular which is never tired of dilating upon the noble supremacy of its own greatness over the spurious imitation. It offers incense obliquely to itself in offering it generically to the class genius. It brings ghee to its own image. There are great men, for example, such as Lord Lytton, Disraeli, Victor Hugo, the Lion Comique, and Mr. Oscar Wilde, who pose perpetually as great men ; they cry aloud to the poor silly public so far beneath them, ' I am a genius ! Admire me ! Worship me ! ' Against this Byronic self-elevation on an aerial pedestal, high above the heads of the blind and battling multitude, we poor common mortals, who are not unfortunately geniuses, are surely entitled to enter occasionally our humble protest. Our contention is that the genius only differs from the man of ability as the man of ability differs from the intelligent man, and the intelligent man from the worthy person of sound common sense. The sliding scale of brains has infinite gradations ; and the gradations merge insensibly into one another. There is no

gulf, no gap, no sudden jump of nature ; here as elsewhere, throughout the whole range of her manifold pro-
ductions, our common mother *saltum non facit*.

The question before the house, then, narrows itself
down finally to this ; what are the conditions under which
exceptional ability or high talent is likely to arise ?

Now, I suppose everybody is ready to admit that
two complete born fools are not at all likely to become the
proud father and happy mother of a Shakespeare or a
Newton. I suppose everybody will unhesitatingly allow
that a great mathematician could hardly by any conceivable
chance arise among the South African Bushmen, who cannot understand the arduous arithmetical proposition that
two and two make four. No amount of education or
careful training, I take it, would suffice to elevate the most
profoundly artistic among the Veddahs of Ceylon, who
cannot even comprehend an English drawing of a dog or
horse, into a respectable president of the Royal Academy.
It is equally unlikely (as it seems to me) that a Mendelssohn
or a Beethoven could be raised in the bosom of a family all
of whose members on either side were incapable (like a
distinguished modern English poet) of discriminating any
one note in an octave from any other. Such leaps as these
would be little short of pure miracles. They would be
equivalent to the sudden creation, without antecedent
cause, of a whole vast system of nerves and nerve-centres
in the prodigious brain of some infant phenomenon.

On the other hand, much of the commonplace, shallow
fashionable talk about hereditary genius—I don't mean, of
course, the talk of our Darwins and Galtons, but the cheap
drawing-room philosophy of easy sciolists who can't understand them—is itself fully as absurd in its own way as the
idea that something can come out of nothing. For it is
no explanation of the existence of genius to say that it is

hereditary. You only put the difficulty one place back.
Granting that young Alastor Jones is a budding poet
because his father, Percy Bysshe Jones, was a poet before
him, why, pray, was Jones the elder a poet at all, to start
with ? This kind of explanation, in fact, explains nothing ;
it begins by positing the existence of one original genius,
absolutely unaccounted for, and then proceeds blandly to
point out that the other geniuses derive their characteristics from him, by virtue of descent, just as all the sons
of a peer are born honourables. The elephant supports
the earth, and the tortoise supports the elephant, but
who, pray, supports the tortoise ? If the first chicken
came out of an egg, what was the origin of the hen that
laid it ?

Besides, the allegation as it stands is not even a true
one. Genius, as we actually know it, is by no means
hereditary. The great man is not necessarily the son of a
great man or the father of a great man : often enough, he
stands quite isolated, a solitary golden link in a chain of
baser metal on either side of him. Mr. John Shakespeare
woolstapler, of Stratford-on-Avon, Warwickshire, was no
doubt an eminently respectable person in his own trade,
and he had sufficient intelligence to be mayor of his native
town once upon a time : but, so far as is known, none of
his literary remains are at all equal to *Macbeth* or *Othello*.
Parson Newton, of the Parish of Woolsthorpe, in Lincoln-
shire, may have preached a great many very excellent and
convincing discourses , but there is no evidence of any sort
that he ever attempted to write the *Principia*. *Per contra*
the Miss Miltons, good young ladies that they were (though
of conflicting memory), do not appear to have differed con-
spicuously in ability from the other Priscillas and Patiences
and Mercies amongst whom their lot was cast ; while the
Marlboroughs and the Wellingtons do not seem to bud out

spontaneously into great commanders in the second generation. True, there are numerous cases such as that of the
Herschels, father and son, or the two Scaligers, or the
Caracci, or the Pitts, or the Scipios, and a dozen more,
where the genius, once developed, has persisted for two
or three, or even four lives : but these instances really cast
no light at all upon our central problem, which is just this
—How does the genius come in the first place to be developed at all from parents in whom individually no particular genius is ultimately to be seen ?

Suppose we take, to start with, a race of hunting savages
in the earliest, lowest, and most undifferentiated stage, we
shall get really next to no personal peculiarities or idiosyncrasies of any sort amongst them. Every one of them
will be a good hunter, a good fisherman, a good scalper and
a good manufacturer of bows and arrows. Division of
labour, and the other troublesome technicalities of our
modern political economy, are as unknown among such
folk as the modern nuisance of dressing for dinner. Each
man performs all the functions of a citizen on his own
account, because there is nobody else to perform them for
him—the medium of exchange known as hard cash has
not, so far as he is concerned, yet been invented ; and he
performs them well, such as they are, because he inherits
from all his ancestors aptitudes of brain and muscle in
these directions, owing to the simple fact that those among
his collateral predecessors who didn't know how to snare a
bird, or were hopelessly stupid in the art of chipping flint
arrowheads, died out of starvation, leaving no representatives. The beneficent institution of the poor law does not
exist among savages, in order to enable the helpless and
ncompetent to bring up families in their own image.
There, survival of the fittest still works out its own ultimately benevolent and useful end in its own directly cruel

and relentless way, cutting off ruthlessly the stupid or the weak, and allowing only the strong and the cunning to become the parents of future generations.

Hence every young savage, being descended on both sides from ancestors who in their own way perfectly fulfilled the ideal of complete savagery—were good hunters, good fishers, good fighters, good craftsmen of bow or boomerang —inherits from these his successful predecessors all those qualities of eye and hand and brain and nervous system which go to make up the abstractly Admirable Crichton of a savage. The qualities in question are ensured in him by two separate means. In the first place, survival of the fittest takes care that he and all his ancestors shall have duly possessed them to some extent to start with ; in the second place, constant practice from boyhood upward increases and develops the original faculty. Thus savages, as a rule, display absolutely astonishing ability and clever-ness in the few lines which they have made their own. Their cunning in hunting, their patience in fishing, their skill in trapping, their infinite dodges for deceiving and cajoling the animals or enemies that they need to outwit, have moved the wonder and admiration of innumerable travellers. The savage, in fact, is not stupid : in his own way his cleverness is extraordinary. But the way is a very narrow and restricted one, and all savages of the same race walk in it exactly alike. Cunning they have, skill they have, instinct they have, to a most marvellous degree ; but of spontaneity, originality, initiative, variability, not a single spark. Know one savage of a tribe and you know them all. Their cleverness is not the cleverness of the individual man : it is the inherited and garnered intelligence or instinct of the entire race.

How, then, do originality, diversity, individuality, genius, begin to come in ? In this way, as it seems to

me, looking at the matter both à *priori* and by the light
of actual experience.

Suppose a country inhabited in its interior by a savage
race of hunters and fighters, and on its seaboard by an
equally savage race of pirates and fishermen, like the
Dyaks of Borneo. Each of these races, if left to itself, will
develop in time its own peculiar and special type of savage
cleverness. Each (in the scientific slang of the day) will
adapt itself to its particular environment. The people
of the interior will acquire and inherit a wonderful facility
in spearing monkeys and knocking down parrots ; while
the people of the sea-coast will become skilful managers of
canoes upon the water, and merciless plunderers of one
another's villages, after the universal fashion of all pirates.
These original differences of position and function will
necessarily entail a thousand minor differences of intelligence and skill in a thousand different ways. For example,
the sea-coast people, having of pure need to make themselves canoes and paddles, will probably learn to decorate
their handicraft with ornamental patterns; and the
æsthetic taste thus aroused will, no doubt, finally lead
them to adorn the façades of their wooden huts with the
grinning skulls of slaughtered enemies, prettily disposed at
measured distances. A thoughtless world may laugh,
indeed, at these naïve expressions of the nascent artistic
and decorative faculties in the savage breast, but the
æsthetic philosopher knows how to appreciate them at
their true worth, and to see in them the earliest ingenuous
precursors of our own Salisbury, Lichfield, and West-
minster.

Now, so long as these two imaginary races of ours
continue to remain distinct and separate, it is not likely
that idiosyncrasies or varieties to any great extent will
arise among them. But, as soon as you permit inter-

marriage to take place, the inherited and developed qualities of the one race will be liable to crop up in the next generation, diversely intermixed in every variety of degree with the inherited and developed qualities of the other. The children may take after either parent in any combination of qualities whatsoever. You have admitted an apparently capricious element of individuality : a power on the part of the half-breeds of differing from one another to an extent quite impossible in the two original homo-geneous societies. In one word, you have made possible the future existence of diversity in character.

If, now, we turn from these perfectly simple savage communities to our own very complex and heterogeneous world, what do we find? An endless variety of soldiers, sailors, tinkers, tailors, butchers, bakers, candlestick makers, and jolly undertakers, most of whom fall into a certain rough number of classes, each with its own deve-loped and inherited traits and peculiarities. Our world is made up, like the world of ancient Egypt and of modern India, of an immense variety of separate castes—not, indeed, rigidly demarcated and strictly limited as in those extremely hierarchical societies, but still very fairly here-ditary in character, and given on the average to a tolerably close system of intermarriage within the caste.

For example, there is the agricultural labourer caste— the Hodge Chawbacon of urban humour, who in his mili-tary avatar also reappears as Tommy Atkins, a little trans-figured, but at bottom identical—the alternative aspect of a single undivided central reality. Hodge for the most part lives and dies in his ancestral village : marries Mary, the daughter of Hodge Secundus of that parish, and begets assorted Hodges and Marys in vast quantities, all of the same pattern, to replenish the earth in the next generation. There you have a very well-marked heredi-

tary caste, little given to intermixture with others, and
from whose members, however recruited by fresh blood,
the object of our quest, the Divine Genius, is very unlikely to find his point of origin. Then there is the town
artisan caste, sprung originally, indeed, from the ranks of
the Hodges, but naturally selected out of its most active,
enterprising, and intelligent individuals, and often of many
generations standing in various forms of handicraft. This
is a far higher and more promising type of humanity, from
the judicious intermixture of whose best elements we are
apt to get our Stephensons, our Arkwrights, our Telfords,
and our Edisons. In a rank of life just above the last, we
find the fixed and immobile farmer caste, which only
rarely blossoms out, under favourable circumstances on
both sides, into a stray Cobbett or an almost miraculous
miller Constable. The shopkeepers are a tribe of more
varied interests and more diversified lives. An immense
variety of brain elements are called into play by their diverse functions in diverse lines; and when we take them
in conjunction with the upper mercantile grades, which are
chiefly composed of their ablest and most successful members, we get considerable chances of those happy blendings of
individual excellences in their casual marriages which go to
make up talent, and, in their final outcome, genius. Last of
all, in the professional and upper classes there is a freedom
and play of faculty everywhere going on, which in the
chances of intermarriage between lawyer-folk and doctor-
folk, scientific people and artistic people, county families
and bishops or law lords, and so forth *ad infinitum*, offers
by far the best opportunities of any for the occasional development of that rare product of the highest humanity,
the genuine genius.

But in every case it is, I believe, essentially intermixture of variously acquired hereditary characteristics that

z

makes the best and truest geniuses.   Left to itself, each
separate line of caste ancestry would tend to produce a
certain fixed Chinese or Japanese perfection of handicraft
in a certain definite, restricted direction, but not probably
anything worth calling real genius.   For example, a family
of artists, starting with some sort of manual dexterity in
imitating natural forms and colours with paint and pencil,
and strictly intermarrying always with other families possessing exactly the same inherited endowments, would probably go on getting more and more woodenly accurate in its
drawing ; more and more conventionally correct in its
grouping ; more and more technically perfect in its perspective and light-and-shade, and so forth, by pure dint of
accumulated hereditary experience from generation to
generation.   It would pass from the Egyptian to the
Chinese style of art by slow degrees and with infinite gradations.   But suppose, instead of thus rigorously con-
fining itself to its own caste, this family of handicraft
artists were to intermarry freely with poetical, or sea-
faring, or candlestick-making stocks.   What would be the
consequence ?   Why, such an infiltration of other hereditary characteristics, otherwise acquired, as might make the
young painters of future generations more wide minded,
more diversified, more individualistic, more vivid and life-
like.   Some divine spark of poetical imagination, some
tenderness of sentiment, some play of fancy, unknown
perhaps, to the hard, dry, matter-of-fact limners of the
ancestral school, might thus be introduced into the original
line of hereditary artists.   In this way one can easily see
how even intermarriage with non-artistic stocks might improve the breed of a family of painters.   For while each
caste, left to itself, is liable to harden down into a mere
technical excellence after its own kind, a wooden facility
for drawing faces, or casting up columns of figures, or

hacking down enemies, or building steam-engines, a healthy cross with other castes is liable to bring in all kinds of new and valuable qualities, each of which, though acquired perhaps in a totally different line of life, is apt to bear a new application in the new complex whereof it now forms a part.

In our very varied modern societies, every man and every woman, in the upper and middle ranks of life at least, has an individuality and an idiosyncrasy so compounded of endless varying stocks and races. Here is one whose father was an Irishman and his mother a Scotchwoman ; here is another whose paternal line were country parsons, while his maternal ancestors were city merchants or distinguished soldiers. Take almost anybody's ' sixteen quarters '—his great-great grandfathers and great-great grandmothers, of whom he has sixteen all told—and what do you often find ? A peer, a cobbler, a barrister, a common sailor, a Welsh doctor, a Dutch merchant, a Huguenot pastor, a cornet of horse, an Irish heiress, a farmer's daughter, a housemaid, an actress, a Devonshire beauty, a rich young lady of sugar-broking extraction, a Lady Carolina, a London lodging-house keeper. This is not by any means an exaggerated case ; it would be easy, indeed, from one's own knowledge of family histories to supply a great many real examples far more startling than this partially imaginary one. With such a variety of racial and professional antecedents behind us, what infinite possibilities are opened before us of children with ability, folly, stupidity, genius ?

Infinite numbers of intermixtures everywhere exist in civilised societies. Most of them are passable ; many of them are execrable ; a few of them are admirable ; and here and there, one of them consists of that happy blending of individual characteristics which we all immediately recognise as genius—at least after somebody else has told us so.

z 2

The ultimate recipe for genius, then, would appear to be somewhat after this fashion. Take a number of good, strong, powerful stocks, mentally or physically, endowed with something more than the average amount of energy and application. Let them be as varied as possible in characteristics ; and, so far as convenient, try to include among them a considerable small-change of races, dispositions, professions, and temperaments. Mix, by marriage, to the proper consistency ; educate the offspring, especially by circumstances and environment, as broadly, freely, and diversely as you can ; let them all intermarry again with other similarly produced, but personally unlike, idiosyncrasies ; and watch the result to find your genius in the fourth or fifth generation. If the experiment has been properly performed, and all the conditions have been decently favourable, you will get among the resultant five hundred persons a considerable sprinkling of average fools, a fair proportion of modest mediocrities, a small number of able people, and (in case you are exceptionally lucky and have shuffled your cards very carefully) perhaps among them all a single genius. But most probably the genius will have died young of scarlet fever, or missed fire through some tiny defect of internal brain structure. Nature herself is trying this experiment unaided every day all around us, and, though she makes a great many misses, occasionally she makes a stray hit and then we get a Shakespeare or a Grimaldi.

' But you haven't proved all this : you have only suggested it.' Does one prove a thesis of deep-reaching importance in a ten-page essay ? And if one proved it in a big book, with classified examples and detailed genealogies of all the geniuses, would anybody on earth except Mr. Francis Galton ever take the trouble to read it ?

DESERT SANDS

IF deserts *have* a fault (which their present biographer is far from admitting), that fault may doubtless be found in the fact that their scenery as a rule tends to be just a trifle monotonous. Though fine in themselves, they lack variety. To be sure, very few of the deserts of real life possess that absolute flatness, sandiness and sameness, which characterises the familiar desert of the poet and of the annual exhibitions—a desert all level yellow expanse, most bilious in its colouring, and relieved by but four allowable academy properties, a palm-tree, a camel, a sphinx, and a pyramid. For foreground, throw in a sheikh in appropriate drapery ; for background, a sky-line and a bleaching skeleton ; stir and mix, and your picture is finished. Most practical deserts one comes across in travelling, however, are a great deal less simple and theatrical than that ; rock preponderates over sand in their composition, and inequalities of surface are often the rule rather than the exception. There is reason to believe, indeed, that the artistic conception of the common or Burlington House desert has been unduly influenced for evil by the accessibility and the poetic adjuncts of the Egyptian sand-waste, which, being situated in a great alluvial river valley is really flat, and, being the most familiar, has therefore distorted to its own shape the mental picture of all its kind elsewhere. But most deserts of actual nature are not all flat, nor all sandy ;

they present a considerable diversity and variety of surface, and their rocks are often unpleasantly obtrusive to the tender feet of the pedestrian traveller.

A desert, in fact, is only a place where the weather is always and uniformly fine. The sand is there merely as what the logicians call, in their cheerful way, ' a separable accident ' ; the essential of a desert, as such, is the absence of vegetation, due to drought. The barometer in those happy, too happy, regions, always stands at Set Fair. At least, it would, if barometers commonly grew in the desert, where, however, in the present condition of science, they are rarely found. It is this dryness of the air, and this alone, that makes a desert; all the rest, like the camels, the sphinx, the skeleton, and the pyramid, is only thrown in to complete the picture.

Now the first question that occurs to the inquiring mind—which is but a graceful periphrasis for the present writer—when it comes to examine in detail the peculiarities of deserts is just this : Why are there places on the earth's surface on which rain never falls ? What makes it so uncommonly dry in Sahara when it's so unpleasantly wet and so unnecessarily foggy in this realm of England? And the obvious answer is, of course, that deserts exist only in those parts of the world where the run of mountain ranges, prevalent winds, and ocean currents conspire to render the average rainfall as small as possible. But, strangely enough, there is a large irregular belt of the great eastern continent where these peculiar conditions occur in an almost unbroken line for thousands of miles together, from the west coast of Africa to the borders of China : and it is in this belt that all the best known deserts of the world are actually situated. In one place it is the Atlas and the Kong mountains (now don't pretend, as David Copperfield's aunt would have said, you don't know the

Kong mountains) ; at another place it is the Arabian coast range, Lebanon, and the Beluchi hills ; at a third, it is the Himalayas and the Chinese heights that intercept and precipitate all the moisture from the clouds. But, from whatever variety of local causes it may arise, the fact still remains the same, that all the great deserts run in this long, almost unbroken series, beginning with the greater and the smaller Sahara, continuing in the Libyan and Egyptian desert, spreading on through the larger part of Arabia, reappearing to the north as the Syrian desert, and to the east as the desert of Rajputana (the Great Indian Desert of the Anglo-Indian mind), while further east again the long line terminates in the desert of Gobi on the Chinese frontier.

In other parts of the world, deserts are less frequent. The peculiar combination of circumstances which goes to produce them does not elsewhere occur over any vast area, on so large a scale. Still, there is one region in western America where the necessary conditions are found to perfection. The high snow-clad peaks of the Rocky Mountains on the one side check and condense all the moisture that comes from the Atlantic ; the Sierra Nevada and the Wahsatch range on the other, running parallel with them to the west, check and condense all the moisture that comes from the Pacific coast. In between these two great lines lies the dry and almost rainless district known to the ambitious western mind as the Great American Desert, enclosing in its midst that slowly evaporating inland sea, the Great Salt Lake, a last relic of some extinct chain of mighty waters once comparable to Superior, Erie, and Ontario. In Mexico, again, where the twin ranges draw closer together, desert conditions once more supervene. But it is in central Australia that the causes which lead to the desert state are, perhaps on the whole, best exemplified.

There, ranges of high mountains extend almost all round the coasts, and so completely intercept the rainfall which ought to fertilise the great central plain that the rivers are almost all short and local, and one thirsty waste spreads for miles and miles together over the whole unexplored interior of the continent.

But why are deserts rocky and sandy? Why aren't they covered, like the rest of the world, with earth, soil, mould, or dust? One can see plainly enough why there should be little or no vegetation where no rain falls, but one can't see quite so easily why there should be only sand and rock instead of arid clay-field.

Well, the answer is that without vegetation there is no such thing as soil on earth anywhere. The top layer of the land in all ordinary and well-behaved countries is composed entirely of vegetable mould, the decaying remains of innumerable generations of weeds and grasses. Earth to earth is the rule of nature. Soil, in fact, consists entirely of dead leaves. And where there are no leaves to die and decay, there can be no mould or soil to speak of. Darwin showed, indeed, in his last great book, that we owe the whole earthy covering of our hills and plains almost entirely to the perennial exertions of that friend of the farmers, the harmless, necessary earthworm. Year after year the silent worker is busy every night pulling down leaves through his tunnelled burrow into his underground nest, and there converting them by means of his castings into the black mould which produces, in the end, for lordly man, all his cultivable fields and pasture-lands and meadows. Where there are no leaves and no earth-worms, therefore, there can be no soil; and under those circumstances we get what we familiarly know as a desert.

The normal course of events where new land rises above the sea is something like this, as oceanic isles have sufficiently demonstrated. The rock when it first emerges from the water rises bare and rugged like a sea-cliff; no living thing, animal or vegetable, is harboured anywhere on its naked surface. In time, however, as rain falls upon its jutting peaks and barren pinnacles, disintegration sets in, or, to speak plainer English, the rock crumbles ; and soon streams wash down tiny deposits of sand and mud thus produced into the valleys and hollows of the upheaved area. At the same time lichens begin to spring in yellow patches upon the bare face of the rock, and feathery ferns, whose spores have been wafted by the wind, or carried by the waves, or borne on the feet of unconscious birds, sprout here and there from the clefts and crannies. These, as they die and decay, in turn form a thin layer of vegetable mould, the first beginning of a local soil, in which the trusty earthworm (imported in the egg on driftwood or floating weeds) straightway sets to work to burrow, and which he rapidly increases by his constant labour. On the soil thus deposited, flowering plants and trees can soon root themselves, as fast as seeds, nuts or fruits are wafted to the island by various accidents from surrounding countries. The new land thrown up by the great eruption of Krakatoa has in this way already clothed itself from head to foot with a luxuriant sheet of ferns, mosses, and other vegetation.

First soil, then plant and animal life, are thus in the last resort wholly dependent for their existence on the amount of rainfall. But in deserts, where rain seldom or never falls (except by accident) the first term in this series is altogether wanting. There can be no rivers, brooks or streams to wash down beds of alluvial deposit from the mountains to the valleys. Denudation (the term, though rather awful, is not an improper one) must therefore take a different turn. Practically speaking, there is no water action; the work is all done by sun and wind. Under these circumstances, the rocks crumble away very slowly by mere exposure into small fragments, which the wind knocks off and blows about the surface, forming sand or dust of them in all convenient hollows. The frequent currents, produced by the heated air that lies upon the basking layer of sand, continually keep the surface agitated, and so blow about the sand and grind one piece against the other till it becomes ever finer and finer. Thus for the most part the hollows or valleys of deserts are filled by plains of bare sand, while their higher portions consist rather of barren, rocky mountains or table-land.

The effect upon whatever animal or vegetable life can manage here and there to survive under such circumstances is very peculiar. Deserts are the most exacting of all known environments, and they compel their inhabitants with profound imperiousness to knuckle under to their prejudices and preconceptions in ten thousand particulars.

To begin with, all the smaller denizens of the desert—whether butterflies, beetles, birds, or lizards—must be quite uniformly isabelline or sand-coloured. This universal determination of the desert-haunting creatures to fall in with the fashion and to harmonise with their surroundings adds considerably to the painfully monotonous effect of desert scenery. A green plant, a blue butterfly, a red and yellow bird, a black or bronze-coloured beetle or lizard would improve the artistic aspect of the desert not a little. But no; the animals will hear nothing of such gaudy hues; with Quaker uniformity they will clothe themselves in dove-colour; they will all wear a sandy pepper-and-salt with as great unanimity as the ladies of the Court (on receipt of orders) wear Court mourning for the late lamented King of the Tongataboo Islands.

In reality, this universal sombre tint of desert animals is a beautiful example of the imperious working of our modern *Deus ex machinâ*, natural selection. The more uniform in hue is the environment of any particular region, the more uniform in hue must be all its inhabitants. In the arctic snows, for example, we find this principle pushed to its furthest logical conclusion. There, everything is and must be white—hares, foxes, and ptarmigans alike; and the reason is obvious—there can be no exception. Any brown or black or reddish animal who ventured north would at once render himself unpleasantly conspicuous in the midst of the uniform arctic whiteness. If he were a brown hare, for example, the foxes and bears and birds of prey of the district would spot him at once on the white fields, and pounce down upon him forthwith on his first appearance. That hare would leave no similar descendants to continue the race of brown hares in arctic regions after him. Or, suppose, on the other hand, it were a brown fox who invaded the domain of eternal snow. All the hares and ptarmigans of his new district would behold him coming from afar and keep well out of his way, while he, poor creature, would never be able to spot them at all among the white snow-fields. He would starve for want of prey, at the very time when the white fox, his neighbour, was stealing unperceived with stealthy tread upon the hares and ptarmigans. In this way, from generation to generation of arctic animals, the blacker or browner have been constantly weeded out, and the greyer and whiter have been constantly encouraged, till now all arctic animals alike are as spotlessly snowy as the snow around them.

In the desert much the same causes operate, in a slightly different way, in favour of a general greyness or brownness as against pronounced shades of black, white,

red, green, or yellow. Desert animals, like intense South
Kensington, go in only for neutral tints. In proportion as
each individual approaches in hue to the sand about it will
it succeed in life in avoiding its enemies or in creeping
upon its prey, according to circumstances. In proportion
as it presents a strikingly vivid or distinct appearance
among the surrounding sand will it make itself a sure
mark for its watchful foes, if it happen to be an unprotected skulker, or will it be seen beforehand and
avoided by its prey, if it happen to be a predatory hunting
or insect-eating beast. Hence on the sandy desert all
species alike are uniformly sand-coloured. Spotty lizards
bask on spotty sands, keeping a sharp look-out for spotty
butterflies and spotty beetles, only to be themselves spotted
and devoured in turn by equally spotty birds, or snakes, or
tortoises. All nature seems to have gone into half-mourn-
ing together, or, converted by a passing Puritan missionary,
to have clad itself incontinently in grey and fawn-colour.

Even the larger beasts that haunt the desert take their
tone not a little from their sandy surroundings. You have
only to compare the desert-haunting lion with the other
great cats to see at once the reason for his peculiar uniform. The tigers and other tropical jungle-cats have their
coats arranged in vertical stripes of black and yellow, which,
though you would hardly believe it unless you saw them in
their native nullahs (good word 'nullah,' gives a convincing Indian tone to a narrative of adventure), harmonise
marvellously with the lights and shades of the bamboos
and cane-brakes through whose depths the tiger moves so
noiselessly.

Looking into the gloom of a tangled jungle, it is almost
impossible to pick out the beast from the yellow stems and
dark shadows in which it hides, save by the baleful gleam
of those wicked eyes, catching the light for one second as

they turn wistfully and bloodthirstily towards the approaching stranger. The jaguar, oncelot, leopard, and other tree-cats, on the other hand, are dappled or spotted—a type of coloration which exactly harmonises with the light and shade of the round sun-spots seen through the foliage of a tropical forest. They, too, are almost indistinguishable from the trees overhead as they creep along cautiously on the trunks and branches. But spots or stripes would at once betray the crouching lion among the bare rocks or desert sands; and therefore the lion is approximately sand-coloured. Seen in a cage at the Zoo, the British lion is a very conspicuous animal indeed ; but spread at full length on a sandy patch or among bare yellow rocks under the Saharan sun, you may walk into his mouth before you are even aware of his august existence.

The three other great desert beasts of Asia or Africa—the ostrich, the giraffe, and the camel—are less protectively coloured, for various reasons. Giraffes and ostriches go in herds ; they trust for safety mainly to their swiftness of foot, and, when driven to bay, like most gregarious animals, they make common cause against the ill-advised intruder. In such cases it is often well, for the sake of stragglers, that the herd should be readily distinguished at a distance ; and it is to insure this advantage, I believe, that giraffes have acquired their strongly marked spots, as zebras have acquired their distinctive stripes, and hyænas their similarly banded or dappled coats. One must always remember that disguise may be carried a trifle too far, and that recognisability in the parents often gives the young and giddy a point in their favour. For example, it seems certain that the general grey-brown tint of European rabbits serves to render them indistinguishable in a field of bracken, stubble, or dry grass. How hard it is, either for man or hawk, to pick out rabbits so long as they sit still, in an English meadow! But as soon as they begin to run towards their burrows the white patch by their tails inevitably betrays them; and this betrayal seems at first sight like a failure of adaptation. Certainly many a rabbit must be spotted and shot, or killed by birds of prey, solely on account of that tell-tale white patch as he makes for his shelter. Nevertheless, when we come to look closer, we can see, as Mr. Wallace acutely suggests, that the tell-tale patch has its function also. On the first alarm the parent rabbits take to their heels at once, and run at any untoward sight or sound toward the safety of the burrow. The white patch and the hoisted tail act as a danger-signal to the little bunnies, and direct them which way to escape the threatened misfortune. The young ones take the hint at once and follow their leader. Thus what may be sometimes a disadvantage to the individual animal becomes in the long run of incalculable benefit to the entire community.

It is interesting to note, too, how much alike in build and gait are these three thoroughbred desert roamers, the giraffe, the ostrich, and the camel or dromedary. In their long legs, their stalking march, their tall necks, and their ungainly appearance they all betoken their common adaptation to the needs and demands of a special environment. Since food is scarce and shelter rare, they have to run about much over large spaces in search of a livelihood or to escape their enemies. Then the burning nature of the sand as well as the need for speed compels them to have long legs which in turn necessitate equally long necks, if they are to reach the ground or the trees overhead for food and drink. Their feet have to be soft and padded to enable them to run over the sand with ease; and hard horny patches must protect their knees and all other portions of the body liable to touch the sweltering surface when they lie down to rest themselves. Finally, they can all endure thirst for long periods together ; and the camel, the most inveterate desert-haunter of the trio, is even provided with a special stomach to take in water for several days at a stretch, besides having a peculiarly tough skin in which perspiration is reduced to a minimum. He carries his own water-supply internally, and wastes as little of it by the way as possible.

What the camel is among animals that is the cactus among plants—the most confirmed and specialised of desert-haunting organisms. It has been wholly developed in, by, and for the desert. I don't mean merely to say that cactuses resemble camels because they are clumsy, ungainly, awkward, and paradoxical ; that would be a point of view almost as far beneath the dignity of science (which in spite of occasional lapses into the sin of levity I endeavour as a rule piously to uphold) as the old and fallacious reason ' because there's a B in both.' But cactuses, like camels, take in their water supply whenever they can get it, and never waste any of it on the way by needless evaporation. As they form the perfect central type of desert vegetation, and are also familiar plants to everyone, they may be taken as a good illustrative example of the effect that desert conditions inevitably produce upon vegetable evolution.

Quaint, shapeless, succulent, jointed, the cactuses look at first sight as if they were all leaves, and had no stem or trunk worth mentioning. Of course, therefore, the exact opposite is really the case ; for, as a late lamented poet has assured us in mournful numbers, things (generally speaking) are not what they seem. The true truth about the cactuses runs just the other way ; they are all stem and no leaves ; what look like leaves being really joints of the trunk or branches, and the foliage being all dwarfed and stunted into the prickly hairs that dot and encumber the surface. All plants of very arid soils—for example, our common English stonecrops—tend to be thick, jointed, and succu-

lent ; the distinction between stem and leaves tends to disappear ; and the whole weed, accustomed at times to long
drought, acquires the habit of drinking in water greedily
at its rootlets after every rain, and storing it away for future
use in its thick, sponge-like, and water-tight tissues.　To
prevent undue evaporation, the surface also is covered with
a thick, shiny skin—a sort of vegetable macintosh, which
effectually checks all unnecessary transpiration.　Of this
desert type, then, the cactus is the furthest possible term.
It has no flat leaves with expanded blades, to wither and
die in the scorching desert air ; but in their stead the thick
and jointed stems do the same work—absorb carbon from
the carbonic acid of the air, and store up water in the driest
of seasons.　Then, to repel the attacks of herbivores, who
would gladly get at the juicy morsel if they could, the
foliage has been turned into sharp defensive spines and
prickles.　The cactus is tenacious of life to a wonderful
degree ; and for reproduction it trusts not merely to its
brilliant flowers, fertilised for the most part by desert moths
or butterflies, and to its juicy fruit, of which the common
prickly pear is a familiar instance, but it has the special
property of springing afresh from any stray bit or fragment
of the stem that happens to fall upon the dry ground anywhere.

True cactuses (in the native state) are confined to
America ; but the unhappy naturalist who ventures to say
so in mixed society is sure to get sat upon (without due
cause) by numberless people who have seen ' the cactus '
wild all the world over.　For one thing, the prickly pear
and a few other common American species, have been
naturalised and run wild throughout North Africa, the
Mediterranean shores, and a great part of India, Arabia,
and Persia.　But what is more interesting and more confus-
ing still, other desert plants which are *not* cactuses, living in

South Africa, Sind, Rajputana, and elsewhere unspecified, have been driven by the nature of their circumstances and the dryness of the soil to adopt precisely the same tactics, and therefore unconsciously to mimic or imitate the cactus tribe in the minutest details of their personal appearance. Most of these fallacious pseudo-cactuses are really spurges or euphorbias by family. They resemble the true Mexican type in externals only ; that is to say, their stems are thick, jointed, and leaf-like, and they grow with clumsy and awkward angularity ; but in the flower, fruit, seed, and in short in all structural peculiarities whatsoever, they differ utterly from the genuine cactus, and closely resemble all their spurge relations. Adaptive likenesses of this sort, due to mere stress of local conditions, have no more weight as indications of real relationship than the wings of the bat or the flippers of the seal, which don't make the one into a skylark, or the other into a mackerel.

In Sahara, on the other hand, the prevailing type of vegetation (wherever there is any) belongs to the kind playfully described by Sir Lambert Playfair as ' salsolaceous,' that is to say, in plainer English, it consists of plants like the glass-wort and the kali-weed, which are commonly burnt to make soda. These fleshy weeds resemble the cactuses in being succulent and thick-skinned but they differ from them in their curious ability to live upon very salt and soda-laden water. All through the great African desert region, in fact, most of the water is more or less brackish ; ' bitter lakes ' are common, and gypsum often covers the ground over immense areas. These districts occupy the beds of vast ancient lakes, now almost dry, of which the existing *chotts*, or very salt pools, are the last shrunken and evanescent relics.

And this point about the water brings me at last to a cardinal fact in the constitution of deserts which is almost

A A

always utterly misconceived in Europe. Most people at home picture the desert to themselves as wholly dead, flat, and sandy. To talk about the fauna and flora of Sahara sounds in their ears like self-contradictory nonsense. But, as a matter of fact, that uniform and lifeless desert of the popular fancy exists only in those sister arts that George II.—good, practical man—so heartily despised, ' boetry and bainting.' The desert of real life, though less impressive, is far more varied. It has its ups and downs, its hills and valleys. It has its sandy plains and its rocky ridges. It has its lakes and ponds, and even its rivers. It has its plants and animals, its oases and palm-groves. In short, like everything else on earth, it's a good deal more complex than people imagine.

One may take Sahara as a very good example of the actual desert of physical geography, in contradistinction to the level and lifeless desert that stretches like the sea over illimitable spaces in verse or canvas. And here, I fear, I am going to dispel another common and cherished illusion. It is my fate to be an iconoclast, and perhaps long practice has made me rather like the trade than otherwise. A popular belief exists all over Europe that the late M. Roudaire —that De Lesseps who never quite ' came off '— proposed to cut a canal from the Mediterranean into the heart of Africa, which was intended, in the stereotyped phrase of journalism, to ' flood Sahara,' and convert the desert into an inland sea. He might almost as well have talked of cutting a canal from Brighton to the Devil's Dyke and ' submerging England,' as the devil wished to do in the old legend. As a matter of fact, good, practical M. Roudaire, sound engineer that he was, never even dreamt of anything so chimerical. What he did really propose was something far milder and simpler in its way, but, as his scheme has given rise to the absurd notion tha

Sahara as a whole lies below sea-level, it may be worth while briefly to explain what it was he really thought of doing.

Some sixty miles south of Biskra, the most fashionable resort in the Algerian Sahara, there is a deep depression two hundred and fifty miles long, partly occupied by three salt lakes of the kind so common over the whole dried-up Saharan area. These three lakes, shrunken remnants of much larger sheets, lie below the level of the Mediterranean, but they are separated from it, and from one another, by upland ranges which rise considerably above the sea line. What M. Roudaire proposed to do was to cut canals through these three barriers, and flood the basins of the salt lakes. The result would have been, not as is commonly said to submerge Sahara, nor even to form anything worth seriously describing as 'an inland sea,' but to substitute three larger salt lakes for the existing three smaller ones. The area so flooded, however, would bear to the whole area of Sahara something like the same proportion that Windsor Park bears to the entire surface of England. This is the true truth about that stupendous undertaking, which is to create a new Mediterranean in the midst of the Dark Continent, and to modify the climate of Northern Europe to something like the condition of the Glacial Epoch. A new Dead Sea would be much nearer the mark, and the only way Northern Europe would feel the change, if it felt it at all, would be in a slight fall in the price of dates in the wholesale market.

No, Sahara as a whole is *not* below sea-level; it is *not* the dry bed of a recent ocean; and it is *not* as flat as the proverbial pancake all over. Part of it, indeed, is very mountainous, and all of it is more or less varied in level. The Upper Sahara consists of a rocky plateau, rising at times into considerable peaks ; the Lower, to which it

descends by a steep slope, is ' a vast depression of clay and
sand,' but still for the most part standing high above sea-
level.   No portion of the Upper Sahara is less than 1,300
feet high—a good deal higher than Dartmoor or Derbyshire.   Most of the Lower reaches from two to three
hundred feet—quite as elevated as Essex or Leicester.
The few spots below sea-level consist of the beds of ancient
lakes, now much shrunk by evaporation, owing to the
present rainless condition of the country ; the soil around
these is deep in gypsum, and the water itself is considerably
salter than the sea.   That, however, is always the case
with freshwater lakes in their last dotage, as American
geologists have amply proved in the case of the Great Salt
Lake of Utah.   Moving sand undoubtedly covers a large
space in both divisions of the desert, but according to Sir
Lambert Playfair, our best modern authority on the subject, it occupies not more than one-third part of the entire
Algerian Sahara.   Elsewhere rock, clay, and muddy lake
are the prevailing features, interspersed with not infrequent
`ate-groves and villages, the product of artesian wells, or
excavated spaces, or river oases.   Even Sahara, in short,
o give it its due, is not by any means so black as it's
painted.